DICTIONARY
THEME – BASED

British English Collection

ENGLISH-
ARABIC

The most useful words
To expand your lexicon and sharpen
your language skills

7000 words

Theme-based dictionary British English-Arabic - 7000 words

By Andrey Taranov

T&P Books vocabularies are intended for helping you learn, memorize and review foreign words. The dictionary is divided into themes, covering all major spheres of everyday activities, business, science, culture, etc.

The process of learning words using T&P Books' theme-based dictionaries gives you the following advantages:

- Correctly grouped source information predetermines success at subsequent stages of word memorization
- Availability of words derived from the same root allowing memorization of word units (rather than separate words)
- Small units of words facilitate the process of establishing associative links needed for consolidation of vocabulary
- Level of language knowledge can be estimated by the number of learned words

T&P Books Publishing
www.tpbooks.com

This book is also available in E-book formats.
Please visit www.tpbooks.com or the major online bookstores.

ARABIC THEME-BASED DICTIONARY
British English collection

T&P Books vocabularies are intended to help you learn, memorize, and review foreign words. The vocabulary contains over 7000 commonly used words arranged thematically.

- Vocabulary contains the most commonly used words
- Recommended as an addition to any language course
- Meets the needs of beginners and advanced learners of foreign languages
- Convenient for daily use, revision sessions, and self-testing activities
- Allows you to assess your vocabulary

Special features of the vocabulary

- Words are organized according to their meaning, not alphabetically
- Words are presented in three columns to facilitate the reviewing and self-testing processes
- Words in groups are divided into small blocks to facilitate the learning process
- The vocabulary offers a convenient and simple transcription of each foreign word

The vocabulary has 198 topics including:

Basic Concepts, Numbers, Colors, Months, Seasons, Units of Measurement, Clothing & Accessories, Food & Nutrition, Restaurant, Family Members, Relatives, Character, Feelings, Emotions, Diseases, City, Town, Sightseeing, Shopping, Money, House, Home, Office, Working in the Office, Import & Export, Marketing, Job Search, Sports, Education, Computer, Internet, Tools, Nature, Countries, Nationalities and more …

TABLE OF CONTENTS

PRONUNCIATION GUIDE

T&P phonetic alphabet	Arabic example	English example
[a]	طفَى [ṭaffa]	shorter than in 'ask'
[ā]	إختار [ixtār]	calf, palm
[e]	هامبورجر [hamburger]	elm, medal
[i]	زفاف [zifāf]	shorter than in 'feet'
[ī]	أبريل [abrīl]	feet, meter
[u]	كلكتا [kalkutta]	book
[ū]	جاموس [ʒāmūs]	fuel, tuna
[b]	بداية [bidāya]	baby, book
[d]	سعادة [sa'āda]	day, doctor
[ḍ]	وضع [waḍ']	[d] pharyngeal
[ʒ]	الأرجنتين [arʒantīn]	forge, pleasure
[ð]	تذكار [tiðkār]	weather, together
[z]	ظهر [zahar]	[z] pharyngeal
[f]	خفيف [xafīf]	face, food
[g]	جولف [gūlf]	game, gold
[h]	إتّجاه [ittiʒāh]	home, have
[ḥ]	أحبّ [aḥabb]	[h] pharyngeal
[y]	ذهبيّ [ðahabiy]	yes, New York
[k]	كرسيّ [kursiy]	clock, kiss
[l]	لمح [lamaḥ]	lace, people
[m]	مرصد [marṣad]	magic, milk
[n]	جنوب [ʒanūb]	sang, thing
[p]	كابتشينو [kaputʃīnu]	pencil, private
[q]	وثّق [waθiq]	king, club
[r]	روح [rūḥ]	rice, radio
[s]	سخريّة [suxriyya]	city, boss
[ṣ]	معصم [mi'ṣam]	[s] pharyngeal
[ʃ]	عشاء [ʻaʃā']	machine, shark
[t]	تنّوب [tannūb]	tourist, trip
[ṭ]	خريطة [xarīṭa]	[t] pharyngeal
[θ]	ماموث [mamūθ]	month, tooth
[v]	فيتنام [vitnām]	very, river
[w]	ودّع [wadda']	vase, winter
[x]	بخيل [baxīl]	as in Scots 'loch'
[ɣ]	تغدّى [taɣadda]	between [g] and [h]
[z]	ماعز [mā'iz]	zebra, please
['] (ayn)	سبعة [sab'a]	voiced pharyngeal fricative
['] (hamza)	سأل [sa'al]	glottal stop

ABBREVIATIONS
used in the dictionary

Arabic abbreviations

du	-	plural noun (double)
f	-	feminine noun
m	-	masculine noun
pl	-	plural

English abbreviations

ab.	-	about
adj	-	adjective
adv	-	adverb
anim.	-	animate
as adj	-	attributive noun used as adjective
e.g.	-	for example
etc.	-	et cetera
fam.	-	familiar
fem.	-	feminine
form.	-	formal
inanim.	-	inanimate
masc.	-	masculine
math	-	mathematics
mil.	-	military
n	-	noun
pl	-	plural
pron.	-	pronoun
sb	-	somebody
sing.	-	singular
sth	-	something
v aux	-	auxiliary verb
vi	-	intransitive verb
vi, vt	-	intransitive, transitive verb
vt	-	transitive verb

BASIC CONCEPTS

Basic concepts. Part 1

1. Pronouns

I, me	ana	أنا
you (masc.)	anta	أنت
you (fem.)	anti	أنت
he	huwa	هو
she	hiya	هي
we	naḥnu	نحن
you (to a group)	antum	أنتم
they	hum	هم

2. Greetings. Salutations. Farewells

Hello! (form.)	as salāmu 'alaykum!	السلام عليكم!
Good morning!	ṣabāḥ al xayr!	صباح الخير!
Good afternoon!	nahārak sa'īd!	نهارك سعيد!
Good evening!	masā' al xayr!	مساء الخير!
to say hello	sallam	سلّم
Hi! (hello)	salām!	سلام!
greeting (n)	salām (m)	سلام
to greet (vt)	sallam 'ala	سلّم على
How are you?	kayfa ḥāluka?	كيف حالك؟
What's new?	ma axbārak?	ما أخبارك؟
Bye-Bye! Goodbye!	ma' as salāma!	مع السلامة!
See you soon!	ilal liqā'!	إلى اللقاء!
Farewell!	ma' as salāma!	مع السلامة!
to say goodbye	wadda'	ودّع
Cheers!	bay bay!	باي باي!
Thank you! Cheers!	ʃukran!	شكرًا!
Thank you very much!	ʃukran ʒazīlan!	شكرًا جزيلًا!
My pleasure!	'afwan	عفوا
Don't mention it!	la ʃukr 'ala wāʒib	لا شكر على واجب
It was nothing	al 'afw	العفو
Excuse me! (fam.)	'an iðnak!	عن أذنك!
Excuse me! (form.)	'afwan!	عفوًا!
to excuse (forgive)	'aðar	عذر
to apologize (vi)	i'taðar	إعتذر
My apologies	ana 'āsif	أنا آسف

I'm sorry!	la tu'āxiðni!	لا تؤاخذني!
to forgive (vt)	'afa	عفا
please (adv)	min faḍlak	من فضلك

Don't forget!	la tansa!	لا تنس!
Certainly!	ṭab'an!	طبعًا!
Of course not!	abadan!	أبدًا!
Okay! (I agree)	ittafaqna!	إتفقنا!
That's enough!	kifāya!	كفاية!

3. Cardinal numbers. Part 1

0 zero	ṣifr	صفر
1 one	wāḥid	واحد
1 one (fem.)	wāḥida	واحدة
2 two	iθnān	إثنان
3 three	θalāθa	ثلاثة
4 four	arba'a	أربعة

5 five	xamsa	خمسة
6 six	sitta	ستّة
7 seven	sab'a	سبعة
8 eight	θamāniya	ثمانية
9 nine	tis'a	تسعة

10 ten	'aʃara	عشرة
11 eleven	aḥad 'aʃar	أحد عشر
12 twelve	iθnā 'aʃar	إثنا عشر
13 thirteen	θalāθat 'aʃar	ثلاثة عشر
14 fourteen	arba'at 'aʃar	أربعة عشر

15 fifteen	xamsat 'aʃar	خمسة عشر
16 sixteen	sittat 'aʃar	ستّة عشر
17 seventeen	sab'at 'aʃar	سبعة عشر
18 eighteen	θamāniyat 'aʃar	ثمانية عشر
19 nineteen	tis'at 'aʃar	تسعة عشر

20 twenty	'iʃrūn	عشرون
21 twenty-one	wāḥid wa 'iʃrūn	واحد وعشرون
22 twenty-two	iθnān wa 'iʃrūn	إثنان وعشرون
23 twenty-three	θalāθa wa 'iʃrūn	ثلاثة وعشرون

30 thirty	θalāθīn	ثلاثون
31 thirty-one	wāḥid wa θalāθūn	واحد وثلاثون
32 thirty-two	iθnān wa θalāθūn	إثنان وثلاثون
33 thirty-three	θalāθa wa θalāθūn	ثلاثة وثلاثون

40 forty	arba'ūn	أربعون
41 forty-one	wāḥid wa arba'ūn	واحد وأربعون
42 forty-two	iθnān wa arba'ūn	إثنان وأربعون
43 forty-three	θalāθa wa arba'ūn	ثلاثة وأربعون

| 50 fifty | xamsūn | خمسون |
| 51 fifty-one | wāḥid wa xamsūn | واحد وخمسون |

52 fifty-two	iθnān wa χamsūn	إثنان وخمسون
53 fifty-three	θalāθa wa χamsūn	ثلاثة وخمسون
60 sixty	sittūn	ستّون
61 sixty-one	wāḥid wa sittūn	واحد وستّون
62 sixty-two	iθnān wa sittūn	إثنان وستّون
63 sixty-three	θalāθa wa sittūn	ثلاثة وستّون
70 seventy	sabʿūn	سبعون
71 seventy-one	wāḥid wa sabʿūn	واحد وسبعون
72 seventy-two	iθnān wa sabʿūn	إثنان وسبعون
73 seventy-three	θalāθa wa sabʿūn	ثلاثة وسبعون
80 eighty	θamānūn	ثمانون
81 eighty-one	wāḥid wa θamānūn	واحد وثمانون
82 eighty-two	iθnān wa θamānūn	إثنان وثمانون
83 eighty-three	θalāθa wa θamānūn	ثلاثة وثمانون
90 ninety	tisʿūn	تسعون
91 ninety-one	wāḥid wa tisʿūn	واحد وتسعون
92 ninety-two	iθnān wa tisʿūn	إثنان وتسعون
93 ninety-three	θalāθa wa tisʿūn	ثلاثة وتسعون

4. Cardinal numbers. Part 2

100 one hundred	miʾa	مائة
200 two hundred	miʾatān	مائتان
300 three hundred	θalāθumiʾa	ثلاثمائة
400 four hundred	rubʿumiʾa	أربعمائة
500 five hundred	χamsumiʾa	خمسمائة
600 six hundred	sittumiʾa	ستّمائة
700 seven hundred	sabʿumiʾa	سبعمائة
800 eight hundred	θamānimiʾa	ثمانمائة
900 nine hundred	tisʿumiʾa	تسعمائة
1000 one thousand	alf	ألف
2000 two thousand	alfān	ألفان
3000 three thousand	θalāθat ʾālāf	ثلاثة آلاف
10000 ten thousand	ʿaʃarat ālāf	عشرة آلاف
one hundred thousand	miʾat alf	مائة ألف
million	milyūn (m)	مليون
billion	milyār (m)	مليار

5. Numbers. Fractions

fraction	kasr (m)	كسر
one half	niṣf	نصف
one third	θulθ	ثلث
one quarter	rubʿ	ربع
one eighth	θumn	ثمن
one tenth	ʿuʃr	عشر

two thirds	θulθān	ثلثان
three quarters	talātit arbāʿ	ثلاثة أرباع

6. Numbers. Basic operations

subtraction	ṭarḥ (m)	طرح
to subtract (vi, vt)	ṭaraḥ	طرح
division	qisma (f)	قسمة
to divide (vt)	qasam	قسم
addition	ʒamʿ (m)	جمع
to add up (vt)	ʒamaʿ	جمع
to add (vi)	ʒamaʿ	جمع
multiplication	ḍarb (m)	ضرب
to multiply (vt)	ḍarab	ضرب

7. Numbers. Miscellaneous

digit, figure	raqm (m)	رقم
number	ʿadad (m)	عدد
numeral	ism al ʿadad (m)	إسم العدد
minus sign	nāqiṣ (m)	ناقص
plus sign	zāʾid (m)	زائد
formula	ṣīɣa (f)	صيغة
calculation	ḥisāb (m)	حساب
to count (vi, vt)	ʿadd	عدّ
to count up	ḥasab	حسب
to compare (vt)	qāran	قارن
How much?	kam?	كم؟
sum, total	maʒmūʿ (m)	مجموع
result	natīʒa (f)	نتيجة
remainder	al bāqi (m)	الباقي
a few (e.g., ~ years ago)	ʿiddat	عدّة
little (I had ~ time)	qalīl	قليل
the rest	al bāqi (m)	الباقي
one and a half	wāḥid wa niṣf (m)	واحد ونصف
dozen	iθnā ʿaʃar (f)	إثنا عشر
in half (adv)	ila ʃaṭrayn	إلى شطرين
equally (evenly)	bit tasāwi	بالتساوى
half	niṣf (m)	نصف
time (three ~s)	marra (f)	مرّة

8. The most important verbs. Part 1

to advise (vt)	naṣaḥ	نصح
to agree (say yes)	ittafaq	إتّفق

to answer (vi, vt)	aʒāb	أجاب
to apologize (vi)	i'taðar	إعتذر
to arrive (vi)	waṣal	وصل
to ask (~ oneself)	sa'al	سأل
to ask (~ sb to do sth)	ṭalab	طلب
to be (vi)	kān	كان
to be afraid	χāf	خاف
to be hungry	arād an ya'kul	أراد أن يأكل
to be interested in ...	ihtamm	إهتمّ
to be needed	kān maṭlūb	كان مطلوبا
to be surprised	indahaʃ	إندهش
to be thirsty	arād an yaʃrab	أراد أن يشرب
to begin (vt)	bada'	بدأ
to belong to ...	χaṣṣ	خصّ
to boast (vi)	tabāha	تباهى
to break (split into pieces)	kasar	كسر
to call (~ for help)	istaɣāθ	إستغاث
can (v aux)	istaṭā'	إستطاع
to catch (vt)	amsak	أمسك
to change (vt)	ɣayyar	غيّر
to choose (select)	iχtār	إختار
to come down (the stairs)	nazil	نزل
to compare (vt)	qāran	قارن
to complain (vi, vt)	ʃaka	شكا
to confuse (mix up)	iχtalaṭ	إختلط
to continue (vt)	istamarr	إستمرّ
to control (vt)	taḥakkam	تحكّم
to cook (dinner)	ḥaḍḍar	حضّر
to cost (vt)	kallaf	كلّف
to count (add up)	'add	عدّ
to count on ...	i'tamad 'ala ...	إعتمد على...
to create (vt)	χalaq	خلق
to cry (weep)	baka	بكى

9. The most important verbs. Part 2

to deceive (vi, vt)	χada'	خدع
to decorate (tree, street)	zayyan	زيّن
to defend (a country, etc.)	dāfa'	دافع
to demand (request firmly)	ṭālib	طالب
to dig (vt)	ḥafar	حفر
to discuss (vt)	nāqaʃ	ناقش
to do (vt)	'amal	عمل
to doubt (have doubts)	ʃakk fi	شكّ في
to drop (let fall)	awqa'	أوقع
to enter (room, house, etc.)	daχal	دخل
to exist (vi)	kān mawʒūd	كان موجودًا

to expect (foresee)	tanabba'	تنبّأ
to explain (vt)	ʃaraḥ	شرح
to fall (vi)	saqaṭ	سقط
to fancy (vt)	aʿʒab	أعجب
to find (vt)	waʒad	وجد
to finish (vt)	atamm	أتمّ
to fly (vi)	ṭār	طار
to follow ... (come after)	tabaʿ	تبع
to forget (vi, vt)	nasiy	نسي
to forgive (vt)	ʿafa	عفا
to give (vt)	aʿṭa	أعطى
to give a hint	aʿṭa talmīḥ	أعطى تلميحًا
to go (on foot)	maʃa	مشى
to go for a swim	sabaḥ	سبح
to go out (for dinner, etc.)	xaraʒ	خرج
to guess (the answer)	xamman	خمّن
to have (vt)	malak	ملك
to have breakfast	afṭar	أفطر
to have dinner	taʿaʃʃa	تعشّى
to have lunch	taɣadda	تغدّى
to hear (vt)	samiʿ	سمع
to help (vt)	sāʿad	ساعد
to hide (vt)	xaba'	خبأ
to hope (vi, vt)	tamanna	تمنّى
to hunt (vi, vt)	iṣṭād	إصطاد
to hurry (vi)	istaʿʒal	إستعجل

10. The most important verbs. Part 3

to inform (vt)	axbar	أخبر
to insist (vi, vt)	aṣarr	أصرّ
to insult (vt)	ahān	أهان
to invite (vt)	daʿa	دعا
to joke (vi)	mazaḥ	مزح
to keep (vt)	ḥafaẓ	حفظ
to keep silent, to hush	sakat	سكت
to kill (vt)	qatal	قتل
to know (sb)	ʿaraf	عرف
to know (sth)	ʿaraf	عرف
to laugh (vi)	ḍaḥik	ضحك
to liberate (city, etc.)	ḥarrar	حرّر
to look for ... (search)	baḥaθ	بحث
to love (sb)	aḥabb	أحبّ
to make a mistake	axṭa'	أخطأ
to manage, to run	adār	أدار
to mean (signify)	ʿana	عنى
to mention (talk about)	ðakar	ذكر

to miss (school, etc.)	ɣāb	غاب
to notice (see)	lāḥaẓ	لاحظ
to object (vi, vt)	i'taraḍ	إعترض

to observe (see)	rāqab	راقب
to open (vt)	fataḥ	فتح
to order (meal, etc.)	ṭalab	طلب
to order (mil.)	amar	أمر
to own (possess)	malak	ملك

to participate (vi)	iʃtarak	إشترك
to pay (vi, vt)	dafaʻ	دفع
to permit (vt)	raxxaṣ	رخّص
to plan (vt)	xaṭṭaṭ	خطّط
to play (children)	laʻib	لعب

to pray (vi, vt)	ṣalla	صلّى
to prefer (vt)	faḍḍal	فضّل
to promise (vt)	waʻad	وعد
to pronounce (vt)	naṭaq	نطق
to propose (vt)	iqtaraḥ	إقترح
to punish (vt)	ʻāqab	عاقب

11. The most important verbs. Part 4

to read (vi, vt)	qara'	قرأ
to recommend (vt)	naṣaḥ	نصح
to refuse (vi, vt)	rafaḍ	رفض
to regret (be sorry)	nadim	ندم
to rent (sth from sb)	ista'ʒar	إستأجر

to repeat (say again)	karrar	كرّر
to reserve, to book	ḥaʒaz	حجز
to run (vi)	ʒara	جرى
to save (rescue)	anqað	أنقذ

to say (~ thank you)	qāl	قال
to scold (vt)	wabbax	وبّخ
to see (vt)	ra'a	رأى
to sell (vt)	bāʻ	باع

to send (vt)	arsal	أرسل
to shoot (vi)	aṭlaq an nār	أطلق النار
to shout (vi)	ṣarax	صرخ
to show (vt)	ʻaraḍ	عرض
to sign (document)	waqqaʻ	وقّع

to sit down (vi)	ʒalas	جلس
to smile (vi)	ibtasam	إبتسم
to speak (vi, vt)	takallam	تكلّم
to steal (money, etc.)	saraq	سرق
to stop (for pause, etc.)	waqaf	وقف
to stop (please ~ calling me)	tawaqqaf	توقّف
to study (vt)	daras	درس

to swim (vi)	sabaḥ	سبح
to take (vt)	aχað	أخذ
to think (vi, vt)	ẓann	ظنّ
to threaten (vt)	haddad	هدّد
to touch (with hands)	lamas	لمس
to translate (vt)	tarʒam	ترجم
to trust (vt)	waθiq	وثق
to try (attempt)	ḥāwal	حاول
to turn (e.g., ~ left)	inʿaṭaf	إنعطف
to underestimate (vt)	istaχaff	إستخفّ
to understand (vt)	fahim	فهم
to unite (vt)	waḥḥad	وحّد
to wait (vt)	inṭazar	إنتظر
to want (wish, desire)	arād	أراد
to warn (vt)	ḥaððar	حذّر
to work (vi)	ʿamal	عمل
to write (vt)	katab	كتب
to write down	katab	كتب

12. Colours

colour	lawn (m)	لون
shade (tint)	daraʒat al lawn (m)	درجة اللون
hue	ṣabγit lūn (f)	لون
rainbow	qaws quzaḥ (m)	قوس قزح
white (adj)	abyaḍ	أبيض
black (adj)	aswad	أسود
grey (adj)	ramādiy	رماديّ
green (adj)	aχḍar	أخضر
yellow (adj)	aṣfar	أصفر
red (adj)	aḥmar	أحمر
blue (adj)	azraq	أزرق
light blue (adj)	azraq fātiḥ	أزرق فاتح
pink (adj)	wardiy	ورديّ
orange (adj)	burtuqāliy	برتقاليّ
violet (adj)	banafsaʒiy	بنفسجيّ
brown (adj)	bunniy	بنّيّ
golden (adj)	ðahabiy	ذهبيّ
silvery (adj)	fiḍḍiy	فضّيّ
beige (adj)	bɛːʒ	بيج
cream (adj)	ʿāʒiy	عاجيّ
turquoise (adj)	fayrūziy	فيروزيّ
cherry red (adj)	karaziy	كرزيّ
lilac (adj)	laylakiy	ليلكيّ
crimson (adj)	qirmiziy	قرمزيّ
light (adj)	fātiḥ	فاتح

dark (adj)	ɣāmiq	غامق
bright, vivid (adj)	zāhi	زاه
coloured (pencils)	mulawwan	ملوّن
colour (e.g. ~ film)	mulawwan	ملوّن
black-and-white (adj)	abyaḍ wa aswad	أبيض وأسود
plain (one-coloured)	waḥīd al lawn, sāda	وحيد اللون, سادة
multicoloured (adj)	muta'addid al alwān	متعدّد الألوان

13. Questions

Who?	man?	من؟
What?	māða?	ماذا؟
Where? (at, in)	ayna?	أين؟
Where (to)?	ila ayna?	إلى أين؟
From where?	min ayna?	من أين؟
When?	mata?	متى؟
Why? (What for?)	li māða?	لماذا؟
Why? (~ are you crying?)	li māða?	لماذا؟
What for?	li māða?	لماذا؟
How? (in what way)	kayfa?	كيف؟
What? (What kind of ...?)	ay?	أي؟
Which?	ay?	أي؟
To whom?	li man?	لمن؟
About whom?	'amman?	عمّن؟
About what?	'amma?	عمّا؟
With whom?	ma' man?	مع من؟
How many? How much?	kam?	كم؟
Whose?	li man?	لمن؟

14. Function words. Adverbs. Part 1

Where? (at, in)	ayna?	أين؟
here (adv)	huna	هنا
there (adv)	hunāk	هناك
somewhere (to be)	fi makānin ma	في مكان ما
nowhere (not in any place)	la fi ay makān	لا في أي مكان
by (near, beside)	bi ʒānib	بجانب
by the window	bi ʒānib aʃ ʃubbāk	بجانب الشبّاك
Where (to)?	ila ayna?	إلى أين؟
here (e.g. come ~!)	huna	هنا
there (e.g. to go ~)	hunāk	هناك
from here (adv)	min huna	من هنا
from there (adv)	min hunāk	من هناك
close (adv)	qarīban	قريبًا
far (adv)	ba'īdan	بعيدًا

near (e.g. ~ Paris)	'ind	عند
nearby (adv)	qarīban	قريبًا
not far (adv)	ɣayr ba'īd	غير بعيد
left (adj)	al yasār	اليسار
on the left	'alaʃ ʃimāl	على الشمال
to the left	ilaʃ ʃimāl	إلى الشمال
right (adj)	al yamīn	اليمين
on the right	'alal yamīn	على اليمين
to the right	llal yamīn	إلى اليمين
in front (adv)	min al amām	من الأمام
front (as adj)	amāmiy	أمامي
ahead (the kids ran ~)	ilal amām	إلى الأمام
behind (adv)	warā'	وراء
from behind	min al warā'	من الوراء
back (towards the rear)	ilal warā'	إلى الوراء
middle	wasaṭ (m)	وسط
in the middle	fil wasat	في الوسط
at the side	bi ʒānib	بجانب
everywhere (adv)	fi kull makān	في كل مكان
around (in all directions)	ḥawl	حول
from inside	min ad dāχil	من الداخل
somewhere (to go)	ila ayy makān	إلى أيّ مكان
straight (directly)	bi aqṣar ṭarīq	بأقصر طريق
back (e.g. come ~)	'īyāban	إيابًا
from anywhere	min ayy makān	من أي مكان
from somewhere	min makānin ma	من مكان ما
firstly (adv)	awwalan	أوّلًا
secondly (adv)	θāniyan	ثانيًا
thirdly (adv)	θāliθan	ثالثًا
suddenly (adv)	faʒ'a	فجأة
at first (in the beginning)	fil bidāya	في البداية
for the first time	li 'awwal marra	لأوّل مرّة
long before …	qabl … bi mudda ṭawīla	قبل...بمدّة طويلة
anew (over again)	min ʒadīd	من جديد
for good (adv)	ilal abad	إلى الأبد
never (adv)	abadan	أبدًا
again (adv)	min ʒadīd	من جديد
now (at present)	al 'ān	الآن
often (adv)	kaθīran	كثيرًا
then (adv)	fi ðalika al waqt	في ذلك الوقت
urgently (quickly)	'āʒilan	عاجلًا
usually (adv)	kal 'āda	كالعادة
by the way, …	'ala fikra …	على فكرة...
possibly	min al mumkin	من الممكن

probably (adv)	la'alla	لَعلّ
maybe (adv)	min al mumkin	من الممكن
besides ...	bil iḍāfa ila ðalik ...	بالإضافة إلى...
that's why ...	li ðalik	لذلك
in spite of ...	bir raɣm min ...	بالرغم من...
thanks to ...	bi faḍl ...	بفضل...

what (pron.)	allaði	الذي
that (conj.)	anna	أنّ
something	ʃay' (m)	شيء
anything (something)	ʃay' (m)	شيء
nothing	la ʃay'	لا شيء

who (pron.)	allaði	الذي
someone	aḥad	أحد
somebody	aḥad	أحد

nobody	la aḥad	لا أحد
nowhere (a voyage to ~)	la ila ay makān	لا إلى أي مكان
nobody's	la yaxuṣṣ aḥad	لا يخص أحدًا
somebody's	li aḥad	لأحد

so (I'm ~ glad)	hakaða	هكذا
also (as well)	kaðalika	كذلك
too (as well)	ayḍan	أيضًا

15. Function words. Adverbs. Part 2

Why?	li māða?	لماذا؟
for some reason	li sababin ma	لسبب ما
because ...	li'anna ...	لأنّ...
for some purpose	li amr mā	لأمر ما

and	wa	و
or	aw	أو
but	lakin	لكن
for (e.g. ~ me)	li	لـ

too (excessively)	kaθīran ʒiddan	كثير جدًا
only (exclusively)	faqaṭ	فقط
exactly (adv)	biḍ ḍabṭ	بالضبط
about (more or less)	naḥw	نحو

approximately (adv)	taqrīban	تقريبًا
approximate (adj)	taqrībiy	تقريبي
almost (adv)	taqrīban	تقريبًا
the rest	al bāqi (m)	الباقي

each (adj)	kull	كلّ
any (no matter which)	ayy	أيّ
many, much (a lot of)	kaθīr	كثير
many people	kaθīr min an nās	كثير من الناس
all (everyone)	kull an nās	كل الناس
in return for ...	muqābil ...	مقابل...

in exchange (adv)	muqābil	مقابل
by hand (made)	bil yad	باليد
hardly (negative opinion)	hayhāt	هيهات
probably (adv)	la'alla	لعلّ
on purpose (intentionally)	qaṣdan	قصدا
by accident (adv)	ṣudfa	صدفة
very (adv)	ʒiddan	جدًا
for example (adv)	maθalan	مثلا
between	bayn	بين
among	bayn	بين
so much (such a lot)	haðihi al kammiyya	هذه الكمية
especially (adv)	χāṣṣa	خاصّة

Basic concepts. Part 2

16. Opposites

rich (adj)	ɣaniy	غنيّ
poor (adj)	faqīr	فقير
ill, sick (adj)	marīḍ	مريض
well (not sick)	salīm	سليم
big (adj)	kabīr	كبير
small (adj)	ṣaɣīr	صغير
quickly (adv)	bi sur'a	بسرعة
slowly (adv)	bi buṭ'	ببطء
fast (adj)	sarī'	سريع
slow (adj)	baṭī'	بطيء
glad (adj)	farḥān	فرحان
sad (adj)	ḥazīn	حزين
together (adv)	ma'an	معًا
separately (adv)	bi mufradih	بمفرده
aloud (to read)	bi ṣawt 'āli	بصوت عال
silently (to oneself)	sirran	سرًّا
tall (adj)	'āli	عال
low (adj)	munχafiḍ	منخفض
deep (adj)	'amīq	عميق
shallow (adj)	ḍaḥl	ضحل
yes	na'am	نعم
no	la	لا
distant (in space)	ba'īd	بعيد
nearby (adj)	qarīb	قريب
far (adv)	ba'īdan	بعيدًا
nearby (adv)	qarīban	قريبًا
long (adj)	ṭawīl	طويل
short (adj)	qaṣīr	قصير
good (kindhearted)	ṭayyib	طيّب
evil (adj)	ʃarīr	شرير

married (adj)	mutazawwiʒ	متزوّج
single (adj)	aʿzab	أعزب
to forbid (vt)	manaʿ	منع
to permit (vt)	samaḥ	سمح
end	nihāya (f)	نهاية
beginning	bidāya (f)	بداية
left (adj)	al yasār	اليسار
right (adj)	al yamīn	اليمين
first (adj)	awwal	أوّل
last (adj)	ʾāχir	آخر
crime	ʒarīma (f)	جريمة
punishment	ʿuqūba (f), ʿiqāb (m)	عقوبة، عقاب
to order (vt)	amar	أمر
to obey (vi, vt)	ṭāʿ	طاع
straight (adj)	mustaqīm	مستقيم
curved (adj)	munḥani	منحن
paradise	al ʒanna (f)	الجنّة
hell	al ʒaḥīm (f)	الجحيم
to be born	wulid	وُلد
to die (vi)	māt	مات
strong (adj)	qawiy	قويّ
weak (adj)	ḍaʿīf	ضعيف
old (adj)	ʿaʒūz	عجوز
young (adj)	ʃābb	شابّ
old (adj)	qadīm	قديم
new (adj)	ʒadīd	جديد
hard (adj)	ṣalb	صلب
soft (adj)	ṭariy	طريّ
warm (tepid)	dāfiʾ	دافئ
cold (adj)	bārid	بارد
fat (adj)	θaχīn	ثخين
thin (adj)	naḥīf	نحيف
narrow (adj)	ḍayyiq	ضيّق
wide (adj)	wāsiʿ	واسع
good (adj)	ʒayyid	جيّد
bad (adj)	sayyiʾ	سيئ
brave (adj)	ʃuʒāʿ	شجاع
cowardly (adj)	ʒabān	جبان

17. Weekdays

Monday	yawm al iθnayn (m)	يوم الإثنين
Tuesday	yawm aθ θulāθā' (m)	يوم الثلاثاء
Wednesday	yawm al arbi'ā (m)	يوم الأربعاء
Thursday	yawm al χamīs (m)	يوم الخميس
Friday	yawm al ʒum'a (m)	يوم الجمعة
Saturday	yawm as sabt (m)	يوم السبت
Sunday	yawm al aḥad (m)	يوم الأحد
today (adv)	al yawm	اليوم
tomorrow (adv)	ɣadan	غدًا
the day after tomorrow	ba'd ɣad	بعد غد
yesterday (adv)	ams	أمس
the day before yesterday	awwal ams	أوّل أمس
day	yawm (m)	يوم
working day	yawm 'amal (m)	يوم عمل
public holiday	yawm al 'uṭla ar rasmiyya (m)	يوم العطلة الرسمية
day off	yawm 'uṭla (m)	يوم عطلة
weekend	ayyām al 'uṭla (pl)	أيام العطلة
all day long	ṭūl al yawm	طول اليوم
the next day (adv)	fil yawm at tāli	في اليوم التالي
two days ago	min yawmayn	قبل يومين
the day before	fil yawm as sābiq	في اليوم السابق
daily (adj)	yawmiy	يومي
every day (adv)	yawmiyyan	يوميًا
week	usbū' (m)	أسبوع
last week (adv)	fil isbū' al māḍi	في الأسبوع الماضي
next week (adv)	fil isbū' al qādim	في الأسبوع القادم
weekly (adj)	usbū'iy	أسبوعي
every week (adv)	usbū'iyyan	أسبوعيًا
twice a week	marratayn fil usbū'	مرّتين في الأسبوع
every Tuesday	kull yawm aθ θulaθā'	كل يوم الثلاثاء

18. Hours. Day and night

morning	ṣabāḥ (m)	صباح
in the morning	fiṣ ṣabāḥ	في الصباح
noon, midday	ʒuhr (m)	ظهر
in the afternoon	ba'd aẓ ẓuhr	بعد الظهر
evening	masā' (m)	مساء
in the evening	fil masā'	في المساء
night	layl (m)	ليل
at night	bil layl	بالليل
midnight	muntaṣif al layl (m)	منتصف الليل
second	θāniya (f)	ثانية
minute	daqīqa (f)	دقيقة
hour	sā'a (f)	ساعة

half an hour	niṣf sā'a (m)	نصف ساعة
a quarter-hour	rub' sā'a (f)	ربع ساعة
fifteen minutes	χamsat 'aʃar daqīqa	خمس عشرة دقيقة
24 hours	yawm kāmil (m)	يوم كامل
sunrise	ʃurūq aʃ ʃams (m)	شروق الشمس
dawn	faʒr (m)	فجر
early morning	ṣabāḥ bākir (m)	صباح باكر
sunset	ɣurūb aʃ ʃams (m)	غروب الشمس
early in the morning	fis ṣabāḥ al bākir	في الصباح الباكر
this morning	al yawm fiṣ ṣabāḥ	اليوم في الصباح
tomorrow morning	ɣadan fiṣ ṣabāḥ	غدًا في الصباح
this afternoon	al yawm ba'd aẓ ẓuhr	اليوم بعد الظهر
in the afternoon	ba'd aẓ ẓuhr	بعد الظهر
tomorrow afternoon	ɣadan ba'd aẓ ẓuhr	غدًا بعد الظهر
tonight (this evening)	al yawm fil masā'	اليوم في المساء
tomorrow night	ɣadan fil masā'	غدًا في المساء
at 3 o'clock sharp	fis sā'a aθ θāliθa tamāman	في الساعة الثالثة تماما
about 4 o'clock	fis sā'a ar rābi'a taqrīban	في الساعة الرابعة تقريبا
by 12 o'clock	ḥattas sā'a aθ θāniya 'aʃara	حتى الساعة الثانية عشرة
in 20 minutes	ba'd 'iʃrīn daqīqa	بعد عشرين دقيقة
in an hour	ba'd sā'a	بعد ساعة
on time (adv)	fi maw'idih	في موعده
a quarter to …	illa rub'	إلا ربع
within an hour	ṭiwāl sā'a	طوال الساعة
every 15 minutes	kull rub' sā'a	كل ربع ساعة
round the clock	layl nahār	ليل نهار

19. Months. Seasons

January	yanāyir (m)	يناير
February	fibrāyir (m)	فبراير
March	māris (m)	مارس
April	abrīl (m)	أبريل
May	māyu (m)	مايو
June	yūnyu (m)	يونيو
July	yūlyu (m)	يوليو
August	aɣusṭus (m)	أغسطس
September	sibtambar (m)	سبتمبر
October	uktūbir (m)	أكتوبر
November	nuvimbar (m)	نوفمبر
December	disimbar (m)	ديسمبر
spring	rabī' (m)	ربيع
in spring	fir rabī'	في الربيع
spring (as adj)	rabī'iy	ربيعي
summer	ṣayf (m)	صيف
in summer	fiṣ ṣayf	في الصيف

summer (as adj)	ṣayfiy	صيفي
autumn	xarīf (m)	خريف
in autumn	fil xarīf	في الخريف
autumn (as adj)	xarīfiy	خريفيّ
winter	ʃitāʾ (m)	شتاء
in winter	fiʃ ʃitāʾ	في الشتاء
winter (as adj)	ʃitawiy	شتويّ
month	ʃahr (m)	شهر
this month	fi haða aʃ ʃahr	في هذا الشهر
next month	fiʃ ʃahr al qādim	في الشهر القادم
last month	fiʃ ʃahr al māḍi	في الشهر الماضي
a month ago	qabl ʃahr	قبل شهر
in a month (a month later)	baʻd ʃahr	بعد شهر
in 2 months (2 months later)	baʻd ʃahrayn	بعد شهرين
the whole month	ṭūl aʃ ʃahr	طول الشهر
all month long	ʃahr kāmil	شهر كامل
monthly (~ magazine)	ʃahriy	شهريّ
monthly (adv)	kull ʃahr	كل شهر
every month	kull ʃahr	كل شهر
twice a month	marratayn fiʃ ʃahr	مرّتين في الشهر
year	sana (f)	سنة
this year	fi haðihi as sana	في هذه السنة
next year	fis sana al qādima	في السنة القادمة
last year	fis sana al māḍiya	في السنة الماضية
a year ago	qabla sana	قبل سنة
in a year	baʻd sana	بعد سنة
in two years	baʻd sanatayn	بعد سنتين
the whole year	ṭūl as sana	طول السنة
all year long	sana kāmila	سنة كاملة
every year	kull sana	كل سنة
annual (adj)	sanawiy	سنويّ
annually (adv)	kull sana	كل سنة
4 times a year	arbaʻ marrāt fis sana	أربع مرّات في السنة
date (e.g. today's ~)	tarīx (m)	تاريخ
date (e.g. ~ of birth)	tarīx (m)	تاريخ
calendar	taqwīm (m)	تقويم
half a year	niṣf sana (m)	نصف سنة
six months	niṣf sana (m)	نصف سنة
season (summer, etc.)	faṣl (m)	فصل
century	qarn (m)	قرن

20. Time. Miscellaneous

| time | waqt (m) | وقت |
| moment | laḥẓa (f) | لحظة |

instant (n)	laḥẓa (f)	لمظة
instant (adj)	χāṭif	خاطف
lapse (of time)	fatra (f)	فترة
life	ḥayāt (f)	حياة
eternity	abadiyya (f)	أبديّة
epoch	'ahd (m)	عهد
era	'aṣr (m)	عصر
cycle	dawra (f)	دورة
period	fatra (f)	فترة
term (short-~)	fatra (f)	فترة
the future	al mustaqbal (m)	المستقبل
future (as adj)	qādim	قادم
next time	fil marra al qādima	في المرّة القادمة
the past	al māḍi (m)	الماضي
past (recent)	māḍi	ماض
last time	fil marra al māḍiya	في المرّة الماضية
later (adv)	fima ba'd	فيما بعد
after (prep.)	ba'd	بعد
nowadays (adv)	fi haðihi al ayyām	في هذه الأيام
now (at this moment)	al 'ān	الآن
immediately (adv)	ḥālan	حالًا
soon (adv)	qarīban	قريبًا
in advance (beforehand)	muqaddaman	مقدّمًا
a long time ago	min zamān	من زمان
recently (adv)	min zaman qarīb	من زمان قريب
destiny	maṣīr (m)	مصير
recollections	ðikra (f)	ذكرى
archives	arʃīf (m)	أرشيف
during ...	aθnā'...	أثناء...
long, a long time (adv)	li mudda ṭawīla	لمدّة طويلة
not long (adv)	li mudda qaṣīra	لمدّة قصيرة
early (in the morning)	bākiran	باكرًا
late (not early)	muta'aχχiran	متأخّرًا
forever (for good)	lil abad	للأبد
to start (begin)	bada'	بدأ
to postpone (vt)	aʒʒal	أجّل
at the same time	fi nafs al waqt	في نفس الوقت
permanently (adv)	dā'iman	دائمًا
constant (noise, pain)	mustamirr	مستمرّ
temporary (adj)	mu'aqqat	مؤقّت
sometimes (adv)	min ḥīn li 'āχar	من حين لآخر
rarely (adv)	nādiran	نادرًا
often (adv)	kaθīran	كثيرًا

21. Lines and shapes

| square | murabba' (m) | مربّع |
| square (as adj) | murabba' | مربّع |

circle	dā'ira (f)	دائرة
round (adj)	mudawwar	مدور
triangle	muθallaθ (m)	مثلث
triangular (adj)	muθallaθ	مثلث
oval	baydawiy (m)	بيضوي
oval (as adj)	baydawiy	بيضوي
rectangle	mustatīl (m)	مستطيل
rectangular (adj)	mustatīliy	مستطيلي
pyramid	haram (m)	هرم
rhombus	mu'ayyan (m)	معين
trapezium	murabba' munharif (m)	مربع منحرف
cube	muka''ab (m)	مكعب
prism	manjūr (m)	منشور
circumference	muhīt munhanan muɣlaq (m)	محيط منحنى مغلق
sphere	kura (f)	كرة
ball (solid sphere)	kura (f)	كرة
diameter	qutr (m)	قطر
radius	nisf qatr (m)	نصف قطر
perimeter (circle's ~)	muhīt (m)	محيط
centre	wasat (m)	وسط
horizontal (adj)	ufuqiy	أفقي
vertical (adj)	'amūdiy	عمودي
parallel (n)	χatt mutawāzi (m)	خط متواز
parallel (as adj)	mutawāzi	متواز
line	χatt (m)	خط
stroke	haraka (m)	حركة
straight line	χatt mustaqīm (m)	خط مستقيم
curve (curved line)	χatt munhani (m)	خط منحن
thin (line, etc.)	rafī'	رقيع
contour (outline)	kuntūr (m)	كنتور
intersection	taqātu' (m)	تقاطع
right angle	zāwya mustaqīma (f)	زاوية مستقيمة
segment	qit'a (f)	قطعة
sector (circular ~)	qitā' (m)	قطاع
side (of a triangle)	dil' (m)	ضلع
angle	zāwiya (f)	زاوية

22. Units of measurement

weight	wazn (m)	وزن
length	tūl (m)	طول
width	'ard (m)	عرض
height	irtifā' (m)	إرتفاع
depth	'umq (m)	عمق
volume	haʒm (m)	حجم
area	misāha (f)	مساحة
gram	grām (m)	جرام
milligram	milliɣrām (m)	مليغرام

kilogram	kiluɣrām (m)	كيلوغرام
ton	ṭunn (m)	طنّ
pound	raṭl (m)	رطل
ounce	ūnṣa (f)	أونصة

metre	mitr (m)	متر
millimetre	millimitr (m)	مليمتر
centimetre	santimitr (m)	سنتيمتر
kilometre	kilumitr (m)	كيلومتر
mile	mīl (m)	ميل

inch	būṣa (f)	بوصة
foot	qadam (f)	قدم
yard	yārda (f)	ياردة

| square metre | mitr murabbaʿ (m) | متر مربّع |
| hectare | hiktār (m) | هكتار |

litre	litr (m)	لتر
degree	daraʒa (f)	درجة
volt	vūlt (m)	فولت
ampere	ambīr (m)	أمبير
horsepower	ḥiṣān (m)	حصان

quantity	kammiyya (f)	كمّيّة
a little bit of ...	qalīl ...	قليل...
half	niṣf (m)	نصف
dozen	iθnā ʿaʃar (f)	إثنا عشر
piece (item)	waḥda (f)	وحدة

| size | ḥaʒm (m) | حجم |
| scale (map ~) | miqyās (m) | مقياس |

minimal (adj)	al adna	الأدنى
the smallest (adj)	al aṣɣar	الأصغر
medium (adj)	mutawassiṭ	متوسّط
maximal (adj)	al aqṣa	الأقصى
the largest (adj)	al akbar	الأكبر

23. Containers

canning jar (glass ~)	barṭamān (m)	برطمان
tin, can	tanaka (f)	تنكة
bucket	ʒardal (m)	جردل
barrel	barmīl (m)	برميل

wash basin (e.g., plastic ~)	ḥawḍ lil ɣasīl (m)	حوض للغسيل
tank (100L water ~)	xazzān (m)	خزّان
hip flask	zamzamiyya (f)	زمزميّة
jerrycan	ʒirikan (m)	جركن
tank (e.g., tank car)	xazzān (m)	خزّان

| mug | māgg (m) | ماجّ |
| cup (of coffee, etc.) | finʒān (m) | فنجان |

saucer	ṭabaq finʒān (m)	طبق فنجان
glass (tumbler)	kubbāya (f)	كبّاية
wine glass	ka's (f)	كأس
stock pot (soup pot)	kassirūlla (f)	كاسرولة
bottle (~ of wine)	zuʒāʒa (f)	زجاجة
neck (of the bottle, etc.)	'unq (m)	عنق
carafe (decanter)	dawraq zuʒāʒiy (m)	دورق زجاجيّ
pitcher	ibrīq (m)	إبريق
vessel (container)	inā' (m)	إناء
pot (crock, stoneware ~)	aṣīṣ (m)	أصيص
vase	vāza (f)	فازة
flacon, bottle (perfume ~)	zuʒāʒa (f)	زجاجة
vial, small bottle	zuʒāʒa (f)	زجاجة
tube (of toothpaste)	umbūba (f)	أنبوبة
sack (bag)	kīs (m)	كيس
bag (paper ~, plastic ~)	kīs (m)	كيس
packet (of cigarettes, etc.)	'ulba (f)	علبة
box (e.g. shoebox)	'ulba (f)	علبة
crate	ṣundū' (m)	صندوق
basket	salla (f)	سلّة

24. Materials

material	mādda (f)	مادّة
wood (n)	xaʃab (m)	خشب
wood-, wooden (adj)	xaʃabiy	خشبيّ
glass (n)	zuʒāʒ (m)	زجاج
glass (as adj)	zuʒāʒiy	زجاجيّ
stone (n)	ḥaʒar (m)	حجر
stone (as adj)	ḥaʒariy	حجريّ
plastic (n)	blastīk (m)	بلاستيك
plastic (as adj)	min al blastīk	من البلاستيك
rubber (n)	maṭṭāṭ (m)	مطّاط
rubber (as adj)	maṭṭāṭiy	مطّاطيّ
cloth, fabric (n)	qumāʃ (m)	قماش
fabric (as adj)	min al qumāʃ	من القماش
paper (n)	waraq (m)	ورق
paper (as adj)	waraqiy	ورقيّ
cardboard (n)	kartūn (m)	كرتون
cardboard (as adj)	kartūniy	كرتونيّ
polyethylene	buli iθilīn (m)	بولي إثيلين
cellophane	silufān (m)	سيلوفان

plywood	ablakāʃ (m)	أبلكاش
porcelain (n)	bursilān (m)	بورسلان
porcelain (as adj)	min il bursilān	من البورسلان
clay (n)	ṭīn (m)	طين
clay (as adj)	faxxāry	فخّاري
ceramic (n)	siramīk (m)	سيراميك
ceramic (as adj)	siramīkiy	سيراميكيّ

25. Metals

metal (n)	maʿdan (m)	معدن
metal (as adj)	maʿdaniy	معدنيّ
alloy (n)	sabīka (f)	سبيكة
gold (n)	ðahab (m)	ذهب
gold, golden (adj)	ðahabiy	ذهبيّ
silver (n)	fiḍḍa (f)	فضة
silver (as adj)	fiḍḍiy	فضّيّ
iron (n)	ḥadīd (m)	حديد
iron-, made of iron (adj)	ḥadīdiy	حديديّ
steel (n)	fūlāð (m)	فولاذ
steel (as adj)	fulāðiy	فولاذيّ
copper (n)	nuḥās (m)	نحاس
copper (as adj)	nuḥāsiy	نحاسيّ
aluminium (n)	alumīniyum (m)	الومينيوم
aluminium (as adj)	alumīniyum	الومينيوم
bronze (n)	brūnz (m)	برونز
bronze (as adj)	brūnziy	برونزيّ
brass	nuḥās aṣfar (m)	نحاس أصفر
nickel	nikil (m)	نيكل
platinum	blatīn (m)	بلاتين
mercury	ziʾbaq (m)	زئبق
tin	qaṣdīr (m)	قصدير
lead	ruṣāṣ (m)	رصاص
zinc	zink (m)	زنك

HUMAN BEING

Human being. The body

26. Humans. Basic concepts

human being	insān (m)	إنسان
man (adult male)	raʒul (m)	رجل
woman	imra'a (f)	إمرأة
child	ṭifl (m)	طفل
girl	bint (f)	بنت
boy	walad (m)	ولد
teenager	murāhiq (m)	مراهق
old man	ʕaʒūz (m)	عجوز
old woman	ʕaʒūza (f)	عجوزة

27. Human anatomy

organism (body)	ʒism (m)	جسم
heart	qalb (m)	قلب
blood	dam (m)	دم
artery	ʃaryān (m)	شريان
vein	ʕirq (m)	عرق
brain	muxx (m)	مخّ
nerve	ʕaṣab (m)	عصب
nerves	aʕṣāb (pl)	أعصاب
vertebra	faqra (f)	فقرة
spine (backbone)	ʕamūd faqriy (m)	عمود فقريّ
stomach (organ)	maʕida (f)	معدة
intestines, bowels	amʕā' (pl)	أمعاء
intestine (e.g. large ~)	miʕan (m)	معى
liver	kibd (f)	كبد
kidney	kilya (f)	كلية
bone	ʕaẓm (m)	عظم
skeleton	haykal ʕaẓmiy (m)	هيكل عظميّ
rib	ḍilʕ (m)	ضلع
skull	ʒumʒuma (f)	جمجمة
muscle	ʕaḍala (f)	عضلة
biceps	ʕaḍala ðāt ra'sayn (f)	عضلة ذات رأسين
triceps	ʕaḍla θulāθiyyat ar ru'ūs (f)	عضلة ثلائيّة الرءوس
tendon	watar (m)	وتر
joint	mafṣil (m)	مفصل

lungs	ri'atān (du)	رئتان
genitals	a'ḍā' ʒinsiyya (pl)	أعضاء جنسيّة
skin	buʃra (m)	بشرة

28. Head

head	ra's (m)	رأس
face	waʒh (m)	وجه
nose	anf (m)	أنف
mouth	fam (m)	فم
eye	'ayn (f)	عين
eyes	'uyūn (pl)	عيون
pupil	ḥadaqa (f)	حدقة
eyebrow	ḥāʒib (m)	حاجب
eyelash	rimʃ (m)	رمش
eyelid	ʒafn (m)	جفن
tongue	lisān (m)	لسان
tooth	sinn (f)	سنّ
lips	ʃifāh (pl)	شفاه
cheekbones	'iẓām waʒhiyya (pl)	عظام وجهيّة
gum	liθθa (f)	لثّة
palate	ḥanak (m)	حنك
nostrils	minxarān (du)	منخران
chin	ðaqan (m)	ذقن
jaw	fakk (m)	فكّ
cheek	xadd (m)	خدّ
forehead	ʒabha (f)	جبهة
temple	ṣudɣ (m)	صدغ
ear	uðun (f)	أذن
back of the head	qafa (m)	قفا
neck	raqaba (f)	رقبة
throat	ḥalq (m)	حلق
hair	ʃa'r (m)	شعر
hairstyle	tasrīḥa (f)	تسريحة
haircut	tasrīḥa (f)	تسريحة
wig	barūka (f)	باروكة
moustache	ʃawārib (pl)	شوارب
beard	liḥya (f)	لحية
to have (a beard, etc.)	'indahu	عنده
plait	ḍifīra (f)	ضفيرة
sideboards	sawālif (pl)	سوالف
red-haired (adj)	aḥmar aʃ ʃa'r	أحمر الشعر
grey (hair)	abyaḍ	أبيض
bald (adj)	aṣla'	أصلع
bald patch	ṣala' (m)	صلع
ponytail	ðayl ḥiṣān (m)	ذيل حصان
fringe	quṣṣa (f)	قصّة

29. Human body

hand	yad (m)	يد
arm	ðirā' (f)	ذراع
finger	iṣba' (m)	إصبع
toe	iṣba' al qadam (m)	إصبع القدم
thumb	ibhām (m)	إبهام
little finger	χunṣur (m)	خنصر
nail	ẓufr (m)	ظفر
fist	qabḍa (f)	قبضة
palm	kaff (f)	كفّ
wrist	mi'ṣam (m)	معصم
forearm	sā'id (m)	ساعد
elbow	mirfaq (m)	مرفق
shoulder	katf (f)	كتف
leg	riʒl (f)	رجل
foot	qadam (f)	قدم
knee	rukba (f)	ركبة
calf	sammāna (f)	سمّانة
hip	faχð (f)	فخذ
heel	'aqb (m)	عقب
body	ʒism (m)	جسم
stomach	baṭn (m)	بطن
chest	ṣadr (m)	صدر
breast	θady (m)	ثدي
flank	ʒamb (m)	جنب
back	ẓahr (m)	ظهر
lower back	asfal aẓ ẓahr (m)	أسفل الظهر
waist	χaṣr (m)	خصر
navel (belly button)	surra (f)	سرّة
buttocks	ardāf (pl)	أرداف
bottom	dubr (m)	دبر
beauty spot	ʃāma (f)	شامة
birthmark (café au lait spot)	waḥma	وحمة
tattoo	waʃm (m)	وشم
scar	nadba (f)	ندبة

Clothing & Accessories

30. Outerwear. Coats

clothes	malābis (pl)	ملابس
outerwear	malābis fawqāniyya (pl)	ملابس فوقانيّة
winter clothing	malābis ʃitawiyya (pl)	ملابس شتويّة

coat (overcoat)	miʿṭaf (m)	معطف
fur coat	miʿṭaf farw (m)	معطف فرو
fur jacket	ʒakīt farw (m)	جاكيت فرو
down coat	haʃiyyat rīʃ (m)	حشية ريش

jacket (e.g. leather ~)	ʒākīt (m)	جاكيت
raincoat (trenchcoat, etc.)	miʿṭaf lil maṭar (m)	معطف للمطر
waterproof (adj)	ṣāmid lil māʾ	صامد للماء

31. Men's & women's clothing

shirt (button shirt)	qamīṣ (m)	قميص
trousers	banṭalūn (m)	بنطلون
jeans	ʒīnz (m)	جينز
suit jacket	sutra (f)	سترة
suit	badla (f)	بدلة

dress (frock)	fustān (m)	فستان
skirt	tannūra (f)	تنّورة
blouse	blūza (f)	بلوزة
knitted jacket (cardigan, etc.)	kardigān (m)	كارديجان
jacket (of a woman's suit)	ʒākīt (m)	جاكيت

T-shirt	ti ʃirt (m)	تي شيرت
shorts (short trousers)	ʃūrt (m)	شورت
tracksuit	badlat at tadrīb (f)	بدلة التدريب
bathrobe	θawb hammām (m)	ثوب حمّام
pyjamas	biʒāma (f)	بيجاما

jumper (sweater)	bulūvir (m)	بلوفر
pullover	bulūvir (m)	بلوفر

waistcoat	ṣudayriy (m)	صديريَ
tailcoat	badlat sahra (f)	بدلة سهرة
dinner suit	smūkin (m)	سموكن

uniform	zayy muwaḥḥad (m)	زي موحّد
workwear	θiyāb al ʿamal (m)	ثياب العمل
boiler suit	uvirūl (m)	اوفرول
coat (e.g. doctor's smock)	θawb (m)	ثوب

32. Clothing. Underwear

underwear	malābis dāχiliyya (pl)	ملابس داخليّة
pants	sirwāl dāχiliy riʒāliy (m)	سروال داخلي رجاليّ
panties	sirwāl dāχiliy nisā'iy (m)	سروال داخلي نسائيّ
vest (singlet)	qamīṣ bila aqmām (m)	قميص بلا أكمام
socks	ʒawārib (pl)	جوارب
nightdress	qamīṣ nawm (m)	قميص نوم
bra	ḥammālat ṣadr (f)	حمّالة صدر
knee highs (knee-high socks)	ʒawārib ṭawīla (pl)	جوارب طويلة
tights	ʒawārib kulūn (pl)	جوارب كولون
stockings (hold ups)	ʒawārib nisā'iyya (pl)	جوارب نسائية
swimsuit, bikini	libās sibāḥa (m)	لباس سباحة

33. Headwear

hat	qubba'a (f)	قبّعة
trilby hat	burnayṭa (f)	برنيطة
baseball cap	kāb baysbūl (m)	كاب بيسبول
flatcap	qubba'a musaṭṭaḥa (f)	قبّعة مسطحة
beret	birīh (m)	بيريه
hood	γiṭā' (m)	غطاء
panama hat	qubba'at banāma (f)	قبّعة بناما
knit cap (knitted hat)	qubbā'a maḥbūka (m)	قبّعة محبوكة
headscarf	ʕiʃārb (m)	إيشارب
women's hat	burnayṭa (f)	برنيطة
hard hat	χūða (f)	خوذة
forage cap	kāb (m)	كاب
helmet	χūða (f)	خوذة
bowler	qubba'at dirbi (f)	قبّعة ديربي
top hat	qubba'a 'āliya (f)	قبّعة عالية

34. Footwear

footwear	aḥðiya (pl)	أحذية
shoes (men's shoes)	ʒazma (f)	جزمة
shoes (women's shoes)	ʒazma (f)	جزمة
boots (e.g., cowboy ~)	būt (m)	بوت
carpet slippers	ʃibʃib (m)	شبشب
trainers	ḥiðā' riyāḍiy (m)	حذاء رياضيّ
trainers	kutʃi (m)	كوتشي
sandals	ṣandal (pl)	صندل
cobbler (shoe repairer)	iskāfiy (m)	إسكافيّ
heel	ka'b (m)	كعب

English	Transcription	Arabic
pair (of shoes)	zawʒ (m)	زوج
lace (shoelace)	ʃarīṭ (m)	شريط
to lace up (vt)	rabaṭ	ربط
shoehorn	labbāsat ḥiðā' (f)	لبّاسة حذاء
shoe polish	warnīʃ al ḥiðā' (m)	ورنيش الحذاء

35. Textile. Fabrics

cotton (n)	quṭn (m)	قطن
cotton (as adj)	min al quṭn	من القطن
flax (n)	kattān (m)	كتّان
flax (as adj)	min il kattān	من الكتّان
silk (n)	ḥarīr (m)	حرير
silk (as adj)	min al ḥarīr	من الحرير
wool (n)	ṣūf (m)	صوف
wool (as adj)	min aṣ ṣūf	من الصوف
velvet	muxmal (m)	مخمل
suede	ʒild ʃāmwāh (m)	جلد شامواه
corduroy	quṭn qaṭīfa (f)	قطن قطيفة
nylon (n)	naylūn (m)	نايلون
nylon (as adj)	min an naylūn	من النيلون
polyester (n)	bulyistir (m)	بوليستر
polyester (as adj)	min al bulyastar	من البوليستر
leather (n)	ʒild (m)	جلد
leather (as adj)	min al ʒild	من الجلد
fur (n)	farw (m)	فرو
fur (e.g. ~ coat)	min al farw	من الفرو

36. Personal accessories

English	Transcription	Arabic
gloves	quffāz (m)	قفّاز
mittens	quffāz muxlaq (m)	قفّاز مغلق
scarf (muffler)	'īʃārb (m)	إيشارب
glasses	naẓẓāra (f)	نظّارة
frame (eyeglass ~)	iṭār (m)	إطار
umbrella	ʃamsiyya (f)	شمسيّة
walking stick	'aṣa (f)	عصا
hairbrush	furʃat ʃaʿr (f)	فرشة شعر
fan	mirwaḥa yadawiyya (f)	مروحة يدويّة
tie (necktie)	karavatta (f)	كرافتة
bow tie	babyūn (m)	ببيون
braces	ḥammāla (f)	حمّالة
handkerchief	mandīl (m)	منديل
comb	miʃṭ (m)	مشط
hair slide	dabbūs (m)	دبّوس

hairpin	bansa (m)	بنسة
buckle	bukla (f)	بكلة
belt	ḥizām (m)	حزام
shoulder strap	ḥammalat al katf (f)	حمّالة الكتف
bag (handbag)	ʃanṭa (f)	شنطة
handbag	ʃanṭat yad (f)	شنطة يد
rucksack	ḥaqībat ẓahr (f)	حقيبة ظهر

37. Clothing. Miscellaneous

fashion	mūḍa (f)	موضة
in vogue (adj)	fil mūḍa	في الموضة
fashion designer	muṣammim azyā' (m)	مصمّم أزياء
collar	yāqa (f)	ياقة
pocket	ʒayb (m)	جيب
pocket (as adj)	ʒayb	جيب
sleeve	kumm (m)	كمّ
hanging loop	'allāqa (f)	علّاقة
flies (on trousers)	lisān (m)	لسان
zip (fastener)	zimām munzaliq (m)	زمام منزلق
fastener	miʃbak (m)	مشبك
button	zirr (m)	زرّ
buttonhole	'urwa (f)	عروة
to come off (ab. button)	waqa'	وقع
to sew (vi, vt)	xāṭ	خاط
to embroider (vi, vt)	ṭarraz	طرّز
embroidery	taṭrīz (m)	تطريز
sewing needle	ibra (f)	إبرة
thread	xayṭ (m)	خيط
seam	darz (m)	درز
to get dirty (vi)	tawassax	توسّخ
stain (mark, spot)	buq'a (f)	بقعة
to crease, to crumple	takarmaʃ	تكرمش
to tear, to rip (vt)	qaṭṭa'	قطّع
clothes moth	'uθθa (f)	عثّة

38. Personal care. Cosmetics

toothpaste	ma'ʒūn asnān (m)	معجون أسنان
toothbrush	furʃat asnān (f)	فرشة أسنان
to clean one's teeth	naẓẓaf al asnān	نظّف الأسنان
razor	mūs ḥilāqa (m)	موس حلاقة
shaving cream	krīm ḥilāqa (m)	كريم حلاقة
to shave (vi)	ḥalaq	حلق
soap	ṣābūn (m)	صابون

shampoo	ʃāmbū (m)	شامبو
scissors	maqaṣṣ (m)	مقص
nail file	mibrad (m)	مبرد
nail clippers	milqaṭ (m)	ملقط
tweezers	milqaṭ (m)	ملقط

cosmetics	mawādd at taʒmīl (pl)	موادُّ التجميل
face mask	mask (m)	ماسك
manicure	manikūr (m)	مانيكور
to have a manicure	'amal manikūr	عمل مانيكور
pedicure	badikīr (m)	باديكير

make-up bag	ḥaqībat adawāt at taʒmīl (f)	حقيبة أدوات التجميل
face powder	budrat waʒh (f)	بودرة وجه
powder compact	'ulbat būdra (f)	علبة بودرة
blusher	aḥmar χudūd (m)	أحمر خدود

perfume (bottled)	'iṭr (m)	عطر
toilet water (lotion)	kulūnya (f)	كولونيا
lotion	lusiyun (m)	لوسيون
cologne	kulūniya (f)	كولونيا

eyeshadow	ay ʃaduw (m)	اي شادو
eyeliner	kuḥl al 'uyūn (m)	كحل العيون
mascara	maskara (f)	ماسكارا

lipstick	aḥmar ʃifāh (m)	أحمر شفاه
nail polish	mulammi' al aẓāfir (m)	ملمّع الاظافر
hair spray	muθabbit aʃ ʃa'r (m)	مثبّت الشعر
deodorant	muzīl rawā'iḥ (m)	مزيل روائح

cream	krīm (m)	كريم
face cream	krīm lil waʒh (m)	كريم للوجه
hand cream	krīm lil yadayn (m)	كريم لليدين
anti-wrinkle cream	krīm muḍādd lit taʒā'īd (m)	كريم مضادٌ للتجاعيد
day cream	krīm an nahār (m)	كريم النهار
night cream	krīm al layl (m)	كريم الليل
day (as adj)	nahāriy	نهاريُ
night (as adj)	layliy	ليلي

tampon	tambūn (m)	تانبون
toilet paper (toilet roll)	waraq ḥammām (m)	ورق حمّام
hair dryer	muʒaffif ʃa'r (m)	مجفّف شعر

39. Jewellery

jewellery, jewels	muʒawharāt (pl)	مجوهرات
precious (e.g. ~ stone)	karīm	كريم
hallmark stamp	damɣa (f)	دمغة

ring	χātim (m)	خاتم
wedding ring	diblat al χuṭūba (m)	دبلة الخطوبة
bracelet	siwār (m)	سوار
earrings	ḥalaq (m)	حلق

necklace (~ of pearls)	ʿaqd (m)	عقد
crown	tāʒ (m)	تاج
bead necklace	ʿaqd xaraz (m)	عقد خرز
diamond	almās (m)	الماس
emerald	zumurrud (m)	زمرّد
ruby	yāqūt aḥmar (m)	ياقوت أحمر
sapphire	yāqūt azraq (m)	ياقوت أزرق
pearl	luʾluʾ (m)	لؤلؤ
amber	kahramān (m)	كهرمان

40. Watches. Clocks

watch (wristwatch)	sāʿa (f)	ساعة
dial	waʒh as sāʿa (m)	وجه الساعة
hand (clock, watch)	ʿaqrab as sāʿa (m)	عقرب الساعة
metal bracelet	siwār sāʿa maʿdaniyya (m)	سوار ساعة معدنية
watch strap	siwār sāʿa (m)	سوار ساعة
battery	battāriyya (f)	بطّاريّة
to be flat (battery)	tafarrax	تفرّغ
to change a battery	xayyar al battāriyya	غيّر البطّاريّة
to run fast	sabaq	سبق
to run slow	taʾaxxar	تأخّر
wall clock	sāʿat ḥāʾiṭ (f)	ساعة حائط
hourglass	sāʿa ramliyya (f)	ساعة رمليّة
sundial	sāʿa ʃamsiyya (f)	ساعة شمسيّة
alarm clock	munabbih (m)	منبّه
watchmaker	saʿātiy (m)	ساعاتيّ
to repair (vt)	aṣlaḥ	أصلح

Food. Nutricion

41. Food

meat	laḥm (m)	لحم
chicken	daʒāʒ (m)	دجاج
poussin	farrūʒ (m)	فروج
duck	baṭṭa (f)	بطّة
goose	iwazza (f)	إوزّة
game	ṣayd (m)	صيد
turkey	daʒāʒ rūmiy (m)	دجاج رومي
pork	laḥm al xinzīr (m)	لحم الخنزير
veal	laḥm il ʻiʒl (m)	لحم العجل
lamb	laḥm aḍ ḍa'n (m)	لحم الضأن
beef	laḥm al baqar (m)	لحم البقر
rabbit	arnab (m)	أرنب
sausage (bologna, etc.)	suʒuq (m)	سجق
vienna sausage (frankfurter)	suʒuq (m)	سجق
bacon	bikūn (m)	بيكون
ham	hām (m)	هام
gammon	faxð xinzīr (m)	فخذ خنزير
pâté	ma'ʒūn laḥm (m)	معجون لحم
liver	kibda (f)	كبدة
mince (minced meat)	ḥaʃwa (f)	حشوة
tongue	lisān (m)	لسان
egg	bayḍa (f)	بيضة
eggs	bayḍ (m)	بيض
egg white	bayāḍ al bayḍ (m)	بياض البيض
egg yolk	ṣafār al bayḍ (m)	صفار البيض
fish	samak (m)	سمك
seafood	fawākih al baḥr (pl)	فواكه البحر
caviar	kaviyār (m)	كافيار
crab	salṭa'ūn (m)	سلطعون
prawn	ʒambari (m)	جمبري
oyster	maḥār (m)	محار
spiny lobster	karkand ʃāik (m)	كركند شائك
octopus	uxṭubūṭ (m)	أخطبوط
squid	kalmāri (m)	كالماري
sturgeon	samak al ḥaʃʃ (m)	سمك الحفش
salmon	salmūn (m)	سلمون
halibut	samak al halbūt (m)	سمك الهلبوت
cod	samak al qudd (m)	سمك القدّ
mackerel	usqumriy (m)	أسقمريّ

tuna	tūna (f)	تونة
eel	ḥankalīs (m)	حنكليس
trout	salmūn muraqqaṭ (m)	سلمون مرقّط
sardine	sardīn (m)	سردين
pike	samak al karāki (m)	سمك الكراكي
herring	rinʒa (f)	رنجة
bread	χubz (m)	خبز
cheese	ʒubna (f)	جبنة
sugar	sukkar (m)	سكّر
salt	milḥ (m)	ملح
rice	urz (m)	أرز
pasta (macaroni)	makarūna (f)	مكرونة
noodles	nūdlis (f)	نودلز
butter	zubda (f)	زبدة
vegetable oil	zayt (m)	زيت
sunflower oil	zayt ʿabīd aʃ ʃams (m)	زيت عبيد الشمس
margarine	marɣarīn (m)	مرغرين
olives	zaytūn (m)	زيتون
olive oil	zayt az zaytūn (m)	زيت الزيتون
milk	ḥalīb (m)	حليب
condensed milk	ḥalīb mukaθθaf (m)	حليب مكثّف
yogurt	yūɣurt (m)	يوغورت
soured cream	krīma ḥāmiḍa (f)	كريمة حامضة
cream (of milk)	krīma (f)	كريمة
mayonnaise	mayunīz (m)	مايونيز
buttercream	krīmat zubda (f)	كريمة زبدة
groats (barley ~, etc.)	ḥubūb (pl)	حبوب
flour	daqīq (m)	دقيق
tinned food	muʿallabāt (pl)	معلّبات
cornflakes	kurn fliks (m)	كورن فليكس
honey	ʿasal (m)	عسل
jam	murabba (m)	مربّى
chewing gum	ʿilk (m)	علك

42. Drinks

water	māʾ (m)	ماء
drinking water	māʾ ʃurb (m)	ماء شرب
mineral water	māʾ maʿdaniy (m)	ماء معدنيّ
still (adj)	bi dūn ɣāz	بدون غاز
carbonated (adj)	mukarban	مكربن
sparkling (adj)	bil ɣāz	بالغاز
ice	θalʒ (m)	ثلج
with ice	biθ θalʒ	بالثلج

non-alcoholic (adj)	bi dūn kuḥūl	بدون كحول
soft drink	maʃrūb ɣāziy (m)	مشروب غازي
refreshing drink	maʃrūb muθallaʒ (m)	مشروب مثلج
lemonade	ʃarāb laymūn (m)	شراب ليمون
spirits	maʃrūbāt kuḥūliyya (pl)	مشروبات كحولية
wine	nabīð (f)	نبيذ
white wine	nibīð abyaḍ (m)	نبيذ أبيض
red wine	nabīð aḥmar (m)	نبيذ أحمر
liqueur	liqiūr (m)	ليكيور
champagne	ʃambāniya (f)	شمبانيا
vermouth	virmut (m)	فيرموث
whisky	wiski (m)	وسكي
vodka	vudka (f)	فودكا
gin	ʒīn (m)	جين
cognac	kunyāk (m)	كونياك
rum	rum (m)	رم
coffee	qahwa (f)	قهوة
black coffee	qahwa sāda (f)	قهوة سادة
white coffee	qahwa bil ḥalīb (f)	قهوة بالحليب
cappuccino	kaputʃīnu (m)	كابتشينو
instant coffee	niskafi (m)	نيسكافيه
milk	ḥalīb (m)	حليب
cocktail	kuktayl (m)	كوكتيل
milkshake	milk ʃiyk (m)	ميلك شيك
juice	ʿaṣīr (m)	عصير
tomato juice	ʿaṣīr ṭamāṭim (m)	عصير طماطم
orange juice	ʿaṣīr burtuqāl (m)	عصير برتقال
freshly squeezed juice	ʿaṣīr ṭāziʒ (m)	عصير طازج
beer	bīra (f)	بيرة
lager	bīra xafīfa (f)	بيرة خفيفة
bitter	bīra ɣāmiqa (f)	بيرة غامقة
tea	ʃāy (m)	شاي
black tea	ʃāy aswad (m)	شاي أسود
green tea	ʃāy axḍar (m)	شاي أخضر

43. Vegetables

vegetables	xuḍār (pl)	خضار
greens	xuḍrawāt waraqiyya (pl)	خضروات ورقية
tomato	ṭamāṭim (f)	طماطم
cucumber	xiyār (m)	خيار
carrot	ʒazar (m)	جزر
potato	baṭāṭis (f)	بطاطس
onion	baṣal (m)	بصل
garlic	θūm (m)	ثوم

cabbage	kurumb (m)	كرنب
cauliflower	qarnabīṭ (m)	قرنبيط
Brussels sprouts	kurumb brūksil (m)	كرنب بروكسل
broccoli	brukuli (m)	بركولي

beetroot	banʒar (m)	بنجر
aubergine	bātinʒān (m)	باذنجان
courgette	kūsa (f)	كوسة
pumpkin	qarʿ (m)	قرع
turnip	lift (m)	لفت

parsley	baqdūnis (m)	بقدونس
dill	ʃabat (m)	شبت
lettuce	χass (m)	خسّ
celery	karafs (m)	كرفس
asparagus	halyūn (m)	هليون
spinach	sabāniχ (m)	سبانخ

pea	bisilla (f)	بسلّة
beans	fūl (m)	فول
maize	ðura (f)	ذرّة
kidney bean	faṣūliya (f)	فاصوليا

sweet paper	filfil (m)	فلفل
radish	fiʒl (m)	فجل
artichoke	χurʃūf (m)	خرشوف

44. Fruits. Nuts

fruit	fākiha (f)	فاكهة
apple	tuffāha (f)	تفّاحة
pear	kummaθra (f)	كمّثرى
lemon	laymūn (m)	ليمون
orange	burtuqāl (m)	برتقال
strawberry (garden ~)	farawla (f)	فراولة

tangerine	yūsufiy (m)	يوسفي
plum	barqūq (m)	برقوق
peach	durrāq (m)	دراق
apricot	miʃmiʃ (f)	مشمش
raspberry	tūt al ʿullayq al ahmar (m)	توت العلّيق الأحمر
pineapple	ananās (m)	أناناس

banana	mawz (m)	موز
watermelon	baṭṭīχ ahmar (m)	بطّيخ أحمر
grape	ʿinab (m)	عنب
cherry	karaz (m)	كرز
melon	baṭṭīχ aṣfar (f)	بطّيخ أصفر

grapefruit	zinbāʿ (m)	زنباع
avocado	avukādu (f)	افوكاتو
papaya	babāya (m)	بابايا
mango	mangu (m)	مانجو
pomegranate	rummān (m)	رمان

redcurrant	kiʃmiʃ aḥmar (m)	كشمش أحمر
blackcurrant	ʿinab aθ θaʿlab al aswad (m)	عنب الثعلب الأسود
gooseberry	ʿinab aθ θaʿlab (m)	عنب الثعلب
bilberry	ʿinab al aḥrāʒ (m)	عنب الأحراج
blackberry	θamar al ʿullayk (m)	ثمر العليّق
raisin	zabīb (m)	زبيب
fig	tīn (m)	تين
date	tamr (m)	تمر
peanut	fūl sudāniy (m)	فول سودانيّ
almond	lawz (m)	لوز
walnut	ʿayn al ʒamal (f)	عين الجمل
hazelnut	bunduq (m)	بندق
coconut	ʒawz al hind (m)	جوز هند
pistachios	fustuq (m)	فستق

45. Bread. Sweets

bakers' confectionery (pastry)	ḥalawiyyāt (pl)	حلويّات
bread	xubz (m)	خبز
biscuits	baskawīt (m)	بسكويت
chocolate (n)	ʃukulāta (f)	شكولاتة
chocolate (as adj)	biʃ ʃukulāṭa	بالشكولاتة
candy (wrapped)	bumbūn (m)	بونبون
cake (e.g. cupcake)	kaʿk (m)	كعك
cake (e.g. birthday ~)	tūrta (f)	تورتة
pie (e.g. apple ~)	faṭīra (f)	فطيرة
filling (for cake, pie)	ḥaʃwa (f)	حشوة
jam (whole fruit jam)	murabba (m)	مربّى
marmalade	marmalād (f)	مرملاد
wafers	wāfil (m)	وافل
ice-cream	muθallaʒāt (pl)	مثلّجات
pudding (Christmas ~)	būding (m)	بودنج

46. Cooked dishes

course, dish	waʒba (f)	وجبة
cuisine	matbax (m)	مطبخ
recipe	waṣfa (f)	وصفة
portion	waʒba (f)	وجبة
salad	sulṭa (f)	سلطة
soup	ʃūrba (f)	شوربة
clear soup (broth)	maraq (m)	مرق
sandwich (bread)	sandawitʃ (m)	ساندويتش
fried eggs	bayḍ maqliy (m)	بيض مقليّ
hamburger (beefburger)	hamburger (m)	هامبورجر

beefsteak	biftīk (m)	بفتيك
side dish	ṭabaq ʒānibiy (m)	طبق جانبيّ
spaghetti	spaɣitti (m)	سباغيتي
mash	harīs baṭāṭis (m)	هريس بطاطس
pizza	bītza (f)	بيتزا
porridge (oatmeal, etc.)	ʿaṣīda (f)	عصيدة
omelette	bayḍ maxfūq (m)	بيض مخفوق

boiled (e.g. ~ beef)	maslūq	مسلوق
smoked (adj)	mudaxxin	مدخّن
fried (adj)	maqliy	مقليّ
dried (adj)	muʒaffaf	مجفّف
frozen (adj)	muʒammad	مجمّد
pickled (adj)	muxallil	مخلّل

sweet (sugary)	musakkar	مسكّر
salty (adj)	māliḥ	مالح
cold (adj)	bārid	بارد
hot (adj)	sāxin	ساخن
bitter (adj)	murr	مرّ
tasty (adj)	laðīð	لذيذ

to cook in boiling water	ṭabax	طبخ
to cook (dinner)	haḍḍar	حضّر
to fry (vt)	qala	قلى
to heat up (food)	saxxan	سخّن

to salt (vt)	mallaḥ	ملّح
to pepper (vt)	falfal	فلفل
to grate (vt)	baʃar	بشر
peel (n)	qiʃra (f)	قشرة
to peel (vt)	qaʃʃar	قشّر

47. Spices

salt	milḥ (m)	ملح
salty (adj)	māliḥ	مالح
to salt (vt)	mallaḥ	ملّح

black pepper	filfil aswad (m)	فلفل أسود
red pepper (milled ~)	filfil aḥmar (m)	فلفل أحمر
mustard	ṣalṣat al xardal (f)	صلصة الخردل
horseradish	fiʒl ḥārr (m)	فجل حارّ

condiment	tābil (m)	تابل
spice	bahār (m)	بهار
sauce	ṣalṣa (f)	صلصة
vinegar	xall (m)	خلّ

anise	yānsūn (m)	يانسون
basil	rīḥān (m)	ريحان
cloves	qurumful (m)	قرنفل
ginger	zanʒabīl (m)	زنجبيل
coriander	kuzbara (f)	كزبرة

cinnamon	qirfa (f)	قرفة
sesame	simsim (m)	سمسم
bay leaf	awrāq al ɣār (pl)	أوراق الغار
paprika	babrika (f)	بابريكا
caraway	karāwiya (f)	كراوية
saffron	za'farān (m)	زعفران

48. Meals

food	akl (m)	أكل
to eat (vi, vt)	akal	أكل
breakfast	futūr (m)	فطور
to have breakfast	aftar	أفطر
lunch	ɣadā' (m)	غداء
to have lunch	taɣadda	تغدّى
dinner	'afā' (m)	عشاء
to have dinner	ta'affa	تعشّى
appetite	fahiyya (f)	شهيّة
Enjoy your meal!	hanī'an marī'an!	هنيئًا مريئًا!
to open (~ a bottle)	fataḥ	فتح
to spill (liquid)	dalaq	دلق
to spill out (vi)	indalaq	إندلق
to boil (vi)	ɣala	غلى
to boil (vt)	ɣala	غلى
boiled (~ water)	maɣliy	مغليّ
to chill, cool down (vt)	barrad	برّد
to chill (vi)	tabarrad	تبرّد
taste, flavour	ṭa'm (m)	طعم
aftertaste	al maðāq al 'āliq fil fam (m)	المذاق العالق فى الفم
to slim down (lose weight)	faqad al wazn	فقد الوزن
diet	ḥimya ɣaðā'iyya (f)	حمية غذائية
vitamin	vitamīn (m)	فيتامين
calorie	su'ra ḥarāriyya (f)	سعرة حرارية
vegetarian (n)	nabātiy (m)	نباتيّ
vegetarian (adj)	nabātiy	نباتيّ
fats (nutrient)	duhūn (pl)	دهون
proteins	brutināt (pl)	بروتينات
carbohydrates	nafawiyyāt (pl)	نشويّات
slice (of lemon, ham)	farīḥa (f)	شريحة
piece (of cake, pie)	qiṭ'a (f)	قطعة
crumb (of bread, cake, etc.)	futāta (f)	فتاتة

49. Table setting

spoon	mil'aqa (f)	ملعقة
knife	sikkīn (m)	سكّين

fork	ʃawka (f)	شوكة
cup (e.g., coffee ~)	finʒān (m)	فنجان
plate (dinner ~)	ṭabaq (m)	طبق
saucer	ṭabaq finʒān (m)	طبق فنجان
serviette	mandīl (m)	منديل
toothpick	χallat asnān (f)	خلة أسنان

50. Restaurant

restaurant	maṭʿam (m)	مطعم
coffee bar	kafé (m), maqha (m)	كافيه، مقهى
pub, bar	bār (m)	بار
tearoom	ṣālun ʃāy (m)	صالون شاي
waiter	nādil (m)	نادل
waitress	nādila (f)	نادلة
barman	bārman (m)	بارمان
menu	qā'imat aṭ ṭaʿām (f)	قائمة طعام
wine list	qā'imat al χumūr (f)	قائمة خمور
to book a table	ḥaʒaz mā'ida	حجز مائدة
course, dish	waʒba (f)	وجبة
to order (meal)	ṭalab	طلب
to make an order	ṭalab	طلب
aperitif	ʃarāb (m)	شراب
starter	muqabbilāt (pl)	مقبّلات
dessert, pudding	ḥalawiyyāt (pl)	حلويّات
bill	ḥisāb (m)	حساب
to pay the bill	dafaʿ al ḥisāb	دفع الحساب
to give change	aʿṭa al bāqi	أعطى الباقي
tip	baqʃīʃ (m)	بقشيش

Family, relatives and friends

51. Personal information. Forms

name (first name)	ism (m)	إسم
surname (last name)	ism al 'ā'ila (m)	إسم العائلة
date of birth	tarīχ al mīlād (m)	تاريخ الميلاد
place of birth	makān al mīlād (m)	مكان الميلاد
nationality	ʒinsiyya (f)	جنسية
place of residence	maqarr al iqāma (m)	مقر الإقامة
country	balad (m)	بلد
profession (occupation)	mihna (f)	مهنة
gender, sex	ʒins (m)	جنس
height	ṭūl (m)	طول
weight	wazn (m)	وزن

52. Family members. Relatives

mother	umm (f)	أمّ
father	ab (m)	أب
son	ibn (m)	إبن
daughter	ibna (f)	إبنة
younger daughter	al ibna aṣ ṣaɣīra (f)	الإبنة الصغيرة
younger son	al ibn aṣ ṣaɣīr (m)	الابن الصغير
eldest daughter	al ibna al kabīra (f)	الإبنة الكبيرة
eldest son	al ibn al kabīr (m)	الإبن الكبير
brother	aχ (m)	أخ
elder brother	al aχ al kabīr (m)	الأخ الكبير
younger brother	al aχ aṣ ṣaɣīr (m)	الأخ الصغير
sister	uχt (f)	أخت
elder sister	al uχt al kabīra (f)	الأخت الكبيرة
younger sister	al uχt aṣ ṣaɣīra (f)	الأخت الصغيرة
cousin (masc.)	ibn 'amm (m), ibn χāl (m)	إبن عمّ, إبن خال
cousin (fem.)	ibnat 'amm (f), ibnat χāl (f)	إبنة عم, إبنة خال
mummy	mama (f)	ماما
dad, daddy	baba (m)	بابا
parents	wālidān (du)	والدان
child	ṭifl (m)	طفل
children	aṭfāl (pl)	أطفال
grandmother	ʒidda (f)	جدّة
grandfather	ʒadd (m)	جدّ
grandson	ḥafīd (m)	حفيد

granddaughter	ḥafīda (f)	حفيدة
grandchildren	aḥfād (pl)	أحفاد
uncle	'amm (m), χāl (m)	عمّ, خال
aunt	'amma (f), χāla (f)	عمة, خالة
nephew	ibn al aχ (m), ibn al uχt (m)	إبن الأخ, إبن الأخت
niece	ibnat al aχ (f), ibnat al uχt (f)	إبنة الأخ, إبنة الأخت
mother-in-law (wife's mother)	ḥamātt (f)	حماة
father-in-law (husband's father)	ḥamm (m)	حم
son-in-law (daughter's husband)	zawʒ al ibna (m)	زوج الأبنة
stepmother	zawʒat al ab (f)	زوجة الأب
stepfather	zawʒ al umm (m)	زوج الأمّ
infant	ṭifl raḍī' (m)	طفل رضيع
baby (infant)	mawlūd (m)	مولود
little boy, kid	walad ṣaɣīr (m)	ولد صغير
wife	zawʒa (f)	زوجة
husband	zawʒ (m)	زوج
spouse (husband)	zawʒ (m)	زوج
spouse (wife)	zawʒa (f)	زوجة
married (masc.)	mutazawwiʒ	متزوّج
married (fem.)	mutazawwiʒa	متزوّجة
single (unmarried)	a'zab	أعزب
bachelor	a'zab (m)	أعزب
divorced (masc.)	muṭallaq (m)	مطلّق
widow	armala (f)	أرملة
widower	armal (m)	أرمل
relative	qarīb (m)	قريب
close relative	nasīb qarīb (m)	نسيب قريب
distant relative	nasīb ba'īd (m)	نسيب بعيد
relatives	aqārib (pl)	أقارب
orphan (boy or girl)	yatīm (m)	يتيم
guardian (of a minor)	waliyy amr (m)	وليّ أمر
to adopt (a boy)	tabanna	تبنّى
to adopt (a girl)	tabanna	تبنّى

53. Friends. Colleagues

friend (masc.)	ṣadīq (m)	صديق
friend (fem.)	ṣadīqa (f)	صديقة
friendship	ṣadāqa (f)	صداقة
to be friends	ṣādaq	صادق
pal (masc.)	ṣāḥib (m)	صاحب
pal (fem.)	ṣaḥiba (f)	صاحبة
partner	rafīq (m)	رفيق
chief (boss)	ra'īs (m)	رئيس

superior (n)	ra'īs (m)	رئيس
owner, proprietor	ṣāḥib (m)	صاحب
subordinate (n)	tābi' (m)	تابع
colleague	zamīl (m)	زميل

acquaintance (person)	ma'ruf (m)	معروف
fellow traveller	rafīq safar (m)	رفيق سفر
classmate	zamīl fiṣ ṣaff (m)	زميل في الصفّ

neighbour (masc.)	ʒār (m)	جار
neighbour (fem.)	ʒāra (f)	جارة
neighbours	ʒirān (pl)	جيران

54. Man. Woman

woman	imra'a (f)	إمرأة
girl (young woman)	fatāt (f)	فتاة
bride	'arūsa (f)	عروسة

beautiful (adj)	ʒamīla	جميلة
tall (adj)	ṭawīla	طويلة
slender (adj)	raʃīqa	رشيقة
short (adj)	qaṣīra	قصيرة

| blonde (n) | ʃaqrā' (f) | شقراء |
| brunette (n) | sawdā' aʃ ʃa'r (f) | سوداء الشعر |

ladies' (adj)	sayyidāt	سيّدات
virgin (girl)	'aðrā' (f)	عذراء
pregnant (adj)	ḥāmil	حامل

man (adult male)	raʒul (m)	رجل
blonde haired man	aʃqar (m)	أشقر
dark haired man	aswad aʃ ʃa'r (m)	أسود الشعر
tall (adj)	ṭawīl	طويل
short (adj)	qaṣīr	قصير

rude (rough)	waqiḥ	وقح
stocky (adj)	malyān	مليان
robust (adj)	matīn	متين
strong (adj)	qawiy	قويّ
strength	quwwa (f)	قوّة

plump, fat (adj)	θaxīn	ثخين
swarthy (dark-skinned)	asmar	أسمر
slender (well-built)	raʃīq	رشيق
elegant (adj)	anīq	أنيق

55. Age

| age | 'umr (m) | عمر |
| youth (young age) | ʃabāb (m) | شباب |

young (adj)	ʃābb	شابّ
younger (adj)	aṣɣar	أصغر
older (adj)	akbar	أكبر
young man	ʃābb (m)	شابّ
teenager	murāhiq (m)	مراهق
guy, fellow	ʃābb (m)	شابّ
old man	ʿaʒūz (m)	عجوز
old woman	ʿaʒūza (f)	عجوزة
adult (adj)	bāliɣ (m)	بالغ
middle-aged (adj)	fi muntaṣaf al ʿumr	في منتصف العمر
elderly (adj)	ʿaʒūz	عجوز
old (adj)	ʿaʒūz	عجوز
retirement	maʿāʃ (m)	معاش
to retire (from job)	uḥīl ʿalal maʿāʃ	أحيل على المعاش
retiree, pensioner	mutaqāʿid (m)	متقاعد

56. Children

child	ṭifl (m)	طفل
children	aṭfāl (pl)	أطفال
twins	tawʾamān (du)	توأمان
cradle	mahd (m)	مهد
rattle	xaʃxīʃa (f)	خشخيشة
nappy	ḥifāẓ aṭfāl (m)	حفاظ أطفال
dummy, comforter	bazzāza (f)	بزّازة
pram	ʿarabat aṭfāl (f)	عربة أطفال
nursery	rawḍat aṭfāl (f)	روضة أطفال
babysitter	murabbiyat aṭfāl (f)	مربّية الأطفال
childhood	ṭufūla (f)	طفولة
doll	dumya (f)	دمية
toy	luʿba (f)	لعبة
construction set (toy)	mukaʿʿabāt (pl)	مكعّبات
well-bred (adj)	muʾaddab	مؤدّب
ill-bred (adj)	qalīl al adab	قليل الأدب
spoilt (adj)	mutdalliʿ	متدلّع
to be naughty	laʿib	لعب
mischievous (adj)	laʿūb	لعوب
mischievousness	izʿāʒ (m)	إزعاج
mischievous child	ṭifl laʿūb (m)	طفل لعوب
obedient (adj)	muṭīʿ	مطيع
disobedient (adj)	ʿāq	عاقّ
docile (adj)	ʿāqil	عاقل
clever (intelligent)	ðakiy	ذكيّ
child prodigy	ṭifl muʿʒiza (m)	طفل معجزة

57. Married couples. Family life

to kiss (vt)	bās	باس
to kiss (vi)	bās	باس
family (n)	'ā'ila (f)	عائلة
family (as adj)	'ā'iliy	عائليّ
couple	zawʒān (du)	زوجان
marriage (state)	zawāʒ (m)	زواج
hearth (home)	bayt (m)	بيت
dynasty	sulāla (f)	سلالة
date	maw'id (m)	موعد
kiss	būsa (f)	بوسة
love (for sb)	ḥubb (m)	حبّ
to love (sb)	aḥabb	أحبّ
beloved	ḥabīb	حبيب
tenderness	ḥanān (m)	حنان
tender (affectionate)	ḥanūn	حنون
faithfulness	iχlāṣ (m)	إخلاص
faithful (adj)	muχliṣ	مخلص
care (attention)	'ināya (f)	عناية
caring (~ father)	muhtamm	مهتمّ
newlyweds	'arūsān (du)	عروسان
honeymoon	ʃahr al 'asal (m)	شهر العسل
to get married (ab. woman)	tazawwaʒ	تزوّج
to get married (ab. man)	tazawwaʒ	تزوّج
wedding	zifāf (m)	زفاف
golden wedding	al yubīl að ðahabiy liz zawāʒ (m)	اليوبيل الذهبي للزواج
anniversary	ðikra sanawiyya (f)	ذكرى سنويّة
lover (masc.)	ḥabīb (m)	حبيب
mistress (lover)	ḥabība (f)	حبيبة
adultery	χiyāna zawʒiyya (f)	خيانة زوجية
to cheat on … (commit adultery)	χān	خان
jealous (adj)	ɣayūr	غيور
to be jealous	ɣār	غار
divorce	ṭalāq (m)	طلاق
to divorce (vi)	ṭallaq	طلّق
to quarrel (vi)	taʃāʒar	تشاجر
to be reconciled (after an argument)	taṣālaḥ	تصالح
together (adv)	ma'an	معًا
sex	ʒins (m)	جنس
happiness	sa'āda (f)	سعادة
happy (adj)	sa'īd	سعيد
misfortune (accident)	muṣība (m)	مصيبة
unhappy (adj)	ta'is	تعس

55

Character. Feelings. Emotions

58. Feelings. Emotions

feeling (emotion)	ʃuʿūr (m)	شعور
feelings	maʃāʿir (pl)	مشاعر
to feel (vt)	ʃaʿar	شعر
hunger	ʒawʿ (m)	جوع
to be hungry	arād an yaʾkul	أراد أن يأكل
thirst	ʿataʃ (m)	عطش
to be thirsty	arād an yaʃrab	أراد أن يشرب
sleepiness	nuʿās (m)	نعاس
to feel sleepy	arād an yanām	أراد أن ينام
tiredness	taʿab (m)	تعب
tired (adj)	taʿbān	تعبان
to get tired	taʿib	تعب
mood (humour)	ḥāla nafsiyya, mazāʒ (m)	حالة نفسيّة، مزاج
boredom	malal (m)	ملل
to be bored	ʃaʿar bil malal	شعر بالملل
seclusion	ʿuzla (f)	عزلة
to seclude oneself	inzawa	إنزوى
to worry (make anxious)	aqlaq	أقلق
to be worried	qalaq	قلق
worrying (n)	qalaq (m)	قلق
anxiety	qalaq (m)	قلق
preoccupied (adj)	maʃɣūl al bāl	مشغول البال
to be nervous	qalaq	قلق
to panic (vi)	uṣīb bið ðaʿr	أصيب بالذعر
hope	amal (m)	أمل
to hope (vi, vt)	tamanna	تمنّى
certainty	yaqīn (m)	يقين
certain, sure (adj)	mutaʾakkid	متأكّد
uncertainty	ʿadam at taʾakkud (m)	عدم التأكّد
uncertain (adj)	ɣayr mutaʾakkid	غير متأكّد
drunk (adj)	sakrān	سكران
sober (adj)	ṣāḥi	صاح
weak (adj)	ḍaʿīf	ضعيف
happy (adj)	saʿīd	سعيد
to scare (vt)	arhab	أرهب
fury (madness)	ɣaḍab ʃadīd (m)	غضب شديد
rage (fury)	ɣaḍab (m)	غضب
depression	iktiʾāb (m)	إكتئاب
discomfort (unease)	ʿadam irtiyāḥ (m)	عدم إرتياح

comfort	rāḥa (f)	راحة
to regret (be sorry)	nadim	ندم
regret	nadam (m)	ندم
bad luck	sū' al ḥaẓẓ (m)	سوء الحظ
sadness	ḥuzn (f)	حزن
shame (remorse)	χaӡal (m)	خجل
gladness	faraḥ (m)	فرح
enthusiasm, zeal	ḥamās (m)	حماس
enthusiast	mutaḥammis (m)	متحمّس
to show enthusiasm	taḥammas	تحمّس

59. Character. Personality

character	ṭab' (m)	طبع
character flaw	'ayb (m)	عيب
mind, reason	'aql (m)	عقل
conscience	ḍamīr (m)	ضمير
habit (custom)	'āda (f)	عادة
ability (talent)	qudra (f)	قدرة
can (e.g. ~ swim)	'araf	عرف
patient (adj)	ṣābir	صابر
impatient (adj)	qalīl aṣ ṣabr	قليل الصبر
curious (inquisitive)	fuḍūliy	فضوليّ
curiosity	fuḍūl (m)	فضول
modesty	tawāḍu' (m)	تواضع
modest (adj)	mutawāḍi'	متواضع
immodest (adj)	ɣayr mutawāḍi'	غير متواضع
laziness	kasal (m)	كسل
lazy (adj)	kaslān	كسلان
lazy person (masc.)	kaslān (m)	كسلان
cunning (n)	makr (m)	مكر
cunning (as adj)	mākir	ماكر
distrust	'adam aθ θiqa (m)	عدم الثقة
distrustful (adj)	ʃakūk	شكوك
generosity	karam (m)	كرم
generous (adj)	karīm	كريم
talented (adj)	mawhūb	موهوب
talent	mawhiba (f)	موهبة
courageous (adj)	ʃuӡā'	شجاع
courage	ʃaӡā'a (f)	شجاعة
honest (adj)	amīn	أمين
honesty	amāna (f)	أمانة
careful (cautious)	ḥāðir	حاذر
brave (courageous)	ʃuӡā'	شجاع
serious (adj)	ӡādd	جادّ

strict (severe, stern)	ṣārim	صارم
decisive (adj)	ḥazīm	حزيم
indecisive (adj)	mutaraddid	متردّد
shy, timid (adj)	χaʒūl	خجول
shyness, timidity	χaʒal (m)	خجل
confidence (trust)	θiqa (f)	ثقة
to believe (trust)	waθiq	وثق
trusting (credulous)	sarīʿ at taṣdīq	سريع التصديق
sincerely (adv)	bi ṣarāḥa	بصراحة
sincere (adj)	muχliṣ	مخلص
sincerity	iχlāṣ (m)	إخلاص
open (person)	ṣarīḥ	صريح
calm (adj)	hādi'	هادئ
frank (sincere)	ṣarīḥ	صريح
naïve (adj)	sāðiʒ	ساذج
absent-minded (adj)	ʃārid al fikr	شارد الفكر
funny (odd)	muḍhik	مضحك
greed, stinginess	buχl (m)	بخل
greedy, stingy (adj)	baχīl	بخيل
stingy (adj)	baχīl	بخيل
evil (adj)	ʃarīr	شرير
stubborn (adj)	'anīd	عنيد
unpleasant (adj)	karīh	كريه
selfish person (masc.)	anāniy (m)	أنانيّ
selfish (adj)	anāniy	أنانيّ
coward	ʒabān (m)	جبان
cowardly (adj)	ʒabān	جبان

60. Sleep. Dreams

to sleep (vi)	nām	نام
sleep, sleeping	nawm (m)	نوم
dream	ḥulm (m)	حلم
to dream (in sleep)	ḥalam	حلم
sleepy (adj)	naʿsān	نعسان
bed	sarīr (m)	سرير
mattress	martaba (f)	مرتبة
blanket (eiderdown)	baṭṭāniyya (f)	بطّانيّة
pillow	wisāda (f)	وسادة
sheet	milāya (f)	ملاية
insomnia	araq (m)	أرق
sleepless (adj)	ariq	أرق
sleeping pill	munawwim (m)	منوّم
to take a sleeping pill	tanāwal munawwim	تناول منوّمًا
to feel sleepy	arād an yanām	أراد أن ينام
to yawn (vi)	taθā'ab	تثاءب

to go to bed	ðahab ila n nawm	ذهب إلى النوم
to make up the bed	a'add as sarīr	أعدّ السرير
to fall asleep	nām	نام

nightmare	kābūs (m)	كابوس
snore, snoring	ʃaxīr (m)	شخير
to snore (vi)	ʃaxxar	شخّر

alarm clock	munabbih (m)	منبّه
to wake (vt)	ayqaẓ	أيقظ
to wake up	istayqaẓ	إستيقظ
to get up (vi)	qām	قام
to have a wash	ɣasal waʒhah	غسل وجهه

61. Humour. Laughter. Gladness

humour (wit, fun)	fukāha (f)	فكاهة
sense of humour	ḥiss (m)	حس
to enjoy oneself	istamta'	إستمتع
cheerful (merry)	farḥān	فرحان
merriment (gaiety)	faraḥ (m)	فرح

smile	ibtisāma (f)	إبتسامة
to smile (vi)	ibtasam	إبتسم
to start laughing	ḍaḥik	ضحك
to laugh (vi)	ḍaḥik	ضحك
laugh, laughter	ḍaḥka (f)	ضحكة

anecdote	ḥikāya muḍḥika (f)	حكاية مضحكة
funny (anecdote, etc.)	muḍḥik	مضحك
funny (odd)	muḍḥik	مضحك

to joke (vi)	mazaḥ	مزح
joke (verbal)	nukta (f)	نكتة
joy (emotion)	sa'āda (f)	سعادة
to rejoice (vi)	mariḥ	مرح
joyful (adj)	sa'īd	سعيد

62. Discussion, conversation. Part 1

communication	tawāṣul (m)	تواصل
to communicate	tawāṣal	تواصل

conversation	muḥādaθa (f)	محادثة
dialogue	ḥiwār (m)	حوار
discussion (discourse)	munāqaʃa (f)	مناقشة
dispute (debate)	munāẓara (f)	مناظرة
to dispute, to debate	xālaf	خالف

interlocutor	muḥāwir (m)	محاور
topic (theme)	mawḍū' (m)	موضوع
point of view	wiʒhat naẓar (f)	وجهة نظر

opinion (point of view)	ra'y (m)	رأي
speech (talk)	xiṭāb (m)	خطاب
discussion (of a report, etc.)	munāqaʃa (f)	مناقشة
to discuss (vt)	nāqaʃ	ناقش
talk (conversation)	ḥadīs (m)	حديث
to talk (to chat)	taḥādaθ	تحادث
meeting (encounter)	liqā' (m)	لقاء
to meet (vi, vt)	qābal	قابل
proverb	maθal (m)	مثل
saying	qawl ma'θūr (m)	قول مأثور
riddle (poser)	luɣz (m)	لغز
to pose a riddle	alqa luɣz	ألقى لغزًا
password	kalimat al murūr (f)	كلمة مرور
secret	sirr (m)	سرّ
oath (vow)	qasam (m)	قسم
to swear (an oath)	aqsam	أقسم
promise	wa'd (m)	وعد
to promise (vt)	wa'ad	وعد
advice (counsel)	naṣīḥa (f)	نصيحة
to advise (vt)	naṣaḥ	نصح
to follow one's advice	intaṣaḥ	إنتصح
to listen to ... (obey)	aṭā'	أطاع
news	xabar (m)	خبر
sensation (news)	daʒʒa (f)	ضجّة
information (report)	ma'lūmāt (pl)	معلومات
conclusion (decision)	istintāʒ (f)	إستنتاج
voice	ṣawt (m)	صوت
compliment	madḥ (m)	مدح
kind (nice)	laṭīf	لطيف
word	kalima (f)	كلمة
phrase	'ibāra (f)	عبارة
answer	ʒawāb (m)	جواب
truth	ḥaqīqa (f)	حقيقة
lie	kiðb (m)	كذب
thought	fikra (f)	فكرة
idea (inspiration)	fikra (f)	فكرة
fantasy	xayāl (m)	خيال

63. Discussion, conversation. Part 2

respected (adj)	muḥtaram	محترم
to respect (vt)	iḥtaram	إحترم
respect	iḥtirām (m)	إحترام
Dear ... (letter)	'azīzi ...	عزيزي...
to introduce (sb to sb)	'arraf	عرّف
to make acquaintance	ta'arraf	تعرّف

intention	niyya (f)	نيّة
to intend (have in mind)	nawa	نوى
wish	tamanni (m)	تمنٍ
to wish (~ good luck)	tamanna	تمنّى
surprise (astonishment)	ʿaʒab (m)	عجب
to surprise (amaze)	adhaʃ	أدهش
to be surprised	indahaʃ	إندهش
to give (vt)	aʿta	أعطى
to take (get hold of)	aχað	أخذ
to give back	radd	ردّ
to return (give back)	arʒaʿ	أرجع
to apologize (vi)	iʿtaðar	إعتذر
apology	iʿtiðār (m)	إعتذار
to forgive (vt)	ʿafa	عفا
to talk (speak)	taḥaddaθ	تحدّث
to listen (vi)	istamaʿ	إستمع
to hear out	samiʿ	سمع
to understand (vt)	fahim	فهم
to show (to display)	ʿaraḍ	عرض
to look at ...	naẓar	نظر
to call (yell for sb)	nāda	نادى
to distract (disturb)	ʃaɣal	شغل
to disturb (vt)	azʿaʒ	أزعج
to pass (to hand sth)	sallam	سلم
demand (request)	ṭalab (m)	طلب
to request (ask)	ṭalab	طلب
demand (firm request)	maṭlab (m)	مطلب
to demand (request firmly)	ṭālib	طالب
to tease (call names)	ɣāẓ	غاظ
to mock (make fun of)	saχar	سخر
mockery, derision	suχriyya (f)	سخرية
nickname	laqab (m)	لقب
insinuation	talmīḥ (m)	تلميح
to insinuate (imply)	lamaḥ	لمح
to mean (vt)	qaṣad	قصد
description	waṣf (m)	وصف
to describe (vt)	waṣaf	وصف
praise (compliments)	madḥ (m)	مدح
to praise (vt)	madaḥ	مدح
disappointment	χaybat amal (f)	خيبة أمل
to disappoint (vt)	χayyab	خيّب
to be disappointed	χābat ʾāmāluh	خابت آماله
supposition	iftirāḍ (m)	إفتراض
to suppose (assume)	iftaraḍ	إفترض
warning (caution)	taḥðīr (m)	تحذير
to warn (vt)	ḥaððar	حذّر

64. Discussion, conversation. Part 3

to talk into (convince)	aqna'	أقنع
to calm down (vt)	ṭam'an	طمأن
silence (~ is golden)	sukūt (m)	سكوت
to be silent (not speaking)	sakat	سكت
to whisper (vi, vt)	hamas	همس
whisper	hamsa (f)	همسة
frankly, sincerely (adv)	bi ṣarāḥa	بصراحة
in my opinion ...	fi ra'yi ...	في رأيي...
detail (of the story)	tafṣīl (m)	تفصيل
detailed (adj)	mufaṣṣal	مفصّل
in detail (adv)	bit tafāṣīl	بالتفاصيل
hint, clue	iʃāra (f), talmīḥ (m)	إشارة, تلميح
to give a hint	a'ṭa talmīḥ	أعطى تلميحاً
look (glance)	naẓra (f)	نظرة
to have a look	alqa naẓra	ألقى نظرة
fixed (look)	θābit	ثابت
to blink (vi)	ramaʃ	رمش
to wink (vi)	ɣamaz	غمز
to nod (in assent)	hazz ra'sah	هزّ رأسه
sigh	tanahhuda (f)	تنهّدة
to sigh (vi)	tanahhad	تنهّد
to shudder (vi)	irta'aʃ	إرتعش
gesture	iʃārat yad (f)	إشارة يد
to touch (one's arm, etc.)	lamas	لمس
to seize (e.g., ~ by the arm)	amsak	أمسك
to tap (on the shoulder)	ṣafaq	صفق
Look out!	ҳuð bālak!	خذ بالك!
Really?	wallahi?	والله؟
Are you sure?	hal anta muta'akkid?	هل أنت متأكّد؟
Good luck!	bit tawfīq!	بالتوفيق!
I see!	wāḍiḥ!	واضح!
What a pity!	ya lil asaf!	يا للأسف!

65. Agreement. Refusal

consent	muwāfaqa (f)	موافقة
to consent (vi)	wāfa'	وافق
approval	istiḥsān (m)	إستحسان
to approve (vt)	istiḥsan	إستحسن
refusal	rafḍ (m)	رفض
to refuse (vi, vt)	rafaḍ	رفض
Great!	'aẓīm!	عظيم!
All right!	ittafaqna!	إتّفقنا!

Okay! (I agree)	ittafaqna!	إتّفقنا!
forbidden (adj)	mamnūʿ	ممنوع
it's forbidden	mamnūʿ	ممنوع
it's impossible	mustaḥīl	مستحيل
incorrect (adj)	ɣalaṭ	غلط
to reject (~ a demand)	rafaḍ	رفض
to support (cause, idea)	ayyad	أيّد
to accept (~ an apology)	qabil	قبل
to confirm (vt)	aθbat	أثبت
confirmation	iθbāt (m)	إثبات
permission	samāḥ (m)	سماح
to permit (vt)	samaḥ	سمح
decision	qarār (m)	قرار
to say nothing (hold one's tongue)	ṣamat	صمت
condition (term)	ʃarṭ (m)	شرط
excuse (pretext)	ʿuðr (m)	عذر
praise (compliments)	madḥ (m)	مدح
to praise (vt)	madaḥ	مدح

66. Success. Good luck. Failure

success	naʒāḥ (m)	نجاح
successfully (adv)	bi naʒāḥ	بنجاح
successful (adj)	nāʒiḥ	ناجح
luck (good luck)	ḥazz (m)	حظّ
Good luck!	bit tawfīq!	بالتوفيق!
lucky (e.g. ~ day)	murawaffiq	متوفّق
lucky (fortunate)	maḥzūz	محظوظ
failure	faʃl (m)	فشل
misfortune	sūʾ al ḥazz (m)	سوء الحظّ
bad luck	sūʾ al ḥazz (m)	سوء الحظّ
unsuccessful (adj)	fāʃil	فاشل
catastrophe	kāriθa (f)	كارثة
pride	faxr (m)	فخر
proud (adj)	faxūr	فخور
to be proud	iftaxar	إفتخر
winner	fāʾiz (m)	فائز
to win (vi)	fāz	فاز
to lose (not win)	xasir	خسر
try	muḥāwala (f)	محاولة
to try (vi)	ḥāwal	حاول
chance (opportunity)	furṣa (f)	فرصة

67. Quarrels. Negative emotions

shout (scream)	ṣarχa (f)	صرخة
to shout (vi)	ṣaraχ	صرخ
to start to cry out	ṣaraχ	صرخ
quarrel	muʃāʒara (f)	مشاجرة
to quarrel (vi)	taʃāʒar	تشاجر
fight (squabble)	muʃāʒara (f)	مشاجرة
to make a scene	taʃāʒar	تشاجر
conflict	χilāf (m)	خلاف
misunderstanding	sū'at tafāhum (m)	سوء التفاهم
insult	ihāna (f)	إهانة
to insult (vt)	ahān	أهان
insulted (adj)	muhān	مهان
resentment	ḍaym (m)	ضيم
to offend (vt)	asā'	أساء
to take offence	istā'	إستاء
indignation	istiyā' (m)	إستياء
to be indignant	istā'	إستاء
complaint	ʃakwa (f)	شكوى
to complain (vi, vt)	ʃaka	شكا
apology	i'tiðār (m)	إعتذار
to apologize (vi)	i'taðar	إعتذر
to beg pardon	i'taðar	إعتذر
criticism	naqd (m)	نقد
to criticize (vt)	naqad	نقد
accusation (charge)	ittihām (m)	إتهام
to accuse (vt)	ittaham	إتهم
revenge	intiqām (m)	إنتقام
to avenge (get revenge)	intaqam	إنتقم
to pay back	radd	ردّ
disdain	ihtiqār (m)	إحتقار
to despise (vt)	ihtaqar	إحتقر
hatred, hate	karāha (f)	كراهة
to hate (vt)	karah	كره
nervous (adj)	'aṣabiy	عصبيّ
to be nervous	qalaq	قلق
angry (mad)	za'lān	زعلان
to make angry	az'al	أزعل
humiliation	iðlāl (m)	إذلال
to humiliate (vt)	ðallal	ذلل
to humiliate oneself	taðallal	تذلل
shock	ṣadma (f)	صدمة
to shock (vt)	ṣadam	صدم
trouble (e.g. serious ~)	muʃkila (f)	مشكلة

unpleasant (adj)	karīh	كريه
fear (dread)	χawf (m)	خوف
terrible (storm, heat)	ʃadīd	شديد
scary (e.g. ~ story)	muχīf	مخيف
horror	ruʿb (m)	رعب
awful (crime, news)	murʿib	مرعب
to begin to tremble	irtaʿaʃ	إرتعش
to cry (weep)	baka	بكى
to start crying	baka	بكى
tear	damaʿa (f)	دمعة
fault	γalṭa (f)	غلطة
guilt (feeling)	ðamb (m)	ذنب
dishonor (disgrace)	ʿār (m)	عار
protest	iḥtiʒāʒ (m)	إحتجاج
stress	tawattur (m)	توتّر
to disturb (vt)	azʿaʒ	أزعج
to be furious	γaḍib	غضب
angry (adj)	γaḍbān	غضبان
to end (~ a relationship)	anha	أنهى
to swear (at sb)	ʃātam	شاتم
to scare (become afraid)	χāf	خاف
to hit (strike with hand)	ḍarab	ضرب
to fight (street fight, etc.)	taʿārak	تعارك
to settle (a conflict)	sawwa	سوّى
discontented (adj)	γayr rāḍi	غير راض
furious (adj)	ʿanīf	عنيف
It's not good!	laysa haða amr ʒayyid!	ليس هذا أمرًا جيّدًا!
It's bad!	haða amr sayyiʾ!	هذا أمر سيّء!

Medicine

68. Diseases

illness	maraḍ (m)	مرض
to be ill	maraḍ	مرض
health	ṣiḥḥa (f)	صحّة
runny nose (coryza)	zukām (m)	زكام
tonsillitis	iltihāb al lawzatayn (m)	التهاب اللوزتين
cold (illness)	bard (m)	برد
to catch a cold	aṣābahu al bard	أصابه البرد
bronchitis	iltihāb al qaṣabāt (m)	إلتهاب القصبات
pneumonia	iltihāb ar ri'atayn (m)	إلتهاب الرئتين
flu, influenza	inflūnza (f)	إنفلونزا
shortsighted (adj)	qaṣīr an naẓar	قصير النظر
longsighted (adj)	ba'īd an naẓar	بعيد النظر
strabismus (crossed eyes)	ḥawal (m)	حول
squint-eyed (adj)	aḥwal	أحول
cataract	katarakt (f)	كاتاراكت
glaucoma	glawkūma (f)	جلوكوما
stroke	sakta (f)	سكتة
heart attack	iḥtiʃā' (m)	إحتشاء
myocardial infarction	nawba qalbiya (f)	نوبة قلبية
paralysis	ʃalal (m)	شلل
to paralyse (vt)	ʃall	شلّ
allergy	ḥassāsiyya (f)	حساسيّة
asthma	rabw (m)	ربو
diabetes	ad dā' as sukkariy (m)	الداء السكريّ
toothache	alam al asnān (m)	ألم الأسنان
caries	naχar al asnān (m)	نخر الأسنان
diarrhoea	ishāl (m)	إسهال
constipation	imsāk (m)	إمساك
stomach upset	'usr al haḍm (m)	عسر الهضم
food poisoning	tasammum (m)	تسمّم
to get food poisoning	tasammam	تسمّم
arthritis	iltihāb al mafāṣil (m)	إلتهاب المفاصل
rickets	kusāḥ al atfāl (m)	كساح الأطفال
rheumatism	riumatizm (m)	روماتزم
atherosclerosis	taṣṣallub aʃ ʃarayīn (m)	تصلّب الشرايين
gastritis	iltihāb al ma'ida (m)	إلتهاب المعدة
appendicitis	iltihāb az zā'ida ad dūdiyya (m)	إلتهاب الزائدة الدوديّة

| cholecystitis | iltihāb al marāra (m) | إلتهاب المرارة |
| ulcer | qurḥa (f) | قرحة |

measles	maraḍ al ḥaṣba (m)	مرض الحصبة
rubella (German measles)	ḥaṣba almāniyya (f)	حصبة ألمانية
jaundice	yaraqān (m)	يرقان
hepatitis	iltihāb al kabd al vayrūsiyَ (m)	إلتهاب الكبد الفيروسيّ

schizophrenia	ʃizufrīniya (f)	شيزوفرينيا
rabies (hydrophobia)	dāʼ al kalb (m)	داء الكلب
neurosis	ʻiṣāb (m)	عصاب
concussion	irtiʒāʒ al muxx (m)	إرتجاج المخ

cancer	saraṭān (m)	سرطان
sclerosis	taṣṣallub (m)	تصلّب
multiple sclerosis	taṣṣallub mutaʻaddid (m)	تصلّب متعدد

alcoholism	idmān al xamr (m)	إدمان الخمر
alcoholic (n)	mudmin al xamr (m)	مدمن الخمر
syphilis	sifilis az zuhariy (m)	سفلس الزهري
AIDS	al aydz (m)	الايدز

tumour	waram (m)	ورم
malignant (adj)	xabīθ	خبيث
benign (adj)	ḥamīd (m)	حميد

fever	ḥumma (f)	حمّى
malaria	malāriya (f)	ملاريا
gangrene	ɣanɣrīna (f)	غنغرينا
seasickness	duwār al baḥr (m)	دوار البحر
epilepsy	maraḍ aṣ ṣarʻ (m)	مرض الصرع

epidemic	wabāʼ (m)	وباء
typhus	tīfus (m)	تيفوس
tuberculosis	maraḍ as sull (m)	مرض السلّ
cholera	kulīra (f)	كوليرا
plague (bubonic ~)	ṭāʻūn (m)	طاعون

69. Symptoms. Treatments. Part 1

symptom	ʻaraḍ (m)	عرض
temperature	ḥarāra (f)	حرارة
high temperature (fever)	ḥumma (f)	حمّى
pulse (heartbeat)	nabḍ (m)	نبض

dizziness (vertigo)	dawxa (f)	دوخة
hot (adj)	ḥārr	حارّ
shivering	nafaḍān (m)	نفضان
pale (e.g. ~ face)	aṣfar	أصفر

cough	suʻāl (m)	سعال
to cough (vi)	saʻal	سعل
to sneeze (vi)	ʻaṭas	عطس
faint	iɣmāʼ (m)	إغماء

to faint (vi)	ɣumiya ʿalayh	غمي عليه
bruise (hématome)	kadma (f)	كدمة
bump (lump)	tawarrum (m)	تورّم
to bang (bump)	iṣṭadam	إصطدم
contusion (bruise)	raḍḍ (m)	رضّ
to get a bruise	taraḍḍaḍ	ترضضّ

to limp (vi)	ʿaraʒ	عرج
dislocation	xalʿ (m)	خلع
to dislocate (vt)	xalaʿ	خلع
fracture	kasr (m)	كسر
to have a fracture	inkasar	إنكسر

cut (e.g. paper ~)	ʒurḥ (m)	جرح
to cut oneself	ʒaraḥ nafsah	جرح نفسه
bleeding	nazf (m)	نزف

burn (injury)	ḥarq (m)	حرق
to get burned	taʃayyat	تشيطً

to prick (vt)	waxaz	وخز
to prick oneself	waxaz nafsah	وخز نفسه
to injure (vt)	aṣāb	أصاب
injury	iṣāba (f)	إصابة
wound	ʒurḥ (m)	جرح
trauma	ṣadma (f)	صدمة

to be delirious	haða	هذى
to stutter (vi)	talaʿsam	تلعثم
sunstroke	ḍarbat ʃams (f)	ضربة شمس

70. Symptoms. Treatments. Part 2

pain, ache	alam (m)	ألمَ
splinter (in foot, etc.)	ʃaẓiyya (f)	شظيّة

sweat (perspiration)	ʿirq (m)	عرق
to sweat (perspire)	ʿariq	عرق
vomiting	taqayyuʿ (m)	تقيؤ
convulsions	taʃannuʒāt (pl)	تشنّجات

pregnant (adj)	ḥāmil	حامل
to be born	wulid	وُلد
delivery, labour	wilāda (f)	ولادة
to deliver (~ a baby)	walad	ولد
abortion	iʒhāḍ (m)	إجهاض

breathing, respiration	tanaffus (m)	تنفّس
in-breath (inhalation)	istinʃāq (m)	إستنشاق
out-breath (exhalation)	zafīr (m)	زفير
to exhale (breathe out)	zafar	زفر
to inhale (vi)	istanʃaq	إستنشق
disabled person	muʿāq (m)	معاق
cripple	muqʿad (m)	مقعد

drug addict	mudmin muχaddirāt (m)	مدمن مخدّرات
deaf (adj)	aṭraʃ	أطرش
mute (adj)	aχras	أخرس
deaf mute (adj)	aṭraʃ aχras	أطرش أخرس
mad, insane (adj)	maʒnūn	مجنون
madman (demented person)	maʒnūn (m)	مجنون
madwoman	maʒnūna (f)	مجنونة
to go insane	ʒunn	جُنّ
gene	ʒīn (m)	جين
immunity	manā'a (f)	مناعة
hereditary (adj)	wirāθiy	وراثيّ
congenital (adj)	χilqiy munð al wilāda	خلقيّ منذ الولادة
virus	virūs (m)	فيروس
microbe	mikrūb (m)	ميكروب
bacterium	ʒurθūma (f)	جرثومة
infection	'adwa (f)	عدوى

71. Symptoms. Treatments. Part 3

hospital	mustaʃfa (m)	مستشفى
patient	marīḍ (m)	مريض
diagnosis	taʃχīṣ (m)	تشخيص
cure	'ilāʒ (m)	علاج
medical treatment	'ilāʒ (m)	علاج
to get treatment	ta'ālaʒ	تعالج
to treat (~ a patient)	'ālaʒ	عالَج
to nurse (look after)	marraḍ	مرّض
care (nursing ~)	'ināya (f)	عناية
operation, surgery	'amaliyya ʒarahiyya (f)	عمليّة جرحيّة
to bandage (head, limb)	ḍammad	ضمّد
bandaging	taḍmīd (m)	تضميد
vaccination	talqīḥ (m)	تلقيح
to vaccinate (vt)	laqqah	لقّح
injection	ḥuqna (f)	حقنة
to give an injection	ḥaqan ibra	حقن إبرة
attack	nawba (f)	نوبة
amputation	batr (m)	بتر
to amputate (vt)	batar	بتر
coma	γaybūba (f)	غيبوبة
to be in a coma	kān fi ḥālat γaybūba	كان في حالة غيبوبة
intensive care	al 'ināya al murakkaza (f)	العناية المركّزة
to recover (~ from flu)	ʃufiy	شفي
condition (patient's ~)	ḥāla (f)	حالة
consciousness	wa'y (m)	وعي
memory (faculty)	ðākira (f)	ذاكرة

to pull out (tooth)	xala'	خلع
filling	ḥaʃw (m)	حشو
to fill (a tooth)	ḥaʃa	حشا

| hypnosis | at tanwīm al maɣnaṭīsiy (m) | التنويم المغناطيسيّ |
| to hypnotize (vt) | nawwam | نوّم |

72. Doctors

doctor	ṭabīb (m)	طبيب
nurse	mumarriḍa (f)	ممرّضة
personal doctor	duktūr ʃaxṣiy (m)	دكتور شخصيّ

dentist	ṭabīb al asnān (m)	طبيب الأسنان
optician	ṭabīb al 'uyūn (m)	طبيب العيون
general practitioner	ṭabīb bāṭiniy (m)	طبيب باطنيّ
surgeon	ʒarrāḥ (m)	جرّاح

psychiatrist	ṭabīb nafsiy (m)	طبيب نفسيّ
paediatrician	ṭabīb al aṭfāl (m)	طبيب الأطفال
psychologist	sikulūʒiy (m)	سيكولوجيّ
gynaecologist	ṭabīb an nisā' (m)	طبيب النساء
cardiologist	ṭabīb al qalb (m)	طبيب القلب

73. Medicine. Drugs. Accessories

medicine, drug	dawā' (m)	دواء
remedy	'ilāʒ (m)	علاج
to prescribe (vt)	waṣaf	وصف
prescription	waṣfa (f)	وصفة

tablet, pill	qurṣ (m)	قرص
ointment	marham (m)	مرهم
ampoule	ambūla (f)	أمبولة
mixture, solution	dawā' ʃarāb (m)	دواء شراب
syrup	ʃarāb (m)	شراب
capsule	ḥabba (f)	حبّة
powder	ðarūr (m)	ذرور

gauze bandage	ḍammāda (f)	ضمادة
cotton wool	quṭn (m)	قطن
iodine	yūd (m)	يود

plaster	blāstir (m)	بلاستر
eyedropper	māṣṣat al bastara (f)	ماصّة البسترة
thermometer	tirmūmitr (m)	ترمومتر
syringe	miḥqana (f)	محقنة

wheelchair	kursiy mutaḥarrik (m)	كرسي متحرّك
crutches	'ukkāzān (du)	عكّازان
painkiller	musakkin (m)	مسكّن
laxative	mulayyin (m)	مليّن

spirits (ethanol)	iθanūl (m)	إيثانول
medicinal herbs	a'ʃāb ṭibbiyya (pl)	أعشاب طبية
herbal (~ tea)	'uʃbiy	عشبي

74. Smoking. Tobacco products

tobacco	tabɣ (m)	تبغ
cigarette	sīʒāra (f)	سيجارة
cigar	sīʒār (m)	سيجار
pipe	ɣalyūn (m)	غليون
packet (of cigarettes)	'ulba (f)	علبة

matches	kibrīt (m)	كبريت
matchbox	'ulbat kibrīt (f)	علبة كبريت
lighter	wallā'a (f)	ولّاعة
ashtray	ṭaqṭūqa (f)	طقطوقة
cigarette case	'ulbat saʒā'ir (f)	علبة سجائر

| cigarette holder | ḥamilat siʒāra (f) | حاملة سيجارة |
| filter (cigarette tip) | filtir (m) | فلتر |

to smoke (vi, vt)	daxxan	دخّن
to light a cigarette	aʃ'al siʒāra	أشعل سيجارة
smoking	tadxīn (m)	تدخين
smoker	mudaxxin (m)	مدخّن

cigarette end	'uqb siʒāra (m)	عقب سيجارة
smoke, fumes	duxān (m)	دخان
ash	ramād (m)	رماد

HUMAN HABITAT

City

city, town	madīna (f)	مدينة
capital city	ʿāṣima (f)	عاصمة
village	qarya (f)	قرية
city map	xarīṭat al madīna (f)	خريطة المدينة
city centre	markaz al madīna (m)	مركز المدينة
suburb	ḍāḥiya (f)	ضاحية
suburban (adj)	aḍ ḍawāḥi	الضواحي
outskirts	aṭrāf al madīna (pl)	أطراف المدينة
environs (suburbs)	ḍawāḥi al madīna (pl)	ضواحي المدينة
city block	ḥayy (m)	حي
residential block (area)	ḥayy sakaniy (m)	حي سكني
traffic	ḥarakat al murūr (f)	حركة المرور
traffic lights	iʃārāt al murūr (pl)	إشارات المرور
public transport	wasāʾil an naql (pl)	وسائل النقل
crossroads	taqāṭuʿ (m)	تقاطع
zebra crossing	maʿbar al muʃāt (m)	معبر المشاة
pedestrian subway	nafaq muʃāt (m)	نفق مشاة
to cross (~ the street)	ʿabar	عبر
pedestrian	māʃi (m)	ماش
pavement	raṣīf (m)	رصيف
bridge	ʒisr (m)	جسر
embankment (river walk)	kurnīʃ (m)	كورنيش
fountain	nāfūra (f)	نافورة
allée (garden walkway)	mamʃa (m)	ممشى
park	ḥadīqa (f)	حديقة
boulevard	bulvār (m)	بولفار
square	maydān (m)	ميدان
avenue (wide street)	ʃāriʿ (m)	شارع
street	ʃāriʿ (m)	شارع
side street	zuqāq (m)	زقاق
dead end	ṭarīq masdūd (m)	طريق مسدود
house	bayt (m)	بيت
building	mabna (m)	مبنى
skyscraper	nāṭiḥat saḥāb (f)	ناطحة سحاب
facade	wāʒiha (f)	واجهة
roof	saqf (m)	سقف

window	ʃubbāk (m)	شبّاك
arch	qaws (m)	قوس
column	ʿamūd (m)	عمود
corner	zāwiya (f)	زاوية

shop window	vatrīna (f)	فترينة
signboard (store sign, etc.)	lāfita (f)	لافتة
poster (e.g., playbill)	mulṣaq (m)	ملصق
advertising poster	mulṣaq iʿlāniy (m)	ملصق إعلاني
hoarding	lawḥat iʿlānāt (f)	لوحة إعلانات

rubbish	zubāla (f)	زبالة
rubbish bin	ṣundūq zubāla (m)	صندوق زبالة
to litter (vi)	rama zubāla	رمى زبالة
rubbish dump	mazbala (f)	مزبلة

telephone box	kuʃk tilifūn (m)	كشك تليفون
lamppost	ʿamūd al miṣbāḥ (m)	عمود المصباح
bench (park ~)	dikka (f), kursiy (m)	دكّة, كرسيّ

police officer	ʃurṭiy (m)	شرطيّ
police	ʃurṭa (f)	شرطة
beggar	ʃaḥḥāð (m)	شحّاذ
homeless (n)	mutaʃarrid (m)	متشرّد

76. Urban institutions

shop	maḥall (m)	محلّ
chemist, pharmacy	ṣaydaliyya (f)	صيدليّة
optician (spectacles shop)	al adawāt al baṣariyya (pl)	الأدوات البصريّة
shopping centre	markaz tiʒāriy (m)	مركز تجاريّ
supermarket	subirmarkit (m)	سوبرماركت

bakery	maxbaz (m)	مخبز
baker	xabbāz (m)	خبّاز
cake shop	dukkān ḥalawāniy (m)	دكّان حلوانيّ
grocery shop	baqqāla (f)	بقّالة
butcher shop	malḥama (f)	ملحمة

| greengrocer | dukkān xuḍār (m) | دكّان خضار |
| market | sūq (f) | سوق |

coffee bar	kafé (m), maqha (m)	كافيه, مقهى
restaurant	matʿam (m)	مطعم
pub, bar	ḥāna (f)	حانة
pizzeria	matʿam pizza (m)	مطعم بيتزا

hairdresser	ṣālūn ḥilāqa (m)	صالون حلاقة
post office	maktab al barīd (m)	مكتب البريد
dry cleaners	tanẓīf ʒāff (m)	تنظيف جافّ
photo studio	istūdiyu taṣwīr (m)	إستوديو تصوير

| shoe shop | maḥall aḥðiya (m) | محلّ أحذية |
| bookshop | maḥall kutub (m) | محلّ كتب |

sports shop	maḥall riyāḍiy (m)	محلّ رياضيّ
clothes repair shop	maḥall ҳiyāṭat malābis (m)	محلّ خياطة ملابس
formal wear hire	maḥall taʾȝīr malābis rasmiyya (m)	محلّ تأجير ملابس رسمية
video rental shop	maḥal taʾȝīr vidiyu (m)	محلّ تأجير فيديو

circus	sirk (m)	سيرك
zoo	ḥadīqat al ḥayawān (f)	حديقة حيوان
cinema	sinima (f)	سينما
museum	matḥaf (m)	متحف
library	maktaba (f)	مكتبة

theatre	masraḥ (m)	مسرح
opera (opera house)	ubra (f)	أوبرا
nightclub	malha layliy (m)	ملهى ليليّ
casino	kazinu (m)	كازينو

mosque	masȝid (m)	مسجد
synagogue	kanīs maʿbad yahūdiy (m)	كنيس معبد يهوديّ
cathedral	katidrāʾiyya (f)	كاتدرائيّة
temple	maʿbad (m)	معبد
church	kanīsa (f)	كنيسة

college	kulliyya (m)	كلّيّة
university	ȝāmiʿa (f)	جامعة
school	madrasa (f)	مدرسة

prefecture	muqāṭaʿa (f)	مقاطعة
town hall	baladiyya (f)	بلديّة
hotel	funduq (m)	فندق
bank	bank (m)	بنك

embassy	safāra (f)	سفارة
travel agency	ʃarikat siyāḥa (f)	شركة سياحة
information office	maktab al istiʿlāmāt (m)	مكتب الإستعلامات
currency exchange	ṣarrāfa (f)	صرّافة

underground, tube	mitru (m)	مترو
hospital	mustaʃfa (m)	مستشفى

petrol station	maḥaṭṭat banzīn (f)	محطّة بنزين
car park	mawqif as sayyārāt (m)	موقف السيّارات

77. Urban transport

bus, coach	bāṣ (m)	باص
tram	trām (m)	ترام
trolleybus	truli bāṣ (m)	ترولّي باص
route (bus ~)	ҳaṭṭ (m)	خطّ
number (e.g. bus ~)	raqm (m)	رقم

to go by ...	rakib ...	ركب...
to get on (~ the bus)	rakib	ركب
to get off ...	nazil min	نزل من

stop (e.g. bus ~)	mawqif (m)	موقف
next stop	al maḥaṭṭa al qādima (f)	المحطّة القادمة
terminus	āxir maḥaṭṭa (f)	آخر محطّة
timetable	ʒadwal (m)	جدول
to wait (vt)	intaẓar	إنتظر

| ticket | taðkira (f) | تذكرة |
| fare | uʒra (f) | أجرة |

cashier (ticket seller)	ṣarrāf (m)	صرّاف
ticket inspection	taftīʃ taðkira (m)	تفتيش تذكرة
ticket inspector	mufattiʃ taðākir (m)	مفتّش تذاكر

to be late (for ...)	ta'axxar	تأخّر
to miss (~ the train, etc.)	ta'axxar	تأخّر
to be in a hurry	istaʿʒal	إستعجل

taxi, cab	taksi (m)	تاكسي
taxi driver	sā'iq taksi (m)	سائق تاكسي
by taxi	bit taksi	بالتاكسي
taxi rank	mawqif taksi (m)	موقف تاكسي
to call a taxi	kallam tāksi	كلّم تاكسي
to take a taxi	axað taksi	أخذ تاكسي

traffic	ḥarakat al murūr (f)	حركة المرور
traffic jam	zaḥmat al murūr (f)	زحمة المرور
rush hour	sāʿat að ðurwa (f)	ساعة الذروة
to park (vi)	awqaf	أوقف
to park (vt)	awqaf	أوقف
car park	mawqif as sayyārāt (m)	موقف السيارات

underground, tube	mitru (m)	مترو
station	maḥaṭṭa (f)	محطّة
to take the tube	rakib al mitru	ركب المترو
train	qiṭār (m)	قطار
train station	maḥaṭṭat qiṭār (f)	محطّة قطار

78. Sightseeing

monument	timθāl (m)	تمثال
fortress	qalʿa (f), ḥiṣn (m)	قلعة، حصن
palace	qaṣr (m)	قصر
castle	qalʿa (f)	قلعة
tower	burʒ (m)	برج
mausoleum	ḍarīḥ (m)	ضريح

architecture	handasa miʿmāriyya (f)	هندسة معماريّة
medieval (adj)	min al qurūn al wusṭa	من القرون الوسطى
ancient (adj)	qadīm	قديم
national (adj)	waṭaniy	وطنيّ
famous (monument, etc.)	maʃhūr	مشهور

| tourist | sā'iḥ (m) | سائح |
| guide (person) | murʃid (m) | مرشد |

excursion, sightseeing tour	ʒawla (f)	جولة
to show (vt)	ʻaraḍ	عرض
to tell (vt)	ḥaddaθ	حدَث
to find (vt)	waʒad	وجد
to get lost (lose one's way)	ḍāʻ	ضاع
map (e.g. underground ~)	χarīṭa (f)	خريطة
map (e.g. city ~)	χarīṭa (f)	خريطة
souvenir, gift	tiðkār (m)	تذكار
gift shop	maḥall hadāya (m)	محلّ هدايا
to take pictures	ṣawwar	صوَّر
to have one's picture taken	taṣawwar	تصوَّر

79. Shopping

to buy (purchase)	iʃtara	إشترى
shopping	ʃay' (m)	شيء
to go shopping	iʃtara	إشترى
shopping	ʃubinɣ (m)	شوبينغ
to be open (ab. shop)	maftūḥ	مفتوح
to be closed	muɣlaq	مغلق
footwear, shoes	aḥðiya (pl)	أحذية
clothes, clothing	malābis (pl)	ملابس
cosmetics	mawādd at taʒmīl (pl)	موادّ التجميل
food products	ma'kūlāt (pl)	مأكولات
gift, present	hadiyya (f)	هديّة
shop assistant (masc.)	bā'iʻ (m)	بائع
shop assistant (fem.)	bā'i'a (f)	بائعة
cash desk	ṣundūʻ ad dafʻ (m)	صندوق الدفع
mirror	mir'āt (f)	مرآة
counter (shop ~)	minḍada (f)	منضدة
fitting room	ɣurfat al qiyās (f)	غرفة القياس
to try on	ʒarrab	جرَّب
to fit (ab. dress, etc.)	nāsab	ناسب
to fancy (vt)	aʻʒab	أعجب
price	siʻr (m)	سعر
price tag	tikit as siʻr (m)	تيكت السعر
to cost (vt)	kallaf	كلَّف
How much?	bikam?	بكم؟
discount	χaṣm (m)	خصم
inexpensive (adj)	ɣayr ɣāli	غير غال
cheap (adj)	raχīṣ	رخيص
expensive (adj)	ɣāli	غال
It's expensive	haða ɣāli	هذا غال
hire (n)	isti'ʒār (m)	إستئجار
to hire (~ a dinner jacket)	ista'ʒar	إستأجر

| credit (trade credit) | i'timān (m) | إئتمان |
| on credit (adv) | bid dayn | بالدين |

80. Money

money	nuqūd (pl)	نقود
currency exchange	taḥwīl ʿumla (m)	تحويل عملة
exchange rate	siʿr aṣ ṣarf (m)	سعر الصرف
cashpoint	ṣarrāf 'āliy (m)	صرّاف آليّ
coin	qiṭʿa naqdiyya (f)	قطعة نقديّة

| dollar | dulār (m) | دولار |
| euro | yuru (m) | يورو |

lira	lira iṭāliyya (f)	ليرة إيطالية
Deutschmark	mark almāniy (m)	مارك ألماني
franc	frank (m)	فرنك
pound sterling	ʒunayh istirlīniy (m)	جنيه استرلينيّ
yen	yīn (m)	ين

debt	dayn (m)	دين
debtor	mudīn (m)	مدين
to lend (money)	sallaf	سلّف
to borrow (vi, vt)	istalaf	إستلف

bank	bank (m)	بنك
account	ḥisāb (m)	حساب
to deposit (vt)	awdaʿ	أودع
to deposit into the account	awdaʿ fil ḥisāb	أودع في الحساب
to withdraw (vt)	saḥab min al ḥisāb	سحب من الحساب

credit card	biṭāqat i'timān (f)	بطاقة إئتمان
cash	nuqūd (pl)	نقود
cheque	ʃīk (m)	شيك
to write a cheque	katab ʃīk	كتب شيكًا
chequebook	daftar ʃīkāt (m)	دفتر شيكات

wallet	maḥfaẓat ʒīb (f)	محفظة جيب
purse	maḥfaẓat fakka (f)	محفظة فكّة
safe	χizāna (f)	خزانة

heir	wāris (m)	وارث
inheritance	wirāθa (f)	وراثة
fortune (wealth)	θarwa (f)	ثروة

lease	'īʒār (m)	إيجار
rent (money)	uʒrat as sakan (f)	أجرة السكن
to rent (sth from sb)	ista'ʒar	إستأجر

price	siʿr (m)	سعر
cost	θaman (m)	ثمن
sum	mablaɣ (m)	مبلغ
to spend (vt)	ṣaraf	صرف
expenses	maṣārīf (pl)	مصاريف

| to economize (vi, vt) | waffar | وفّر |
| economical | muwaffir | موفّر |

to pay (vi, vt)	dafa'	دفع
payment	daf' (m)	دفع
change (give the ~)	al bāqi (m)	الباقي

tax	ḍarība (f)	ضريبة
fine	γarāma (f)	غرامة
to fine (vt)	faraḍ γarāma	فرض غرامة

81. Post. Postal service

post office	maktab al barīd (m)	مكتب البريد
post (letters, etc.)	al barīd (m)	البريد
postman	sā'i al barīd (m)	ساعي البريد
opening hours	awqāt al 'amal (pl)	أوقات العمل

letter	risāla (f)	رسالة
registered letter	risāla musaʒʒala (f)	رسالة مسجّلة
postcard	biṭāqa barīdiyya (f)	بطاقة بريديّة
telegram	barqiyya (f)	برقيّة
parcel	ṭard (m)	طرد
money transfer	ḥawāla māliyya (f)	حوالة ماليّة

to receive (vt)	istalam	إستلم
to send (vt)	arsal	أرسل
sending	irsāl (m)	إرسال

address	'unwān (m)	عنوان
postcode	raqm al barīd (m)	رقم البريد
sender	mursil (m)	مرسل
receiver	mursal ilayh (m)	مرسل إليه

| name (first name) | ism (m) | إسم |
| surname (last name) | ism al 'ā'ila (m) | إسم العائلة |

postage rate	ta'rīfa (f)	تعريفة
standard (adj)	'ādiy	عاديّ
economical (adj)	muwaffir	موفّر

weight	wazn (m)	وزن
to weigh (~ letters)	wazan	وزن
envelope	ẓarf (m)	ظرف
postage stamp	ṭābi' (m)	طابع
to stamp an envelope	alṣaq ṭābi'	ألصق طابعا

Dwelling. House. Home

82. House. Dwelling

house	bayt (m)	بيت
at home (adv)	fil bayt	في البيت
yard	finā' (m)	فناء
fence (iron ~)	sūr (m)	سور
brick (n)	ṭūb (m)	طوب
brick (as adj)	min aṭ ṭūb	من الطوب
stone (n)	ḥaʒar (m)	حجر
stone (as adj)	ḥaʒariy	حجريّ
concrete (n)	xarasāna (f)	خرسانة
concrete (as adj)	xarasāniy	خرسانيّ
new (new-built)	ʒadīd	جديد
old (adj)	qadīm	قديم
decrepit (house)	'āyil lis suqūṭ	آيل للسقوط
modern (adj)	mu'āṣir	معاصر
multistorey (adj)	muta'addid aṭ ṭawābiq	متعدّد الطوابق
tall (~ building)	'āli	عال
floor, storey	ṭābiq (m)	طابق
single-storey (adj)	ðu ṭābiq wāḥid	ذو طابق واحد
ground floor	ṭābiq sufliy (m)	طابق سفليّ
top floor	ṭābiq 'ulwiy (m)	طابق علويّ
roof	saqf (m)	سقف
chimney	madxana (f)	مدخنة
roof tiles	qirmīd (m)	قرميد
tiled (adj)	min al qirmīd	من القرميد
loft (attic)	'ullayya (f)	علّية
window	ʃubbāk (m)	شبّاك
glass	zuʒāʒ (m)	زجاج
window ledge	raff ʃubbāk (f)	رف شبّاك
shutters	darf ʃubbāk (m)	درف شبّاك
wall	ḥā'iṭ (m)	حائط
balcony	ʃurfa (f)	شرفة
downpipe	masūrat at taṣrīf (f)	ماسورة التصريف
upstairs (to be ~)	fawq	فوق
to go upstairs	ṣa'ad	صعد
to come down (the stairs)	nazil	نزل
to move (to new premises)	intaqal	إنتقل

83. House. Entrance. Lift

entrance	madχal (m)	مدخل
stairs (stairway)	sullam (m)	سلّم
steps	daraʒāt (pl)	درجات
banisters	drabizīn (m)	درابزين
lobby (hotel ~)	ṣāla (f)	صالة
postbox	ṣundūq al barīd (m)	صندوق البريد
waste bin	ṣundūq az zubāla (m)	صندوق الزبالة
refuse chute	manfaθ aθ θubāla (m)	منفذ الزبالة
lift	miṣ'ad (m)	مصعد
goods lift	miṣ'ad aʃ ʃaḥn (m)	مصعد الشحن
lift cage	kabīna (f)	كابينة
to take the lift	rakib al miṣ'ad	ركب المصعد
flat	ʃaqqa (f)	شقّة
residents (~ of a building)	sukkān al 'imāra (pl)	سكّان العمارة
neighbour (masc.)	ʒār (m)	جار
neighbour (fem.)	ʒāra (f)	جارة
neighbours	ʒirān (pl)	جيران

84. House. Doors. Locks

door	bāb (m)	باب
gate (vehicle ~)	bawwāba (f)	بوّابة
handle, doorknob	qabḍat al bāb (f)	قبضة الباب
to unlock (unbolt)	fataḥ	فتح
to open (vt)	fataḥ	فتح
to close (vt)	aɣlaq	أغلق
key	miftāḥ (m)	مفتاح
bunch (of keys)	rabṭa (f)	ربطة
to creak (door, etc.)	ṣarr	صرّ
creak	ṣarīr (m)	صرير
hinge (door ~)	mufaṣṣala (f)	مفصّلة
doormat	siʒāda (f)	سجادة
door lock	qifl al bāb (m)	قفل الباب
keyhole	θaqb al bāb (m)	ثقب الباب
crossbar (sliding bar)	tirbās (m)	ترباس
door latch	mizlāʒ (m)	مزلاج
padlock	qifl (m)	قفل
to ring (~ the door bell)	rann	رنّ
ringing (sound)	ranīn (m)	رنين
doorbell	ʒaras (m)	جرس
doorbell button	zirr (m)	زرّ
knock (at the door)	ṭarq, daqq (m)	طرق، دقّ
to knock (vi)	daqq	دقّ

code	kūd (m)	كود
combination lock	kūd (m)	كود
intercom	ʒaras al bāb (m)	جرس الباب
number (on the door)	raqm (m)	رقم
doorplate	lawḥa (f)	لوحة
peephole	al ʻayn as siḥriyya (m)	العين السحرية

85. Country house

village	qarya (f)	قرية
vegetable garden	bustān xuḍār (m)	بستان خضار
fence	sūr (m)	سور
picket fence	sūr (m)	سور
wicket gate	bawwāba farʻiyya (f)	بوّابة فرعيّة

granary	ʃawna (f)	شونة
cellar	sirdāb (m)	سرداب
shed (garden ~)	saqīfa (f)	سقيفة
water well	biʼr (m)	بئر

stove (wood-fired ~)	furn (m)	فرن
to stoke the stove	awqad	أوقد
firewood	ḥaṭab (m)	حطب
log (firewood)	qiṭʻat ḥaṭab (f)	قطعة حطب

veranda	virānda (f)	فيراندة
deck (terrace)	ʃurfa (f)	شرفة
stoop (front steps)	sullam (m)	سلّم
swing (hanging seat)	urʒūḥa (f)	أرجوحة

86. Castle. Palace

castle	qalʻa (f)	قلعة
palace	qaṣr (m)	قصر
fortress	qalʻa (f), ḥiṣn (m)	قلعة، حصن

wall (round castle)	sūr (m)	سور
tower	burʒ (m)	برج
keep, donjon	burʒ raʼīsiy (m)	برج رئيسيّ

portcullis	bāb mutaḥarrik (m)	باب متحرّك
subterranean passage	sirdāb (m)	سرداب
moat	xandaq māʼiy (m)	خندق مائيّ

| chain | silsila (f) | سلسلة |
| arrow loop | mazɣal (m) | مزغل |

| magnificent (adj) | rāʼiʻ | رائع |
| majestic (adj) | muhīb | مهيب |

| impregnable (adj) | manīʻ | منيع |
| medieval (adj) | min al qurūn al wusṭa | من القرون الوسطى |

87. Flat

flat	ʃaqqa (f)	شقّة
room	ɣurfa (f)	غرفة
bedroom	ɣurfat an nawm (f)	غرفة النوم
dining room	ɣurfat il akl (f)	غرفة الأكل
living room	sālat al istiqbāl (f)	صالة الإستقبال
study (home office)	maktab (m)	مكتب
entry room	madχal (m)	مدخل
bathroom	ḥammām (m)	حمّام
water closet	ḥammām (m)	حمّام
ceiling	saqf (m)	سقف
floor	arḍ (f)	أرض
corner	zāwiya (f)	زاوية

88. Flat. Cleaning

to clean (vi, vt)	naẓẓaf	نظّف
to put away (to stow)	ʃāl	شال
dust	ɣubār (m)	غبار
dusty (adj)	muɣabbar	مغبّر
to dust (vt)	masaḥ al ɣubār	مسح الغبار
vacuum cleaner	miknasa kahrabā'iyya (f)	مكنسة كهربائيّة
to vacuum (vt)	naẓẓaf bi miknasa kahrabā'iyya	نظّف بمكنسة كهربائيّة
to sweep (vi, vt)	kanas	كنس
sweepings	qumāma (f)	قمامة
order	niẓām (m)	نظام
disorder, mess	'adam an niẓām (m)	عدم النظام
mop	mimsaḥa ṭawīla (f)	ممسحة طويلة
duster	mimsaḥa (f)	ممسحة
short broom	miqaʃʃa (f)	مقشّة
dustpan	ʒārūf (m)	جاروف

89. Furniture. Interior

furniture	aθāθ (m)	أثاث
table	maktab (m)	مكتب
chair	kursiy (m)	كرسيّ
bed	sarīr (m)	سرير
sofa, settee	kanaba (f)	كنبة
armchair	kursiy (m)	كرسيّ
bookcase	χizānat kutub (f)	خزانة كتب
shelf	raff (m)	رفّ
wardrobe	dūlāb (m)	دولاب
coat rack (wall-mounted ~)	ʃammā'a (f)	شمّاعة

coat stand	ʃammāʿa (f)	شمّاعة
chest of drawers	dulāb adrāʒ (m)	دولاب أدراج
coffee table	ṭāwilat al qahwa (f)	طاولة القهوة

mirror	mir'āt (f)	مرآة
carpet	siʒāda (f)	سجادة
small carpet	siʒāda (f)	سجادة

fireplace	midfa'a ḥā'iṭiyya (f)	مدفأة حائطيّة
candle	ʃamʿa (f)	شمعة
candlestick	ʃamʿadān (m)	شمعدان

drapes	satā'ir (pl)	ستائر
wallpaper	waraq ḥīṭān (m)	ورق حيطان
blinds (jalousie)	haṣīrat ʃubbāk (f)	حصيرة شبّاك

table lamp	miṣbāḥ aṭ ṭāwila (m)	مصباح الطاولة
wall lamp (sconce)	miṣbāḥ al ḥā'iṭ (f)	مصباح الحائط
standard lamp	miṣbāḥ ardiy (m)	مصباح أرضيّ
chandelier	naʒafa (f)	نجفة

leg (of a chair, table)	riʒl (f)	رجل
armrest	masnad (m)	مسند
back (backrest)	masnad (m)	مسند
drawer	durʒ (m)	درج

90. Bedding

bedclothes	bayāḍāt as sarīr (pl)	بياضات السرير
pillow	wisāda (f)	وسادة
pillowslip	kīs al wisāda (m)	كيس الوسادة
duvet	baṭṭāniyya (f)	بطّانيّة
sheet	milāya (f)	ملاية
bedspread	ɣiṭā' as sarīr (m)	غطاء السرير

91. Kitchen

kitchen	maṭbax (m)	مطبخ
gas	ɣāz (m)	غاز
gas cooker	butuɣāz (m)	بوتوغاز
electric cooker	furn kaharabā'iy (m)	فرن كهربائيّ
oven	furn (m)	فرن
microwave oven	furn al mikruwayv (m)	فرن الميكروويف

refrigerator	θallāʒa (f)	ثلاجة
freezer	frīzir (m)	فريزير
dishwasher	ɣassāla (f)	غسّالة

mincer	farrāmat laḥm (f)	فرّامة لحم
juicer	ʿaṣṣāra (f)	عصّارة
toaster	maḥmaṣat xubz (f)	محمصة خبز
mixer	xallāṭ (m)	خلّاط

coffee machine	mākinat ṣan' al qahwa (f)	ماكينة صنع القهوة
coffee pot	kanaka (f)	كنكة
coffee grinder	maṭḥanat qahwa (f)	مطحنة قهوة
kettle	barrād (m)	برّاد
teapot	barrād aʃ ʃāy (m)	برّاد الشاي
lid	ɣiṭā' (m)	غطاء
tea strainer	miṣfāt (f)	مصفاة
spoon	mil'aqa (f)	ملعقة
teaspoon	mil'aqat ʃāy (f)	ملعقة شاي
soup spoon	mil'aqa kabīra (f)	ملعقة كبيرة
fork	ʃawka (f)	شوكة
knife	sikkīn (m)	سكين
tableware (dishes)	ṣuḥūn (pl)	صحون
plate (dinner ~)	ṭabaq (m)	طبق
saucer	ṭabaq finʒān (m)	طبق فنجان
shot glass	ka's (f)	كأس
glass (tumbler)	kubbāya (f)	كبّاية
cup	finʒān (m)	فنجان
sugar bowl	sukkariyya (f)	سكّريّة
salt cellar	mamlaḥa (f)	مملحة
pepper pot	mabhara (f)	مبهرة
butter dish	ṣuḥn zubda (m)	صحن زبدة
stock pot (soup pot)	kassirūlla (f)	كاسرولة
frying pan (skillet)	ṭāsa (f)	طاسة
ladle	miɣrafa (f)	مغرفة
colander	miṣfāt (f)	مصفاة
tray (serving ~)	ṣīniyya (f)	صينيّة
bottle	zuʒāʒa (f)	زجاجة
jar (glass)	barṭamān (m)	برطمان
tin (can)	tanaka (f)	تنكة
bottle opener	fattāḥa (f)	فتّاحة
tin opener	fattāḥa (f)	فتّاحة
corkscrew	barrīma (f)	بريمة
filter	filtir (m)	فلتر
to filter (vt)	ṣaffa	صفّى
waste (food ~, etc.)	zubāla (f)	زبالة
waste bin (kitchen ~)	ṣundūq az zubāla (m)	صندوق الزبالة

92. Bathroom

bathroom	ḥammām (m)	حمّام
water	mā' (m)	ماء
tap	ḥanafiyya (f)	حنفيّة
hot water	mā' sāxin (m)	ماء ساخن
cold water	mā' bārid (m)	ماء بارد

toothpaste	ma'ʒūn asnān (m)	معجون أسنان
to clean one's teeth	naẓẓaf al asnān	نظّف الأسنان
toothbrush	furʃat asnān (f)	فرشة أسنان

to shave (vi)	ḥalaq	حلق
shaving foam	raɣwa lil ḥilāqa (f)	رغوة للحلاقة
razor	mūs ḥilāqa (m)	موس حلاقة

to wash (one's hands, etc.)	ɣasal	غسل
to have a bath	istaḥamm	إستحمّ
shower	dūʃ (m)	دوش
to have a shower	aχaðʼ ad duʃ	أخذ الدش

bath	ḥawḍ istiḥmām (m)	حوض استحمام
toilet (toilet bowl)	mirḥāḍ (m)	مرحاض
sink (washbasin)	ḥawḍ (m)	حوض

| soap | ṣābūn (m) | صابون |
| soap dish | ṣabbāna (f) | صبّانة |

sponge	līfa (f)	ليفة
shampoo	ʃāmbū (m)	شامبو
towel	fūṭa (f)	فوطة
bathrobe	θawb ḥammām (m)	ثوب حمّام

laundry (laundering)	ɣasīl (m)	غسيل
washing machine	ɣassāla (f)	غسّالة
to do the laundry	ɣasal al malābis	غسل الملابس
washing powder	mashūq ɣasīl (m)	مسحوق غسيل

93. Household appliances

TV, telly	tilivizyūn (m)	تليفزيون
tape recorder	ʒihāz tasʒīl (m)	جهاز تسجيل
video	ʒihāz tasʒīl vidiyu (m)	جهاز تسجيل فيديو
radio	ʒihāz radiyu (m)	جهاز راديو
player (CD, MP3, etc.)	blayir (m)	بلير

video projector	'āriḍ vidiyu (m)	عارض فيديو
home cinema	sinima manziliyya (f)	سينما منزلية
DVD player	di vi di (m)	دي في دي
amplifier	mukabbir aṣ ṣawt (m)	مكبّر الصوت
video game console	'atāri (m)	أتاري

video camera	kamira vidiyu (f)	كاميرا فيديو
camera (photo)	kamira (f)	كاميرا
digital camera	kamira diʒital (f)	كاميرا ديجيتال

vacuum cleaner	miknasa kahrabā'iyya (f)	مكنسة كهربائية
iron (e.g. steam ~)	makwāt (f)	مكواة
ironing board	lawḥat kayy (f)	لوحة كيّ

| telephone | hātif (m) | هاتف |
| mobile phone | hātif maḥmūl (m) | هاتف محمول |

typewriter	'āla katiba (f)	آلة كاتبة
sewing machine	'ālat al χiyāṭa (f)	آلة الخياطة
microphone	mikrufūn (m)	ميكروفون
headphones	sammā'āt ra'siya (pl)	سمّاعات رأسيّة
remote control (TV)	rimuwt kuntrūl (m)	ريموت كنترول
CD, compact disc	si di (m)	سي دي
cassette, tape	ʃarīṭ (m)	شريط
vinyl record	usṭuwāna (f)	أسطوانة

94. Repairs. Renovation

renovations	taʒdīdāt (m)	تجديدات
to renovate (vt)	ʒaddad	جدّد
to repair, to fix (vt)	aṣlaḥ	أصلح
to put in order	naẓẓam	نظم
to redo (do again)	a'ād	أعاد
paint	dihān (m)	دهان
to paint (~ a wall)	dahan	دهن
house painter	dahhān (m)	دهّان
paintbrush	furʃat lit talwīn (f)	فرشة للتلوين
whitewash	maḥlūl mubayyiḍ (m)	محلول مبيّض
to whitewash (vt)	bayyaḍ	بيّض
wallpaper	waraq ḥīṭān (m)	ورق حيطان
to wallpaper (vt)	laṣaq waraq al ḥīṭān	لصق ورق الحيطان
varnish	warnīʃ (m)	ورنيش
to varnish (vt)	ṭala bil warnīʃ	طلى بالورنيش

95. Plumbing

water	mā' (m)	ماء
hot water	mā' sāχin (m)	ماء ساخن
cold water	mā' bārid (m)	ماء بارد
tap	ḥanafiyya (f)	حنفيّة
drop (of water)	qaṭara (f)	قطرة
to drip (vi)	qaṭar	قطر
to leak (ab. pipe)	sarab	سرب
leak (pipe ~)	tasarrub (m)	تسرّب
puddle	birka (f)	بركة
pipe	māsūra (f)	ماسورة
valve (e.g., ball ~)	ṣimām (m)	صمام
to be clogged up	kān masdūdan	كان مسدودًا
tools	adawāt (pl)	أدوات
adjustable spanner	miftāḥ inʒlīziy (m)	مفتاح إنجليزيّ
to unscrew (lid, filter, etc.)	fataḥ	فتح

to screw (tighten)	aḥkam aʃ ʃadd	أحكم الشدّ
to unclog (vt)	sallak	سلّك
plumber	sabbāk (m)	سبّاك
basement	sirdāb (m)	سرداب
sewerage (system)	ʃabakit il maʒāry (f)	شبكة مياه المجاري

96. Fire. Conflagration

fire (accident)	ḥarīq (m)	حريق
flame	ʃuʿla (f)	شعلة
spark	ʃarāra (f)	شرارة
smoke (from fire)	duxān (m)	دخان
torch (flaming stick)	ʃuʿla (f)	شعلة
campfire	nār muxayyam (m)	نار مخيّم
petrol	banzīn (m)	بنزين
paraffin	kirusīn (m)	كيروسين
flammable (adj)	qābil lil iḥtirāq	قابل للإحتراق
explosive (adj)	mutafaʒʒir	متفجّر
NO SMOKING	mamnūʿ at tadxīn	ممنوع التدخين
safety	amn (m)	أمن
danger	xaṭar (m)	خطر
dangerous (adj)	xaṭīr	خطير
to catch fire	iʃtaʿal	إشتعل
explosion	infiʒār (m)	إنفجار
to set fire	aʃʿal an nār	أشعل النار
arsonist	muʃʿil ḥarīq (m)	مشعل حريق
arson	iḥrāq (m)	إحراق
to blaze (vi)	talahhab	تلهّب
to burn (be on fire)	iḥtaraq	إحترق
to burn down	iḥtaraq	إحترق
to call the fire brigade	istadʿa qism al ḥarīq	إستدعى قسم الحريق
firefighter, fireman	raʒul iṭfāʾ (m)	رجل إطفاء
fire engine	sayyārat iṭfāʾ (f)	سيّارة إطفاء
fire brigade	qism iṭfāʾ (m)	قسم إطفاء
fire engine ladder	sullam iṭfāʾ (m)	سلّم إطفاء
fire hose	xarṭūm al māʾ (m)	خرطوم الماء
fire extinguisher	miṭfaʾat ḥarīq (f)	مطفأة حريق
helmet	xūða (f)	خوذة
siren	ṣaffārat inðār (f)	صفّارة إنذار
to cry (for help)	ṣarax	صرخ
to call for help	istaɣāθ	إستغاث
rescuer	munqið (m)	منقذ
to rescue (vt)	anqað	أنقذ
to arrive (vi)	waṣal	وصل
to extinguish (vt)	aṭfaʾ	أطفأ
water	māʾ (m)	ماء

sand	raml (m)	رمل
ruins (destruction)	hitām (pl)	حطام
to collapse (building, etc.)	inhār	إنهار
to fall down (vi)	inhār	إنهار
to cave in (ceiling, floor)	inhār	إنهار
piece of debris	hitma (f)	حطمة
ash	ramād (m)	رماد
to suffocate (die)	ixtanaq	إختنق
to be killed (perish)	halak	هلك

HUMAN ACTIVITIES

Job. Business. Part 1

97. Banking

bank	bank (m)	بنك
branch (of a bank)	far' (m)	فرع
consultant	muwaẓẓaf bank (m)	موظّف بنك
manager (director)	mudīr (m)	مدير
bank account	ḥisāb (m)	حساب
account number	raqm al ḥisāb (m)	رقم الحساب
current account	ḥisāb ǧāri (m)	حساب جار
deposit account	ḥisāb tawfīr (m)	حساب توفير
to open an account	fataḥ ḥisāb	فتح حسابا
to close the account	aɣlaq ḥisāb	أغلق حسابا
to deposit into the account	awda' fil ḥisāb	أودع في الحساب
to withdraw (vt)	saḥab min al ḥisāb	سحب من الحساب
deposit	wadī'a (f)	وديعة
to make a deposit	awda'	أودع
wire transfer	ḥawāla (f)	حوالة
to wire, to transfer	ḥawwal	حوّل
sum	mablaɣ (m)	مبلغ
How much?	kam?	كم؟
signature	tawqī' (m)	توقيع
to sign (vt)	waqqa'	وقّع
credit card	biṭāqat i'timān (f)	بطاقة ائتمان
code (PIN code)	kūd (m)	كود
credit card number	raqm biṭāqat i'timān (m)	رقم بطاقة إئتمان
cashpoint	ṣarrāf 'āliy (m)	صرّاف آليّ
cheque	ʃīk (m)	شيك
to write a cheque	katab ʃīk	كتب شيكًا
chequebook	daftar ʃīkāt (m)	دفتر شيكات
loan (bank ~)	qarḍ (m)	قرض
to apply for a loan	qaddam ṭalab lil ḥuṣūl 'ala qarḍ	قدّم طلبا للحصول على قرض
to get a loan	ḥaṣal 'ala qarḍ	حصل على قرض
to give a loan	qaddam qarḍ	قدّم قرضا
guarantee	ḍamān (m)	ضمان

98. Telephone. Phone conversation

telephone	hātif (m)	هاتف
mobile phone	hātif maḥmūl (m)	هاتف محمول
answerphone	muʒīb al hātif (m)	مجيب الهاتف

| to call (by phone) | ittaṣal | إتّصل |
| call, ring | mukālama tilifuniyya (f) | مكالمة تليفونية |

to dial a number	ittaṣal bi raqm	إتّصل برقم
Hello!	alu!	ألو!
to ask (vt)	sa'al	سأل
to answer (vi, vt)	radd	ردّ

to hear (vt)	sami'	سمع
well (adv)	ʒayyidan	جيّداً
not well (adv)	sayyi'an	سيّئاً
noises (interference)	taʃwīʃ (m)	تشويش

receiver	sammā'a (f)	سمّاعة
to pick up (~ the phone)	rafa' as sammā'a	رفع السمّاعة
to hang up (~ the phone)	qafal as sammā'a	قفل السمّاعة

busy (engaged)	maʃɣūl	مشغول
to ring (ab. phone)	rann	رنّ
telephone book	dalīl at tilifūn (m)	دليل التليفون

| local (adj) | maḥalliyya | ة محلّيّة |
| local call | mukālama hātifiyya maḥalliyya (f) | مكالمة هاتفيّة محلّيّة |

trunk (e.g. ~ call)	ba'īd al mada	بعيد المدى
trunk call	mukālama ba'īdat al mada (f)	مكالمة بعيدة المدى
international (adj)	duwaliy	دوليّ
international call	mukālama duwaliyya (f)	مكالمة دوليّة

99. Mobile telephone

mobile phone	hātif maḥmūl (m)	هاتف محمول
display	ʒihāz 'arḍ (m)	جهاز عرض
button	zirr (m)	زرّ
SIM card	sim kart (m)	سيم كارت

battery	baṭṭāriyya (f)	بطّاريّة
to be flat (battery)	xalaṣat	خلصت
charger	ʃāḥin (m)	شاحن

menu	qā'ima (f)	قائمة
settings	awḍā' (pl)	أوضاع
tune (melody)	naɣma (f)	نغمة
to select (vt)	ixtār	إختار

| calculator | 'āla ḥāsiba (f) | آلة حاسبة |
| voice mail | barīd ṣawtiy (m) | بريد صوتيّ |

alarm clock	munabbih (m)	منبّه
contacts	ʒihāt al ittiṣāl (pl)	جهات الإتّصال
SMS (text message)	risāla qaṣīra ɛsɛmɛs (f)	sms رسالة قصيرة
subscriber	muʃtarik (m)	مشترك

100. Stationery

ballpoint pen	qalam ʒāf (m)	قلم جاف
fountain pen	qalam rīʃa (m)	قلم ريشة
pencil	qalam ruṣāṣ (m)	قلم رصاص
highlighter	markir (m)	ماركر
felt-tip pen	qalam xaṭṭāṭ (m)	قلم خطاط
notepad	muðakkira (f)	مذكّرة
diary	ʒadwal al aʿmāl (m)	جدول الأعمال
ruler	masṭara (f)	مسطرة
calculator	ʾāla ḥāsiba (f)	آلة حاسبة
rubber	astīka (f)	استيكة
drawing pin	dabbūs (m)	دبّوس
paper clip	dabbūs waraq (m)	دبّوس ورق
glue	ṣamɣ (m)	صمغ
stapler	dabbāsa (f)	دبّاسة
hole punch	xarrāma (m)	خرّامة
pencil sharpener	mibrāt (f)	مبراة

Job. Business. Part 2

101. Mass Media

newspaper	ӡarīda (f)	جريدة
magazine	maӡalla (f)	مجلّة
press (printed media)	ṣiḥāfa (f)	صحافة
radio	iðā'a (f)	إذاعة
radio station	maḥaṭṭat iðā'a (f)	محطّة إذاعة
television	tilivizyūn (m)	تليفزيون
presenter, host	mu'addim (m)	مقدّم
newsreader	muðīʿ (m)	مذيع
commentator	mu'alliq (m)	معلّق
journalist	ṣuḥufiy (m)	صحفيّ
correspondent (reporter)	murāsil (m)	مراسل
press photographer	muṣawwir ṣuḥufiy (m)	مصوّر صحفيّ
reporter	ṣuḥufiy (m)	صحفيّ
editor	muḥarrir (m)	محرّر
editor-in-chief	raʾīs taḥrīr (m)	رئيس تحرير
to subscribe (to …)	iʃtarak	إشترك
subscription	iʃtirāk (m)	إشتراك
subscriber	muʃtarik (m)	مشترك
to read (vi, vt)	qara'	قرأ
reader	qāri' (m)	قارئ
circulation (of a newspaper)	tadāwul (m)	تداول
monthly (adj)	ʃahriy	شهريّ
weekly (adj)	usbū'iy	أسبوعيّ
issue (edition)	'adad (m)	عدد
new (~ issue)	ӡadīd	جديد
headline	'unwān (m)	عنوان
short article	maqāla qaṣīra (f)	مقالة قصيرة
column (regular article)	'amūd (m)	عمود
article	maqāla (f)	مقالة
page	ṣafḥa (f)	صفحة
reportage, report	taqrīr (m)	تقرير
event (happening)	ḥadaθ (m)	حدث
sensation (news)	ḍaӡӡa (f)	ضجّة
scandal	faḍīḥa (f)	فضيحة
scandalous (adj)	fāḍiḥ	فاضح
great (~ scandal)	ʃahīr	شهير
programme (e.g. cooking ~)	barnāmaӡ (m)	برنامج
interview	muqābala (f)	مقابلة

| live broadcast | iðā'a mubāʃira (f) | إذاعة مباشرة |
| channel | qanāt (f) | قناة |

102. Agriculture

agriculture	zirā'a (f)	زراعة
peasant (masc.)	fallāħ (m)	فلّاح
peasant (fem.)	fallāħa (f)	فلّاحة
farmer	muzāri' (m)	مزارع

| tractor | ʒarrār (m) | جرّار |
| combine, harvester | ħaṣṣāda (f) | حصّادة |

plough	miħrāθ (m)	محراث
to plough (vi, vt)	ħaraθ	حرث
ploughland	ħaql maħrūθ (m)	حقل محروث
furrow (in field)	talam (m)	تلم

to sow (vi, vt)	baðar	بذر
seeder	baððāra (f)	بذّارة
sowing (process)	zar' (m)	زرع

| scythe | miħaʃ (m) | محشّ |
| to mow, to scythe | ħaʃʃ | حشّ |

| spade (tool) | karīk (m) | مجرفة |
| to till (vt) | ħafar | حفر |

hoe	mi'zaqa (f)	معزقة
to hoe, to weed	ista'ṣal nabātāt	إستأصل نباتات
weed (plant)	ħaʃʃa (m)	حشيشة

watering can	miraʃʃa al miyāh (f)	مرشّة المياه
to water (plants)	saqa	سقى
watering (act)	saqy (m)	سقي

| pitchfork | maðrāt (f) | مذراة |
| rake | midamma (f) | مدمّة |

fertiliser	samād (m)	سماد
to fertilise (vt)	sammad	سمّد
manure (fertiliser)	zibd (m)	زبل

field	ħaql (m)	حقل
meadow	marʒ (m)	مرج
vegetable garden	bustān xuḍār (m)	بستان خضار
orchard (e.g. apple ~)	bustān (m)	بستان

to graze (vt)	ra'a	رعى
herdsman	rā'i (m)	راع
pasture	mar'a (m)	مرعى

| cattle breeding | tarbiyat al mawāʃi (f) | تربية المواشي |
| sheep farming | tarbiyat aɣnām (f) | تربية أغنام |

plantation	mazra'a (f)	مزرعة
row (garden bed ~s)	ḥawḍ (m)	حوض
hothouse	daffʼa (f)	دفيئة
drought (lack of rain)	ʒafāf (m)	جفاف
dry (~ summer)	ʒāff	جافّ
grain	ḥubūb (pl)	حبوب
cereal crops	maḥāṣīl al ḥubūb (pl)	محاصيل الحبوب
to harvest, to gather	ḥaṣad	حصد
miller (person)	ṭaḥḥān (m)	طحّان
mill (e.g. gristmill)	ṭāḥūna (f)	طاحونة
to grind (grain)	ṭaḥan al ḥubūb	طحن الحبوب
flour	daqīq (m)	دقيق
straw	qaʃʃ (m)	قشّ

103. Building. Building process

building site	arḍ bināʼ (f)	أرض بناء
to build (vt)	bana	بنى
building worker	'āmil bināʼ (m)	عامل بناء
project	maʃrūʻ (m)	مشروع
architect	muhandis miʻmāriy (m)	مهندس معماريّ
worker	'āmil (m)	عامل
foundations (of a building)	asās (m)	أساس
roof	saqf (m)	سقف
foundation pile	watad al asās (f)	وتد الأساس
wall	ḥāʼiṭ (m)	حائط
reinforcing bars	ḥadīd taslīḥ (m)	حديد تسليح
scaffolding	saqāla (f)	سقالة
concrete	xarasāna (f)	خرسانة
granite	granīt (m)	جرانيت
stone	ḥaʒar (m)	حجر
brick	ṭūb (m)	طوب
sand	raml (m)	رمل
cement	ismant (m)	إسمنت
plaster (for walls)	qiṣāra (m)	قصارة
to plaster (vt)	ṭala bil ʒiṣṣ	طلى بالجصّ
paint	dihān (m)	دهان
to paint (~ a wall)	dahhan	دهّن
barrel	barmīl (m)	برميل
crane	rāfiʻa (f)	رافعة
to lift, to hoist (vt)	rafaʻ	رفع
to lower (vt)	anzal	أنزل
bulldozer	ʒarrāfa (f)	جرّافة
excavator	ḥaffāra (f)	حفّارة

scoop, bucket	dalw (m)	دلو
to dig (excavate)	ḥafar	حفر
hard hat	χūða (f)	خوذة

Professions and occupations

104. Job search. Dismissal

job	'amal (m)	عمل
staff (work force)	kawādir (pl)	كوادر
personnel	ṭāqim al 'āmilīn (m)	طاقم العاملين
career	masār mihniy (m)	مسار مهنيّ
prospects (chances)	'āfāq (pl)	آفاق
skills (mastery)	mahārāt (pl)	مهارات
selection (screening)	iχtiyār (m)	إختيار
employment agency	wikālat tawẓīf (f)	وكالة توظيف
curriculum vitae, CV	sīra ðātiyya (f)	سيرة ذاتيّة
job interview	mu'ābalat 'amal (f)	مقابلة عمل
vacancy	waẓīfa χāliya (f)	وظيفة خالية
salary, pay	murattab (m)	مرتّب
fixed salary	rātib θābit (m)	راتب ثابت
pay, compensation	uʒra (f)	أجرة
position (job)	manṣib (m)	منصب
duty (of an employee)	wāʒib (m)	واجب
range of duties	maʒmū'a min al wāʒibāt (f)	مجموعة من الواجبات
busy (I'm ~)	maʃɣūl	مشغول
to fire (dismiss)	aqāl	أقال
dismissal	iqāla (m)	إقالة
unemployment	biṭāla (f)	بطالة
unemployed (n)	'āṭil (m)	عاطل
retirement	ma'āʃ (m)	معاش
to retire (from job)	uḥīl 'alal ma'āʃ	أحيل على المعاش

105. Business people

director	mudīr (m)	مدير
manager (director)	mudīr (m)	مدير
boss	mudīr (m), raʔīs (m)	مدير، رئيس
superior	raʔīs (m)	رئيس
superiors	ru'asā' (pl)	رؤساء
president	raʔīs (m)	رئيس
chairman	raʔīs (m)	رئيس
deputy (substitute)	nā'ib (m)	نائب
assistant	musā'id (m)	مساعد

| secretary | sikirtīr (m) | سكرتير |
| personal assistant | sikritīr χāṣṣ (m) | سكرتير خاصّ |

businessman	raȝul aʿmāl (m)	رجل أعمال
entrepreneur	rāʾid aʿmāl (m)	رائد أعمال
founder	muʾassis (m)	مؤسّس
to found (vt)	assas	أسّس

founding member	muʾassis (m)	مؤسّس
partner	ʃarīk (m)	شريك
shareholder	musāhim (m)	مساهم

millionaire	milyunīr (m)	مليونير
billionaire	milyardīr (m)	ملياردير
owner, proprietor	ṣāḥib (m)	صاحب
landowner	ṣāḥib al arḍ (m)	صاحب الأرض

client	ʿamīl (m)	عميل
regular client	ʿamīl dāʾim (m)	عميل دائم
buyer (customer)	muʃtari (m)	مشتر
visitor	zāʾir (m)	زائر

professional (n)	muḥtarif (m)	محترف
expert	χabīr (m)	خبير
specialist	mutaχaṣṣiṣ (m)	متخصّص

| banker | ṣāḥib maṣraf (m) | صاحب مصرف |
| broker | simsār (m) | سمسار |

cashier	ṣarrāf (m)	صرّاف
accountant	muḥāsib (m)	محاسب
security guard	ḥāris amn (m)	حارس أمن

investor	mustaθmir (m)	مستثمر
debtor	mudīn (m)	مدين
creditor	dāʾin (m)	دائن
borrower	muqtariḍ (m)	مقترض

| importer | mustawrid (m) | مستورد |
| exporter | muṣaddir (m) | مصدّر |

manufacturer	aʃ ʃarika al muṣniʿa (f)	الشركة المصنعة
distributor	muwazziʿ (m)	موزّع
middleman	wasīṭ (m)	وسيط

consultant	mustaʃār (m)	مستشار
sales representative	mandūb mabiʿāt (m)	مندوب مبيعات
agent	wakīl (m)	وكيل
insurance agent	wakīl at taʾmīn (m)	وكيل التأمين

106. Service professions

| cook | ṭabbāχ (m) | طبّاخ |
| chef (kitchen chef) | ʃāf (m) | شاف |

baker	χabbāz (m)	خبّاز
barman	bārman (m)	بارمان
waiter	nādil (m)	نادل
waitress	nādila (f)	نادلة
lawyer, barrister	muḥāmi (m)	محام
lawyer (legal expert)	muḥāmi (m)	محام
notary public	muwaθθaq (m)	موثّق
electrician	kahrabā'iy (m)	كهربائيّ
plumber	sabbāk (m)	سبّاك
carpenter	naʒʒār (m)	نجّار
masseur	mudallik (m)	مدلّك
masseuse	mudallika (f)	مدلّكة
doctor	ṭabīb (m)	طبيب
taxi driver	sā'iq taksi (m)	سائق تاكسي
driver	sā'iq (m)	سائق
delivery man	sā'i (m)	ساع
chambermaid	'āmilat tanẓīf γuraf (f)	عاملة تنظيف غرف
security guard	ḥāris amn (m)	حارس أمن
flight attendant (fem.)	muḍīfat ṭayarān (f)	مضيفة طيران
schoolteacher	mudarris madrasa (m)	مدرّس مدرسة
librarian	amīn maktaba (m)	أمين مكتبة
translator	mutarʒim (m)	مترجم
interpreter	mutarʒim fawriy (m)	مترجم فوريّ
guide	murʃid (m)	مرشد
hairdresser	ḥallāq (m)	حلّاق
postman	sā'i al barīd (m)	ساعي البريد
salesman (store staff)	bā'i' (m)	بائع
gardener	bustāniy (m)	بستانيّ
domestic servant	χādim (m)	خادم
maid (female servant)	χādima (f)	خادمة
cleaner (cleaning lady)	'āmilat tanẓīf (f)	عاملة تنظيف

107. Military professions and ranks

private	ʒundiy (m)	جنديّ
sergeant	raqīb (m)	رقيب
lieutenant	mulāzim (m)	ملازم
captain	naqīb (m)	نقيب
major	rā'id (m)	رائد
colonel	'aqīd (m)	عقيد
general	ʒinirāl (m)	جنرال
marshal	mārʃāl (m)	مارشال
admiral	amirāl (m)	أميرال
military (n)	'askariy (m)	عسكريّ
soldier	ʒundiy (m)	جنديّ

officer	ḍābiṭ (m)	ضابط
commander	qāʼid (m)	قائد
border guard	ḥāris ḥudūd (m)	حارس حدود
radio operator	ʼāmil lāsilkiy (m)	عامل لاسلكيّ
scout (searcher)	mustakʃif (m)	مستكشف
pioneer (sapper)	muhandis ʼaskariy (m)	مهندس عسكريّ
marksman	rāmi (m)	رام
navigator	mallāḥ (m)	ملّاح

108. Officials. Priests

king	malik (m)	ملك
queen	malika (f)	ملكة
prince	amīr (m)	أمير
princess	amīra (f)	أميرة
czar	qayṣar (m)	قيصر
czarina	qayṣara (f)	قيصرة
president	raʼīs (m)	رئيس
Secretary (minister)	wazīr (m)	وزير
prime minister	raʼīs wuzarāʼ (m)	رئيس وزراء
senator	ʼuḍw maʒlis aʃ ʃuyūχ (m)	عضو مجلس الشيوخ
diplomat	diblumāsiy (m)	دبلوماسيّ
consul	qunṣul (m)	قنصل
ambassador	safīr (m)	سفير
counselor (diplomatic officer)	mustaʃār (m)	مستشار
official, functionary (civil servant)	muwazzaf (m)	موظّف
prefect	raʼīs idārat al ḥayy (m)	رئيس إدارة الحيّ
mayor	raʼīs al baladiyya (m)	رئيس البلديّة
judge	qāḍi (m)	قاض
prosecutor	muddaʼi (m)	مدعٍ
missionary	mubaʃʃir (m)	مبشّر
monk	rāhib (m)	راهب
abbot	raʼīs ad dayr (m)	رئيس الدير
rabbi	ḥāχām (m)	حاخام
vizier	wazīr (m)	وزير
shah	ʃāh (m)	شاه
sheikh	ʃɛyχ (m)	شيخ

109. Agricultural professions

beekeeper	naḥḥāl (m)	نحّال
shepherd	rāʼi (m)	راع

agronomist	muhandis zirā'iy (m)	مهندس زراعيّ
cattle breeder	murabbi al mawāʃi (m)	مربّي المواشي
veterinary surgeon	ṭabīb bayṭariy (m)	طبيب بيطريّ
farmer	muzāri' (m)	مزارع
winemaker	ṣāni' an nabīð (m)	صانع النبيذ
zoologist	χabīr fi 'ilm al ḥayawān (m)	خبير في علم الحيوان
cowboy	rā'i al baqar (m)	راعي البقر

110. Art professions

actor	mumaθθil (m)	ممثّل
actress	mumaθθila (f)	ممثّلة
singer (masc.)	muɣanni (m)	مغنّ
singer (fem.)	muɣanniya (f)	مغنّية
dancer (masc.)	rāqiṣ (m)	راقص
dancer (fem.)	rāqiṣa (f)	راقصة
performer (masc.)	fannān (m)	فنّان
performer (fem.)	fannāna (f)	فنّانة
musician	'āzif (m)	عازف
pianist	'āzif biyānu (m)	عازف بيانو
guitar player	'āzif gitār (m)	عازف جيتار
conductor (orchestra ~)	qā'id urkistra (m)	قائد أركسترا
composer	mulaḥḥin (m)	ملحّن
impresario	mudīr firqa (m)	مدير فرقة
film director	muχriʒ (m)	مخرج
producer	muntiʒ (m)	منتج
scriptwriter	kātib sināriyu (m)	كاتب سيناريو
critic	nāqid (m)	ناقد
writer	kātib (m)	كاتب
poet	ʃā'ir (m)	شاعر
sculptor	naḥḥāt (m)	نحّات
artist (painter)	rassām (m)	رسّام
juggler	bahlawān (m)	بهلوان
clown	muharriʒ (m)	مهرّج
acrobat	bahlawān (m)	بهلوان
magician	sāḥir (m)	ساحر

111. Various professions

doctor	ṭabīb (m)	طبيب
nurse	mumarriḍa (f)	ممرّضة
psychiatrist	ṭabīb nafsiy (m)	طبيب نفسيّ
dentist	ṭabīb al asnān (m)	طبيب الأسنان

surgeon	ʒarrāḥ (m)	جرّاح
astronaut	rā'id faḍā' (m)	رائد فضاء
astronomer	'ālim falak (m)	عالم فلك
pilot	ṭayyār (m)	طيّار
driver (of a taxi, etc.)	sā'iq (m)	سائق
train driver	sā'iq (m)	سائق
mechanic	mikanīkiy (m)	ميكانيكيّ
miner	'āmil manʒam (m)	عامل منجم
worker	'āmil (m)	عامل
locksmith	qaffāl (m)	قفّال
joiner (carpenter)	naʒʒār (m)	نجّار
turner (lathe operator)	χarrāṭ (m)	خرّاط
building worker	'āmil binā' (m)	عامل بناء
welder	laḥḥām (m)	لحّام
professor (title)	brufissūr (m)	بروفيسور
architect	muhandis mi'māriy (m)	مهندس معماريّ
historian	mu'arriχ (m)	مؤرّخ
scientist	'ālim (m)	عالم
physicist	fizyā'iy (m)	فيزيائيّ
chemist (scientist)	kimyā'iy (m)	كيميائيّ
archaeologist	'ālim'āθār (m)	عالم آثار
geologist	ʒiulūʒiy (m)	جيولوجيّ
researcher (scientist)	bāḥiθ (m)	باحث
babysitter	murabbiyat aṭfāl (f)	مربّية الأطفال
teacher, educator	mu'allim (m)	معلّم
editor	muḥarrir (m)	محرّر
editor-in-chief	ra'īs taḥrīr (m)	رئيس تحرير
correspondent	murāsil (m)	مراسل
typist (fem.)	kātiba 'alal 'āla al kātiba (f)	كاتبة على الآلة الكاتبة
designer	muṣammim (m)	مصمّم
computer expert	mutaχaṣṣiṣ bil kumbyūtir (m)	متخصّص بالكمبيوتر
programmer	mubarmiʒ (m)	مبرمج
engineer (designer)	muhandis (m)	مهندس
sailor	baḥḥār (m)	بحّار
seaman	baḥḥār (m)	بحّار
rescuer	munqið (m)	منقذ
firefighter	raʒul iṭfā' (m)	رجل إطفاء
police officer	ʃurṭiy (m)	شرطيّ
watchman	ḥāris (m)	حارس
detective	muḥaqqiq (m)	محقّق
customs officer	muwazzaf al ʒamārik (m)	موظّف الجمارك
bodyguard	ḥāris ʃaχṣiy (m)	حارس شخصيّ
prison officer	ḥāris siʒn (m)	حارس سجن
inspector	mufattiʃ (m)	مفتّش
sportsman	riyāḍiy (m)	رياضيّ
trainer, coach	mudarrib (m)	مدرّب

butcher	ʒazzār (m)	جزّار
cobbler (shoe repairer)	iskāfiy (m)	إسكافيّ
merchant	tāʒir (m)	تاجر
loader (person)	ḥammāl (m)	حمّال
fashion designer	muṣammim azyā' (m)	مصمّم أزياء
model (fem.)	mudīl (f)	موديل

112. Occupations. Social status

schoolboy	tilmīð (m)	تلميذ
student (college ~)	ṭālib (m)	طالب
philosopher	faylasūf (m)	فيلسوف
economist	iqtiṣādiy (m)	إقتصاديّ
inventor	muxtariʿ (m)	مخترع
unemployed (n)	ʿāṭil (m)	عاطل
retiree, pensioner	mutaqāʿid (m)	متقاعد
spy, secret agent	ʒāsūs (m)	جاسوس
prisoner	saʒīn (m)	سجين
striker	muḍrib (m)	مضرب
bureaucrat	buruqrāṭiy (m)	بيوروقراطيّ
traveller (globetrotter)	raḥḥāla (m)	رحّالة
gay, homosexual (n)	miθliy ʒinsiyyan (m)	مثليّ جنسيًا
hacker	hākir (m)	هاكر
hippie	hippi (m)	هيبيّ
bandit	qāṭiʿ ṭarīq (m)	قاطع طريق
hit man, killer	qātil ma'ʒūr (m)	قاتل مأجور
drug addict	mudmin muxaddirāt (m)	مدمن مخدّرات
drug dealer	tāʒir muxaddirāt (m)	تاجر مخدّرات
prostitute (fem.)	ʿāhira (f)	عاهرة
pimp	qawwād (m)	قوّاد
sorcerer	sāḥir (m)	ساحر
sorceress (evil ~)	sāḥira (f)	ساحرة
pirate	qurṣān (m)	قرصان
slave	ʿabd (m)	عبد
samurai	samurāy (m)	ساموراي
savage (primitive)	mutawaḥḥiʃ (m)	متوحّش

Sports

113. Kinds of sports. Sportspersons

sportsman	riyāḍiy (m)	رياضيّ
kind of sport	nawʿ min ar riyāḍa (m)	نوع من الرياضة
basketball	kurat as salla (f)	كرة السلّة
basketball player	lāʿib kūrat as salla (m)	لاعب كرة السلّة
baseball	kurat al qāʿida (f)	كرة القاعدة
baseball player	lāʿib kurat al qāʿida (m)	لاعب كرة القاعدة
football	kurat al qadam (f)	كرة القدم
football player	lāʿib kurat al qadam (m)	لاعب كرة القدم
goalkeeper	ḥāris al marma (m)	حارس المرمى
ice hockey	huki (m)	هوكي
ice hockey player	lāʿib huki (m)	لاعب هوكي
volleyball	al kura aṭ ṭāʾira (m)	الكرة الطائرة
volleyball player	lāʿib al kura aṭ ṭāʾira (m)	لاعب الكرة الطائرة
boxing	mulākama (f)	ملاكمة
boxer	mulākim (m)	ملاكم
wrestling	muṣāraʿa (f)	مصارعة
wrestler	muṣāriʿ (m)	مصارع
karate	karatī (m)	كاراتيه
karate fighter	lāʿib karatī (m)	لاعب كاراتيه
judo	ʒudu (m)	جودو
judo athlete	lāʿib ʒudu (m)	لاعب جودو
tennis	tinis (m)	تنس
tennis player	lāʿib tinnis (m)	لاعب تنس
swimming	sibāḥa (f)	سباحة
swimmer	sabbāḥ (m)	سبّاح
fencing	musāyafa (f)	مسايفة
fencer	mubāriz (m)	مبارز
chess	ʃatranʒ (m)	شطرنج
chess player	lāʿib ʃatranʒ (m)	لاعب شطرنج
alpinism	tasalluq al ʒibāl (m)	تسلّق الجبال
alpinist	mutasalliq al ʒibāl (m)	متسلّق الجبال
running	ʒary (m)	جري

runner	'addā' (m)	عدّاء
athletics	al'āb al qiwa (pl)	ألعاب القوى
athlete	lā'ib riyāḍiy (m)	لاعب رياضيّ
horse riding	riyāḍat al furūsiyya (f)	رياضة الفروسيّة
horse rider	fāris (m)	فارس
figure skating	tazalluʒ fanniy 'alal ʒalīd (m)	تزلج فنّيّ على الجليد
figure skater (masc.)	mutazalliʒ fanniy (m)	متزلّج فنّي
figure skater (fem.)	mutazalliʒa fanniyya (f)	متزلّجة فنّيّة
powerlifting	raf' al aθqāl (m)	رفع الأثقال
powerlifter	rāfi' al aθqāl (m)	رافع الأثقال
car racing	sibāq as sayyārāt (m)	سباق السيّارات
racer (driver)	sā'iq sibāq (m)	سائق سباق
cycling	sibāq ad darrāʒāt (m)	سباق الدرّاجات
cyclist	lā'ib ad darrāʒāt (m)	لاعب الدرّاجات
long jump	al qafz aṭ ṭawīl (m)	القفز الطويل
pole vaulting	al qafz biz zāna (m)	القفز بالزانة
jumper	qāfiz (m)	قافز

114. Kinds of sports. Miscellaneous

American football	kurat al qadam (f)	كرة القدم
badminton	kurat ar rīʃa (f)	كرة الريشة
biathlon	al biatlūn (m)	البياثلون
billiards	bilyārdu (m)	بلياردو
bobsleigh	zallāʒa ʒama'iyya (f)	زلّاجة جماعيّة
bodybuilding	kamāl aʒsām (m)	كمال أجسام
water polo	kurat al mā' (f)	كرة الماء
handball	kurat al yad (f)	كرة اليد
golf	gūlf (m)	جولف
rowing	taʒdīf (m)	تجذيف
scuba diving	al ɣaws taḥt al mā' (m)	الغوص تحت الماء
cross-country skiing	riyāḍat al iski (f)	رياضة الإسكي
table tennis (ping-pong)	kurat aṭ ṭāwila (f)	كرة الطاولة
sailing	riyāḍa ibḥar al marākib (f)	رياضة إبحار المراكب
rally	sibāq as sayyārāt (m)	سباق السيّارات
rugby	raɣbi (m)	رغبي
snowboarding	tazalluʒ 'laθ θulūʒ (m)	تزلّج على الثلوج
archery	rimāya (f)	رماية

115. Gym

barbell	ḥadīda (f)	حديدة
dumbbells	dambilz (m)	دمبلز

training machine	ʒihāz tadrīb (m)	جهاز تدريب
exercise bicycle	darrāʒat tadrīb (f)	درّاجة تدريب
treadmill	ʒihāz al maʃy (m)	جهاز المشي
horizontal bar	ʿuqla (f)	عقلة
parallel bars	al mutawāzi (m)	المتوازي
vault (vaulting horse)	hisān al maqābiḍ (m)	حصان المقابض
mat (exercise ~)	ḥaṣīra (f)	حصيرة
skipping rope	ḥabl an naṭṭ (m)	حبل النطّ
aerobics	at tamrīnāt al hiwāʾiyya (pl)	التمرينات الهوائية
yoga	yūga (f)	يوجا

116. Sports. Miscellaneous

Olympic Games	alʿāb ulumbiyya (pl)	ألعاب أولمبيّة
winner	fāʾiz (m)	فائز
to be winning	fāz	فاز
to win (vi)	fāz	فاز
leader	zaʿīm (m)	زعيم
to lead (vi)	taqaddam	تقدّم
first place	al martaba al ūla (f)	المرتبة الأولى
second place	al martaba aθ θāniya (f)	المرتبة الثانية
third place	al martaba aθ θāliθa (f)	المرتبة الثالثة
medal	midāliyya (f)	ميداليّة
trophy	ʒāʾiza (f)	جائزة
prize cup (trophy)	kaʾs (m)	كأس
prize (in game)	ʒāʾiza (f)	جائزة
main prize	akbar ʒāʾiza (f)	أكبر جائزة
record	raqm qiyāsiy (m)	رقم قياسيّ
to set a record	fāz bi raqm qiyāsiy	فاز برقم قياسيّ
final	mubarāt nihāʾiyya (f)	مباراة نهائيّة
final (adj)	nihāʾiy	نهائيّ
champion	baṭal (m)	بطل
championship	buṭūla (f)	بطولة
stadium	malʿab (m)	ملعب
terrace	mudarraʒ (m)	مدرّج
fan, supporter	muʃaʒʒiʿ (m)	مشجّع
opponent, rival	ʿaduww (m)	عدوّ
start (start line)	xaṭṭ al bidāya (m)	خطّ البداية
finish line	xaṭṭ an nihāya (m)	خطّ النهاية
defeat	hazīma (f)	هزيمة
to lose (not win)	xasir	خسر
referee	ḥakam (m)	حكم
jury (judges)	hayʾat al ḥukm (f)	هيئة الحكم

score	natīʒa (f)	نتيجة
draw	ta'ādul (m)	تعادل
to draw (vi)	ta'ādal	تعادل
point	nuqta (f)	نقطة
result (final score)	natīʒa nihā'iyya (f)	نتيجة نهائية
period	ʃawṭ (m)	شوط
half-time	istirāḥa ma bayn aʃ ʃawṭayn (f)	إستراحة ما بين الشوطين
doping	munaʃʃiṭāt (pl)	منشّطات
to penalise (vt)	'āqab	عاقب
to disqualify (vt)	ḥaram	حرم
apparatus	ma'add riyāḍiy (f)	معدّ رياضيّ
javelin	rumḥ (m)	رمح
shot (metal ball)	ʒulla (f)	جلّة
ball (snooker, etc.)	kura (f)	كرة
aim (target)	hadaf (m)	هدف
target	hadaf (m)	هدف
to shoot (vi)	aṭlaq an nār	أطلق النار
accurate (~ shot)	maḍbūṭ	مضبوط
trainer, coach	mudarrib (m)	مدرّب
to train (sb)	darrab	درّب
to train (vi)	tadarrab	تدرّب
training	tadrīb (m)	تدريب
gym	markaz li liyāqa badaniyya (m)	مركز للياقة بدنيّة
exercise (physical)	tamrīn (m)	تمرين
warm-up (athlete ~)	tasχīn (m)	تسخين

Education

117. School

school	madrasa (f)	مدرسة
headmaster	mudīr madrasa (m)	مدير مدرسة
student (m)	tilmīð (m)	تلميذ
student (f)	tilmīða (f)	تلميذة
schoolboy	tilmīð (m)	تلميذ
schoolgirl	tilmīða (f)	تلميذة
to teach (sb)	ʿallam	علّم
to learn (language, etc.)	taʿallam	تعلّم
to learn by heart	ḥafaẓ	حفظ
to learn (~ to count, etc.)	taʿallam	تعلّم
to be at school	daras	درس
to go to school	ðahab ilal madrasa	ذهب إلى المدرسة
alphabet	alifbā' (m)	الفباء
subject (at school)	mādda (f)	مادّة
classroom	faṣl (m)	فصل
lesson	dars (m)	درس
playtime, break	istirāḥa (f)	إستراحة
school bell	ʒaras al madrasa (m)	جرس المدرسة
school desk	taxta lil madrasa (m)	تخته للمدرسة
blackboard	sabbūra (f)	سبّورة
mark	daraʒa (f)	درجة
good mark	daraʒa ʒayyida (f)	درجة جيّدة
bad mark	daraʒa ɣayr ʒayyida (f)	درجة غير جيّدة
to give a mark	aʿṭa daraʒa	أعطى درجة
mistake, error	xaṭa' (m)	خطأ
to make mistakes	axṭa'	أخطأ
to correct (an error)	ṣaḥḥaḥ	صحّح
crib	waraqat ɣaʃʃ (f)	ورقة غشّ
homework	wāʒib manziliy (m)	واجب منزليّ
exercise (in education)	tamrīn (m)	تمرين
to be present	ḥaḍar	حضر
to be absent	ɣāb	غاب
to miss school	taɣayyab ʿan al madrasa	تغيّب عن المدرسة
to punish (vt)	ʿāqab	عاقب
punishment	ʿuqūba (f), ʿiqāb (m)	عقوبة، عقاب
conduct (behaviour)	sulūk (m)	سلوك

school report	at taqrīr al madrasiy (m)	التقرير المدرسيّ
pencil	qalam ruṣāṣ (m)	قلم رصاص
rubber	astīka (f)	استيكة
chalk	ṭabāʃīr (m)	طباشير
pencil case	maqlama (f)	مقلمة

schoolbag	ʃanṭat al madrasa (f)	شنطة المدرسة
pen	qalam (m)	قلم
exercise book	daftar (m)	دفتر
textbook	kitāb taʻlīm (m)	كتاب تعليم
compasses	barʒal (m)	برجل

| to make technical drawings | rasam rasm taqniy | رسم رسمًا تقنيًا |
| technical drawing | rasm taqniy (m) | رسم تقنيّ |

poem	qaṣīda (f)	قصيدة
by heart (adv)	ʻan ẓahr qalb	عن ظهر قلب
to learn by heart	ḥafaẓ	حفظ

school holidays	ʻuṭla madrasiyya (f)	عطلة مدرسيّة
to be on holiday	ʻindahu ʻuṭla	عنده عطلة
to spend holidays	qaḍa al ʻuṭla	قضى العطلة

test (at school)	imtiḥān (m)	إمتحان
essay (composition)	inʃāʾ (m)	إنشاء
dictation	imlāʾ (m)	إملاء
exam (examination)	imtiḥān (m)	إمتحان
to do an exam	marr al imtiḥān	مرّ الإمتحان
experiment (e.g., chemistry ~)	taʒriba (f)	تجربة

118. College. University

academy	akadīmiyya (f)	أكاديميّة
university	ʒāmiʻa (f)	جامعة
faculty (e.g., ~ of Medicine)	kulliyya (f)	كلّيّة

student (masc.)	ṭālib (m)	طالب
student (fem.)	ṭāliba (f)	طالبة
lecturer (teacher)	muḥāḍir (m)	محاضر

| lecture hall, room | mudarraʒ (m) | مدرّج |
| graduate | mutaxarriʒ (m) | متخرّج |

| diploma | diblūma (f) | دبلومة |
| dissertation | risāla ʻilmiyya (f) | رسالة علميّة |

| study (report) | dirāsa (f) | دراسة |
| laboratory | muxtabar (m) | مختبر |

lecture	muḥāḍara (f)	محاضرة
coursemate	zamīl fiṣ ṣaff (m)	زميل في الصفّ
scholarship, bursary	minḥa dirāsiyya (f)	منحة دراسيّة
academic degree	daraʒa ʻilmiyya (f)	درجة علميّة

119. Sciences. Disciplines

mathematics	riyāḍīyyāt (pl)	رياضيّات
algebra	al ʒabr (m)	الجبر
geometry	handasa (f)	هندسة
astronomy	'ilm al falak (m)	علم الفلك
biology	'ilm al aḥyā' (m)	علم الأحياء
geography	ʒuɣrāfiya (f)	جغرافيا
geology	ʒiulūʒiya (f)	جيولوجيا
history	tarīχ (m)	تاريخ
medicine	ṭibb (m)	طبّ
pedagogy	'ilm at tarbiya (f)	علم التربية
law	qānūn (m)	قانون
physics	fizyā' (f)	فيزياء
chemistry	kimyā' (f)	كيمياء
philosophy	falsafa (f)	فلسفة
psychology	'ilm an nafs (m)	علم النفس

120. Writing system. Orthography

grammar	an naḥw waṣ ṣarf (m)	النحو والصرف
vocabulary	mufradāt al luɣa (pl)	مفردات اللغة
phonetics	ṣawtīyyāt (pl)	صوتيّات
noun	ism (m)	إسم
adjective	ṣifa (f)	صفة
verb	fi'l (m)	فعل
adverb	ẓarf (m)	ظرف
pronoun	ḍamīr (m)	ضمير
interjection	ḥarf nidā' (m)	حرف نداء
preposition	ḥarf al ʒarr (m)	حرف الجرّ
root	ʒiðr al kalima (m)	جذر الكلمة
ending	nihāya (f)	نهاية
prefix	sābiqa (f)	سابقة
syllable	maqta' lafẓiy (m)	مقطع لفظيّ
suffix	lāḥiqa (f)	لاحقة
stress mark	nabra (f)	نبرة
apostrophe	'alāmat ḥaðf (f)	علامة حذف
full stop	nuqṭa (f)	نقطة
comma	fāṣila (f)	فاصلة
semicolon	nuqṭa wa fāṣila (f)	نقطة وفاصلة
colon	nuqṭatān ra'siyyatān (du)	نقطتان رأسيتان
ellipsis	θalāθ nuqaṭ (pl)	ثلاث نقط
question mark	'alāmat istifhām (f)	علامة إستفهام
exclamation mark	'alāmat ta'aʒʒub (f)	علامة تعجّب

inverted commas	'alāmāt al iqtibās (pl)	علامات الإقتباس
in inverted commas	bayn 'alāmatay al iqtibās	بين علامتي الإقتباس
parenthesis	qawsān (du)	قوسان
in parenthesis	bayn al qawsayn	بين القوسين

hyphen	'alāmat waṣl (f)	علامة وصل
dash	ʃurṭa (f)	شرطة
space (between words)	farāɣ (m)	فراغ

| letter | ḥarf (m) | حرف |
| capital letter | ḥarf kabīr (m) | حرف كبير |

| vowel (n) | ḥarf ṣawtiy (m) | حرف صوتيّ |
| consonant (n) | ḥarf sākin (m) | حرف ساكن |

sentence	ʒumla (f)	جملة
subject	fā'il (m)	فاعل
predicate	musnad (m)	مسند

line	saṭr (m)	سطر
on a new line	min bidāyat as saṭr	من بداية السطر
paragraph	fiqra (f)	فقرة

word	kalima (f)	كلمة
group of words	maʒmū'a min al kalimāt (pl)	مجموعة من الكلمات
expression	'ibāra (f)	عبارة
synonym	murādif (m)	مرادف
antonym	mutaḍādd luɣawiy (m)	متضادّ

rule	qā'ida (f)	قاعدة
exception	istiθnā' (m)	إستثناء
correct (adj)	ṣaḥīḥ	صحيح

conjugation	ṣarf (m)	صرف
declension	taṣrīf al asmā' (m)	تصريف الأسماء
nominal case	ḥāla ismiyya (f)	حالة إسميّة
question	su'āl (m)	سؤال
to underline (vt)	waḍa' χaṭṭ taḥt	وضع خطًا تحت
dotted line	χaṭṭ munaqqaṭ (m)	خط منقّط

121. Foreign languages

language	luɣa (f)	لغة
foreign (adj)	aʒnabiy	أجنبيّ
foreign language	luɣa aʒnabiyya (f)	لغة أجنبيّة
to study (vt)	daras	درس
to learn (language, etc.)	ta'allam	تعلّم

to read (vi, vt)	qara'	قرأ
to speak (vi, vt)	takallam	تكلّم
to understand (vt)	fahim	فهم
to write (vt)	katab	كتب
fast (adv)	bi sur'a	بسرعة
slowly (adv)	bi buṭ'	ببطء

fluently (adv)	bi ṭalāqa	بطلاقة
rules	qawā'id (pl)	قواعد
grammar	an naḥw waṣ ṣarf (m)	النحو والصرف
vocabulary	mufradāt al luɣa (pl)	مفردات اللغة
phonetics	ṣawtīyyāt (pl)	صوتيّات
textbook	kitāb ta'līm (m)	كتاب تعليم
dictionary	qāmūs (m)	قاموس
teach-yourself book	kitāb ta'līm ðātiy (m)	كتاب تعليم ذاتيّ
phrasebook	kitāb lil 'ibārāt aʃ ʃā'i'a (m)	كتاب للعبارت الشائعة
cassette, tape	ʃarīṭ (m)	شريط
videotape	ʃarīṭ vidiyu (m)	شريط فيديو
CD, compact disc	si di (m)	سي دي
DVD	di vi di (m)	دي في دي
alphabet	alifbā' (m)	الفباء
to spell (vt)	tahaȝȝa	تهجّى
pronunciation	nuṭq (m)	نطق
accent	lukna (f)	لكنة
with an accent	bi lukna	بلكنة
without an accent	bi dūn lukna	بدون لكنة
word	kalima (f)	كلمة
meaning	ma'na (m)	معنى
course (e.g. a French ~)	dawra (f)	دورة
to sign up	saȝȝal ismahu	سجّل إسمه
teacher	mudarris (m)	مدرس
translation (process)	tarȝama (f)	ترجمة
translation (text, etc.)	tarȝama (f)	ترجمة
translator	mutarȝim (m)	مترجم
interpreter	mutarȝim fawriy (m)	مترجم فوريّ
polyglot	'alīm bi 'iddat luɣāt (m)	عليم بعدّة لغات
memory	ðākira (f)	ذاكرة

122. Fairy tale characters

Father Christmas	baba nuwīl (m)	بابا نويل
Cinderella	sindrīla	سيندريلا
mermaid	ḥūriyyat al baḥr (f)	حوريّة البحر
Neptune	nibtūn (m)	نبتون
magician, wizard	sāḥir (m)	ساحر
fairy	sāḥira (f)	ساحرة
magic (adj)	siḥriy	سحريّ
magic wand	'aṣa siḥriyya (f)	عصا سحريّة
fairy tale	ḥikāya xayāliyya (f)	حكاية خياليّة
miracle	mu'ȝiza (f)	معجزة
dwarf	qazam (m)	قزم

to turn into ...	taḥawwal ila ...	...تحوّل إلى
ghost	ʃabaḥ (m)	شبح
phantom	ʃabaḥ (m)	شبح
monster	waḥʃ (m)	وحش
dragon	tinnīn (m)	تنّين
giant	ʿimlāq (m)	عملاق

123. Zodiac Signs

Aries	burʒ al ḥamal (m)	برج الحمل
Taurus	burʒ aθ θawr (m)	برج الثور
Gemini	burʒ al ʒawzā' (m)	برج الجوزاء
Cancer	burʒ as saraṭān (m)	برج السرطان
Leo	burʒ al asad (m)	برج الأسد
Virgo	burʒ al ʿaðrā' (m)	برج العذراء
Libra	burʒ al mīzān (m)	برج الميزان
Scorpio	burʒ al ʿaqrab (m)	برج العقرب
Sagittarius	burʒ al qaws (m)	برج القوس
Capricorn	burʒ al ʒaday (m)	برج الجدي
Aquarius	burʒ ad dalw (m)	برج الدلو
Pisces	burʒ al ḥūt (m)	برج الحوت
character	ṭabʿ (m)	طبع
character traits	aṣ ṣifāt aʃ ʃaxṣiyya (pl)	الصفات الشخصيّة
behaviour	sulūk (m)	سلوك
to tell fortunes	tanabba'	تنبّأ
fortune-teller	ʿarrāfa (f)	عرّافة
horoscope	tawaqquʿāt al abrāʒ (pl)	توقّعات الأبراج

Arts

theatre	masraḥ (m)	مسرح
opera	ubra (f)	أوبرا
operetta	ubirīt (f)	أوبريت
ballet	balīh (m)	باليه
theatre poster	mulṣaq (m)	ملصق
theatre company	firqa (f)	فرقة
tour	ʒawlat fannānīn (f)	جولة فنّانين
to be on tour	taʒawwal	تجوّل
to rehearse (vi, vt)	aʒra bruvāt	أجرى بروفات
rehearsal	brūva (f)	بروفة
repertoire	barnāmaʒ al masraḥ (m)	برنامج المسرح
performance	adā' fanniy (m)	أداء فنّي
theatrical show	'arḍ masraḥiy (m)	عرض مسرحيّ
play	masraḥiyya (f)	مسرحيّة
ticket	taðkira (f)	تذكرة
booking office	ʃubbāk at taðākir (m)	شبّاك التذاكر
lobby, foyer	ṣāla (f)	صالة
coat check (cloakroom)	ɣurfat al ma'āṭif (f)	غرفة المعاطف
cloakroom ticket	biṭāqat 'īdā' al ma'āṭif (f)	بطاقة إيداع المعاطف
binoculars	minẓār (m)	منظار
usher	ḥāʒib (m)	حاجب
stalls (orchestra seats)	karāsi al urkistra (pl)	كراسي الأوركسترا
balcony	balakūna (f)	بلكونة
dress circle	ʃurfa (f)	شرفة
box	lūʒ (m)	لوج
row	ṣaff (m)	صفّ
seat	maq'ad (m)	مقعد
audience	ʒumhūr (m)	جمهور
spectator	muʃāhid (m)	مشاهد
to clap (vi, vt)	ṣaffaq	صفّق
applause	taṣfīq (m)	تصفيق
ovation	taṣfīq ḥārr (m)	تصفيق حارّ
stage	xaʃabat al masraḥ (f)	خشبة المسرح
curtain	sitāra (f)	ستارة
scenery	dikūr (m)	ديكور
backstage	kawalīs (pl)	كواليس
scene (e.g. the last ~)	maʃhad (m)	مشهد
act	faṣl (m)	فصل
interval	istirāḥa (f)	إستراحة

125. Cinema

actor	mumaθθil (m)	ممثّل
actress	mumaθθila (f)	ممثّلة
cinema (industry)	sinima (f)	سينما
film	film sinimā'iy (m)	فيلم سينمائيّ
episode	ӡuz' min al film (m)	جزء من الفيلم
detective film	film bulīsiy (m)	فيلم بوليسيّ
action film	film ḥaraka (m)	فيلم حركة
adventure film	film muɣāmarāt (m)	فيلم مغامرات
science fiction film	film ҳayāl 'ilmiy (m)	فيلم خيال علميّ
horror film	film ru'b (m)	فيلم رعب
comedy film	film kumīdiya (f)	فيلم كوميديا
melodrama	miludrāma (m)	ميلودراما
drama	drāma (f)	دراما
fictional film	film fanniy (m)	فيلم فنّيّ
documentary	film waθā'iqiy (m)	فيلم وثائقيّ
cartoon	film kartūn (m)	فيلم كرتون
silent films	sinima ṣāmita (f)	سينما صامتة
role (part)	dawr (m)	دور
leading role	dawr ra'īsi (m)	دور رئيسي
to play (vi, vt)	maθθal	مثّل
film star	naӡm sinimā'iy (m)	نجم سينمائيّ
well-known (adj)	ma'rūf	معروف
famous (adj)	maʃhūr	مشهور
popular (adj)	maḥbūb	محبوب
script (screenplay)	sināriyu (m)	سيناريو
scriptwriter	kātib sināriyu (m)	كاتب سيناريو
film director	muҳriӡ (m)	مخرج
producer	muntiӡ (m)	منتج
assistant	musā'id (m)	مساعد
cameraman	muṣawwir (m)	مصوّر
stuntman	mu'addi maʃahid ҳaṭīra (m)	مؤدّي مشاهد خطيرة
double (body double)	mumaθθil badīl (m)	ممثّل بديل
to shoot a film	ṣawwar film	صوّر فيلمًا
audition, screen test	taӡribat adā' (f)	تجربة أداء
shooting	taṣwīr (m)	تصوير
film crew	ṭāqim al film (m)	طاقم الفيلم
film set	mintaqat at taṣwīr (f)	منطقة التصوير
camera	kamira sinimā'iyya (f)	كاميرا سينمائيّة
cinema	sinima (f)	سينما
screen (e.g. big ~)	ʃāʃa (f)	شاشة
to show a film	'araḍ film	عرض فيلمًا
soundtrack	musīqa taṣwīriyya (f)	موسيقى تصويريّة
special effects	mu'aθθirāt ҳāṣṣa (pl)	مؤثّرات خاصّة

subtitles	tarʒamat al ḥiwār (f)	ترجمة الحوار
credits	ʃārat an nihāya (f)	شارة النهاية
translation	tarʒama (f)	ترجمة

126. Painting

art	fann (m)	فنّ
fine arts	funūn ʒamīla (pl)	فنون جميلة
art gallery	maʿraḍ fanniy (m)	معرض فنّيّ
art exhibition	maʿraḍ fanniy (m)	معرض فنّيّ
painting (art)	taṣwīr (m)	تصوير
graphic art	rusūmiyyāt (pl)	رسوميّات
abstract art	fann taʒrīdiy (m)	فنّ تجريديّ
impressionism	al intibāʿiyya (f)	الإنطباعيّة
picture (painting)	lawḥa (f)	لوحة
drawing	rasm (m)	رسم
poster	mulṣaq iʿlāniy (m)	ملصق إعلانيّ
illustration (picture)	rasm tawḍīḥiy (m)	رسم توضيحيّ
miniature	ṣūra muṣaʒʒara (f)	صورة مصغّرة
copy (of painting, etc.)	nusχa (f)	نسخة
reproduction	nusχa ṭibq al aṣl (f)	نسخة طبق الأصل
mosaic	fusayfisāʾ (f)	فسيفساء
stained glass window	zuʒāʒ muʿaʃʃaq (m)	زجاج معشّق
fresco	taṣwīr ʒiṣṣiy (m)	تصوير جصّيّ
engraving	naqʃ (m)	نقش
bust (sculpture)	timθāl niṣfiy (m)	تمثال نصفيّ
sculpture	naḥt (m)	نحت
statue	timθāl (m)	تمثال
plaster of Paris	ʒībs (m)	جيس
plaster (as adj)	min al ʒībs	من الجيس
portrait	burtrī (m)	بورتريه
self-portrait	burtrīh ðātiy (m)	بورتريه ذاتيّ
landscape painting	lawḥat manẓar ṭabīʿiy (f)	لوحة منظر طبيعيّ
still life	ṭabīʿa ṣāmita (f)	طبيعة صامتة
caricature	ṣūra karikaturiyya (f)	صورة كاريكاتوريّة
sketch	rasm tamhīdiy (m)	رسم تمهيديّ
paint	lawn (m)	لون
watercolor paint	alwān māʾiyya (m)	ألوان مائية
oil (paint)	zayt (m)	زيت
pencil	qalam ruṣāṣ (m)	قلم رصاص
Indian ink	ḥibr hindiy (m)	حبر هنديّ
charcoal	faḥm (m)	فحم
to draw (vi, vt)	rasam	رسم
to paint (vi, vt)	rasam	رسم
to pose (vi)	qaʿad	قعد
artist's model (masc.)	mudil ḥay (m)	موديل حيّ

artist's model (fem.)	mudil ḥay (m)	موديل حيّ
artist (painter)	rassām (m)	رسّام
work of art	'amal fanniy (m)	عمل فنّيّ
masterpiece	tuḥfa fanniyya (f)	تحفة فنية
studio (artist's workroom)	warʃa (f)	ورشة
canvas (cloth)	kanava (f)	كانفا
easel	musnad ar rasm (m)	مسند الرسم
palette	lawḥat al alwān (f)	لوحة الألوان
frame (picture ~, etc.)	iṭār (m)	إطار
restoration	tarmīm (m)	ترميم
to restore (vt)	rammam	رمم

127. Literature & Poetry

literature	adab (m)	أدب
author (writer)	mu'allif (m)	مؤلّف
pseudonym	ism musta'ār (m)	إسم مستعار
book	kitāb (m)	كتاب
volume	muʒallad (m)	مجلّد
table of contents	fihris (m)	فهرس
page	ṣafḥa (f)	صفحة
main character	aʃ ʃaχṣiyya ar ra'īsiyya (f)	الشخصيّة الرئيسيّة
autograph	tawqī' al mu'allif (m)	توقيع المؤلف
short story	qiṣṣa qaṣīra (f)	قصّة قصيرة
story (novella)	qiṣṣa (f)	قصّة
novel	riwāya (f)	رواية
work (writing)	mu'allif (m)	مؤلّف
fable	ḥikāya (f)	حكاية
detective novel	riwāya bulīsiyya (f)	رواية بوليسيّة
poem (verse)	qaṣīda (f)	قصيدة
poetry	ʃi'r (m)	شعر
poem (epic, ballad)	qaṣīda (f)	قصيدة
poet	ʃā'ir (m)	شاعر
fiction	adab ʒamīl (m)	أدب جميل
science fiction	χayāl 'ilmiy (m)	خيال علميّ
adventures	adab al muʒāmarāt (m)	أدب المغامرات
educational literature	adab tarbawiy (m)	أدب تربويّ
children's literature	adab al aṭfāl (m)	أدب الأطفال

128. Circus

circus	sirk (m)	سيرك
travelling circus	sirk mutanaqqil (m)	سيرك متنقّل
programme	barnāmaʒ (m)	برنامج
performance	adā' fanniy (m)	أداء فنّيّ
act (circus ~)	dawr (m)	دور

circus ring	ḥalbat as sirk (f)	حلبة السيرك
pantomime (act)	'arḍ 'īmā'y (m)	عرض إيمائي
clown	muharriʒ (m)	مهرّج
acrobat	bahlawān (m)	بهلوان
acrobatics	al'āb bahlawāniyya (f)	ألعاب بهلوانيّة
gymnast	lā'ib ʒumbāz (m)	لاعب جنباز
acrobatic gymnastics	ʒumbāz (m)	جنباز
somersault	ʃaqlaba (f)	شقلبة
strongman	lā'ib riyāḍiy (m)	لاعب رياضيّ
tamer (e.g., lion ~)	murawwiḍ (m)	مروّض
rider (circus horse ~)	fāris (m)	فارس
assistant	musā'id (m)	مساعد
stunt	al'āb bahlawāniyya (f)	ألعاب بهلوانيّة
magic trick	xid'a siḥriyya (f)	خدعة سحريّة
conjurer, magician	sāḥir (m)	ساحر
juggler	bahlawān (m)	بهلوان
to juggle (vi, vt)	la'ib bi kurāt 'adīda	لعب بكرات عديدة
animal trainer	mudarrib ḥayawānāt (m)	مدرّب حيوانات
animal training	tadrīb al ḥayawānāt (m)	تدريب الحيوانات
to train (animals)	darrab	درّب

129. Music. Pop music

music	musīqa (f)	موسيقى
musician	'āzif (m)	عازف
musical instrument	'āla musiqiyya (f)	آلة موسيقيّة
to play ...	'azaf ...	عزف...
guitar	gitār (m)	جيتار
violin	kamān (m)	كمان
cello	tʃīlu (m)	تشيلو
double bass	kamān aʒhar (m)	كمان أجهر
harp	qiθār (m)	قيثار
piano	biānu (m)	بيانو
grand piano	biānu kibīr (m)	بيانو كبير
organ	arɣan (m)	أرغن
wind instruments	'ālāt nafxiyya (pl)	آلات نفخيّة
oboe	ubwa (m)	أوبوا
saxophone	saksufūn (m)	ساكسوفون
clarinet	klarnīt (m)	كلارنيت
flute	flut (m)	فلوت
trumpet	būq (m)	بوق
accordion	ukurdiūn (m)	أكورديون
drum	ṭabla (f)	طبلة
duo	θunā'iy (m)	ثنائيّ
trio	θulāθy (m)	ثلاثي

quartet	rubā'iy (m)	رباعيّ
choir	xūrus (m)	خورس
orchestra	urkistra (f)	أوركسترا
pop music	musīqa al bub (f)	موسيقى البوب
rock music	musīqa ar rūk (f)	موسيقى الروك
rock group	firqat ar rūk (f)	فرقة الروك
jazz	ʒāz (m)	جاز
idol	ma'būd (m)	معبود
admirer, fan	mu'ʒab (m)	معجب
concert	ḥafla mūsiqiyya (f)	حفلة موسيقيّة
symphony	simfūniyya (f)	سمفونيّة
composition	qiṭ'a mūsiqiyya (f)	قطعة موسيقيّة
to compose (write)	allaf	ألّف
singing (n)	ɣinā' (m)	غناء
song	uɣniyya (f)	أغنيّة
tune (melody)	laḥn (m)	لحن
rhythm	'īqā' (m)	إيقاع
blues	musīqa al blūz (f)	موسيقى البلوز
sheet music	nutāt (pl)	نوتات
baton	'aṣa al mayistru (m)	عصا المايسترو
bow	qaws (m)	قوس
string	watar (m)	وتر
case (e.g. guitar ~)	ʃanṭa (f)	شنطة

Rest. Entertainment. Travel

130. Trip. Travel

tourism, travel	siyāḥa (f)	سياحة
tourist	sā'iḥ (m)	سائح
trip, voyage	riḥla (f)	رحلة
adventure	muɣāmara (f)	مغامرة
trip, journey	riḥla (f)	رحلة
holiday	ʿutla (f)	عطلة
to be on holiday	ʿindahu ʿutla	عنده عطلة
rest	istirāḥa (f)	إستراحة
train	qiṭār (m)	قطار
by train	bil qiṭār	بالقطار
aeroplane	ṭā'ira (f)	طائرة
by aeroplane	biṭ ṭā'ira	بالطائرة
by car	bis sayyāra	بالسيّارة
by ship	bis safīna	بالسفينة
luggage	aʃ ʃunaṭ (pl)	الشنط
suitcase	ḥaqība safar (f)	حقيبة سفر
luggage trolley	ʿarabat ʃunaṭ (f)	عربة شنط
passport	ʒawāz as safar (m)	جواز السفر
visa	ta'ʃīra (f)	تأشيرة
ticket	taðkira (f)	تذكرة
air ticket	taðkirat ṭā'ira (f)	تذكرة طائرة
guidebook	dalīl (m)	دليل
map (tourist ~)	xarīṭa (f)	خريطة
area (rural ~)	mintaqa (f)	منطقة
place, site	makān (m)	مكان
exotica (n)	ɣarāba (f)	غرابة
exotic (adj)	ɣarīb	غريب
amazing (adj)	mudhiʃ	مدهش
group	maʒmūʿa (f)	مجموعة
excursion, sightseeing tour	ʒawla (f)	جولة
guide (person)	murʃid (m)	مرشد

131. Hotel

hotel	funduq (m)	فندق
motel	mutīl (m)	موتيل
three-star (~ hotel)	θalāθat nuʒūm	ثلاثة نجوم

| five-star | xamsat nuʒūm | خمسة نجوم |
| to stay (in a hotel, etc.) | nazal | نزل |

room	ɣurfa (f)	غرفة
single room	ɣurfa li ʃaxṣ wāḥid (f)	غرفة لشخص واحد
double room	ɣurfa li ʃaxṣayn (f)	غرفة لشخصين
to book a room	ḥaʒaz ɣurfa	حجز غرفة

| half board | waʒbitān fil yawm (du) | وجبتان في اليوم |
| full board | θalāθ waʒabāt fil yawm | ثلاث وجبات في اليوم |

with bath	bi ḥawḍ al istiḥmām	بحوض الإستحمام
with shower	bid duʃ	بالدوش
satellite television	tilivizyūn faḍā'iy (m)	تلفزيون فضائيّ
air-conditioner	takyīf (m)	تكييف
towel	fūṭa (f)	فوطة
key	miftāḥ (m)	مفتاح

administrator	mudīr (m)	مدير
chambermaid	'āmilat tanẓīf ɣuraf (f)	عاملة تنظيف غرف
porter	ḥammāl (m)	حمّال
doorman	bawwāb (m)	بوّاب

restaurant	maṭ'am (m)	مطعم
pub, bar	bār (m)	بار
breakfast	fuṭūr (m)	فطور
dinner	'aʃā' (m)	عشاء
buffet	bufīh (m)	بوفيه

| lobby | radha (f) | ردهة |
| lift | miṣ'ad (m) | مصعد |

| DO NOT DISTURB | ar raʒā' 'adam al iz'āʒ | الرجاء عدم الإزعاج |
| NO SMOKING | mamnū' at tadxīn | ممنوع التدخين |

132. Books. Reading

book	kitāb (m)	كتاب
author	mu'allif (m)	مؤلّف
writer	kātib (m)	كاتب
to write (~ a book)	allaf	ألّف

reader	qāri' (m)	قارئ
to read (vi, vt)	qara'	قرأ
reading (activity)	qirā'a (f)	قراءة

| silently (to oneself) | sirran | سرًّا |
| aloud (adv) | bi ṣawt 'āli | بصوت عال |

to publish (vt)	naʃar	نشر
publishing (process)	naʃr (m)	نشر
publisher	nāʃir (m)	ناشر
publishing house	dār aṭ ṭibā'a wan naʃr (f)	دار الطباعة والنشر
to come out (be released)	ṣadar	صدر

release (of a book)	ṣudūr (m)	صدور
print run	'adad an nusaχ (m)	عدد النسخ
bookshop	maḥall kutub (m)	محلّ كتب
library	maktaba (f)	مكتبة
story (novella)	qiṣṣa (f)	قصّة
short story	qiṣṣa qaṣīra (f)	قصّة قصيرة
novel	riwāya (f)	رواية
detective novel	riwāya bulīsiyya (f)	رواية بوليسيّة
memoirs	muðakkirāt (pl)	مذكّرات
legend	usṭūra (f)	أسطورة
myth	χurāfa (f)	خرافة
poetry, poems	ʃiʿr (m)	شعر
autobiography	sīrat ḥayāt (f)	سيرة حياة
selected works	muχtārāt (pl)	مختارات
science fiction	χayāl 'ilmiy (m)	خيال علميّ
title	'unwān (m)	عنوان
introduction	muqaddima (f)	مقدّمة
title page	ṣafḥat al 'unwān (f)	صفحة العنوان
chapter	faṣl (m)	فصل
extract	qiṭ'a (f)	قطعة
episode	maʃhad (m)	مشهد
plot (storyline)	mawdūʿ (m)	موضوع
contents	muḥtawayāt (pl)	محتويات
table of contents	fihris (m)	فهرس
main character	aʃ ʃaχṣiyya ar raʔīsiyya (f)	الشخصيّة الرئيسيّة
volume	muʒallad (m)	مجلّد
cover	ɣilāf (m)	غلاف
binding	taʒlīd (m)	تجليد
bookmark	ʃarīṭ (m)	شريط
page	ṣafḥa (f)	صفحة
to page through	qallab aṣ ṣafaḥāt	قلّب الصفحات
margins	hāmiʃ (m)	هامش
annotation	mulāḥaza (f)	ملاحظة
(marginal note, etc.)		
footnote	mulāḥaza (f)	ملاحظة
text	naṣṣ (m)	نصّ
type, fount	nawʿ al χaṭṭ (m)	نوع الخطّ
misprint, typo	χaṭaʔ matbaʿiy (m)	خطأ مطبعيّ
translation	tarʒama (f)	ترجمة
to translate (vt)	tarʒam	ترجم
original (n)	aṣliy (m)	أصليّ
famous (adj)	maʃhūr	مشهور
unknown (not famous)	ɣayr maʿrūf	غير معروف
interesting (adj)	mumtiʿ	ممتع

bestseller	akθar mabīʿan (m)	أكثر مبيعًا
dictionary	qāmūs (m)	قاموس
textbook	kitāb taʿlīm (m)	كتاب تعليم
encyclopedia	mawsūʿa (f)	موسوعة

133. Hunting. Fishing

hunting	ṣayd (m)	صيد
to hunt (vi, vt)	iṣṭād	إصطاد
hunter	ṣayyād (m)	صيّاد

to shoot (vi)	aṭlaq an nār	أطلق النار
rifle	bunduqiyya (f)	بندقيّة
bullet (shell)	ruṣāṣa (f)	رصاصة
shot (lead balls)	raʃʃ (m)	رشّ

steel trap	maṣyada (f)	مصيدة
snare (for birds, etc.)	faχχ (m)	فخّ
to fall into the steel trap	waqaʿ fi faχχ	وقع في فخّ
to lay a steel trap	naṣab faχχ	نصب فخّا

poacher	sāriq aṣ ṣayd (m)	سارق الصيد
game (in hunting)	ṣayd (m)	صيد
hound dog	kalb ṣayd (m)	كلب صيد
safari	safāri (m)	سفاري
mounted animal	ḥayawān muhannaṭ (m)	حيوان محنّط

fisherman	ṣayyād as samak (m)	صيّاد السمك
fishing (angling)	ṣayd as samak (m)	صيد السمك
to fish (vi)	iṣṭād as samak	إصطاد السمك

fishing rod	ṣannāra (f)	صنّارة
fishing line	χayṭ (m)	خيط
hook	ʃaṣṣ aṣ ṣayd (m)	شصّ الصيد
float	ʿawwāma (f)	عوّامة
bait	ṭuʿm (m)	طعم

| to cast a line | ṭaraḥ aṣ ṣinnāra | طرح الصنّارة |
| to bite (ab. fish) | ʿaḍḍ | عضّ |

| catch (of fish) | as samak al muṣṭād (m) | السمك المصطاد |
| ice-hole | fatḥa fil ʒalīd (f) | فتحة في الجليد |

fishing net	ʃabakat aṣ ṣayd (f)	شبكة الصيد
boat	markab (m)	مركب
to net (to fish with a net)	iṣṭād biʃ ʃabaka	إصطاد بالشبكة
to cast[throw] the net	rama ʃabaka	رمى شبكة

| to haul the net in | aχraʒ ʃabaka | أخرج شبكة |
| to fall into the net | waqaʿ fi ʃabaka | وقع في شبكة |

whaler (person)	ṣayyād al ḥūt (m)	صيّاد الحوت
whaleboat	safinat ṣayd al ḥītān (f)	سفينة صيد الحيتان
harpoon	ḥarba (f)	حربة

134. Games. Billiards

billiards	bilyārdu (m)	بلياردو
billiard room, hall	qā'at bilyārdu (m)	قاعة بلياردو
ball (snooker, etc.)	kura (f)	كرة
to pocket a ball	aṣqaṭ kura	أصقط كرة
cue	'aṣa bilyardu (f)	عصا بلياردو
pocket	ʒayb bilyārdu (m)	جيب بلياردو

135. Games. Playing cards

diamonds	ad dināriy (m)	الديناريّ
spades	al bastūniy (m)	البستونيّ
hearts	al kūba (f)	الكوبة
clubs	as sibātiy (m)	السباتيّ
ace	'ās (m)	آس
king	malik (m)	ملك
queen	malika (f)	ملكة
jack, knave	walad (m)	ولد
playing card	waraqa (f)	ورقة
cards	waraq (m)	ورق
trump	waraqa rābiḥa (f)	ورقة رابحة
pack of cards	dasta waraq al la'b (f)	دستة ورق اللعب
point	nuqṭa (f)	نقطة
to deal (vi, vt)	farraq	فرّق
to shuffle (cards)	xallaṭ	خلط
lead, turn (n)	dawr (m)	دور
cardsharp	muḥtāl fil qimār (m)	محتال في القمار

136. Rest. Games. Miscellaneous

to stroll (vi, vt)	tanazzah	تنزّه
stroll (leisurely walk)	tanazzuh (m)	تنزّه
car ride	ʒawla bis sayyāra (f)	جولة بالسيّارة
adventure	muɣāmara (f)	مغامرة
picnic	nuzha (f)	نزهة
game (chess, etc.)	lu'ba (f)	لعبة
player	lā'ib (m)	لاعب
game (one ~ of chess)	dawr (m)	دور
collector (e.g. philatelist)	ʒāmi' (m)	جامع
to collect (stamps, etc.)	ʒama'	جمع
collection	maʒmū'a (f)	مجموعة
crossword puzzle	kalimāt mutaqāṭi'a (pl)	كلمات متقاطعة
racecourse (hippodrome)	ḥalbat sibāq al xuyūl (f)	حلبة سباق الخيول

disco (discotheque)	disku (m)	ديسكو
sauna	sāuna (f)	ساونا
lottery	yanaṣīb (m)	يانصيب
camping trip	riḥlat taxyīm (f)	رحلة تخييم
camp	muxayyam (m)	مخيّم
tent (for camping)	xayma (f)	خيمة
compass	būṣila (f)	بوصلة
camper	muxayyim (m)	مخيّم
to watch (film, etc.)	ʃāhid	شاهد
viewer	muʃāhid (m)	مشاهد
TV show (TV program)	barnāmaʒ tiliviziyūniy (m)	برنامج تليفزيونيّ

137. Photography

camera (photo)	kamira (f)	كاميرا
photo, picture	ṣūra (f)	صورة
photographer	muṣawwir (m)	مصوّر
photo studio	istūdiyu taṣwīr (m)	إستوديو تصوير
photo album	albūm aṣ ṣuwar (m)	ألبوم الصور
camera lens	ʿadasa (f)	عدسة
telephoto lens	ʿadasa tiliskūpiyya (f)	عدسة تلسكوبيّة
filter	filtir (m)	فلتر
lens	ʿadasa (f)	عدسة
optics (high-quality ~)	aʒhiza baṣariyya (pl)	أجهزة بصريّة
diaphragm (aperture)	buʾra (f)	بؤرة
exposure time (shutter speed)	muddat at taʿrīḍ (f)	مدة التعريض
viewfinder	al ʿayn al fāḥiṣa (f)	العين الفاحصة
digital camera	kamira raqmiyya (f)	كاميرا رقميّة
tripod	ḥāmil θulāθiy (m)	حامل ثلاثيّ
flash	flāʃ (m)	فلاش
to photograph (vt)	ṣawwar	صوّر
to take pictures	ṣawwar	صوّر
to have one's picture taken	taṣawwar	تصوّر
focus	buʾrat al ʿadasa (f)	بؤرة العدسة
to focus	rakkaz	ركّز
sharp, in focus (adj)	wāḍiḥ	واضح
sharpness	wuḍūḥ (m)	وضوح
contrast	tabāyun (m)	تباين
contrast (as adj)	mutabāyin	متباين
picture (photo)	ṣūra (f)	صورة
negative (n)	ṣūra ṣāliba (f)	صورة سالبة
film (a roll of ~)	film (m)	فيلم
frame (still)	iṭār (m)	إطار
to print (photos)	ṭabaʿ	طبع

138. Beach. Swimming

beach	ʃāṭiʾ (m)	شاطئ
sand	raml (m)	رمل
deserted (beach)	mahʒūr	مهجور
suntan	sumrat al baʃara (f)	سمرة البشرة
to get a tan	taʃammas	تشمس
tanned (adj)	asmar	أسمر
sunscreen	krīm wāqi aʃ ʃams (m)	كريم واقي الشمس
bikini	bikini (m)	بكيني
swimsuit, bikini	libās sibāḥa (m)	لباس سباحة
swim trunks	libās sibāḥa riʒāliy (m)	لباس سباحة رجاليّ
swimming pool	masbaḥ (m)	مسبح
to swim (vi)	sabaḥ	سبح
shower	dūʃ (m)	دوش
to change (one's clothes)	ɣayyar libāsuh	غيّر لباسه
towel	fūṭa (f)	فوطة
boat	markab (m)	مركب
motorboat	lanʃ (m)	لنش
water ski	tazalluʒ ʿalal māʾ (m)	تزلج على الماء
pedalo	ʿaʒala māʾiyya (f)	عجلة مائية
surfing	rukūb al amwāʒ (m)	ركوب الأمواج
surfer	rākib al amwāʒ (m)	راكب الأمواج
scuba set	ʒihāz at tanaffus (m)	جهاز التنفس
flippers (swim fins)	zaʿānif as sibāḥa (pl)	زعانف السباحة
mask (diving ~)	kimāma (f)	كمامة
diver	ɣawwāṣ (m)	غوّاص
to dive (vi)	ɣāṣ	غاص
underwater (adv)	taḥt al māʾ	تحت الماء
beach umbrella	ʃamsiyya (f)	شمسيّة
beach chair (sun lounger)	kursiy blāʒ (m)	كرسيّ بلاج
sunglasses	nazzārat ʃams (f)	نظّارة شمس
air mattress	martaba hawāʾiyya (f)	مرتبة هوائيّة
to play (amuse oneself)	laʿib	لعب
to go for a swim	sabaḥ	سبح
beach ball	kura (f)	كرة
to inflate (vt)	nafaχ	نفخ
inflatable, air (adj)	qābil lin nafχ	قابل للنفخ
wave	mawʒa (f)	موجة
buoy (line of ~s)	ʃamandūra (f)	شمندورة
to drown (ab. person)	ɣariq	غرق
to save, to rescue	anqað	أنقذ
life jacket	sutrat naʒāt (f)	سترة نجاة
to observe, to watch	rāqab	راقب
lifeguard	ḥāris ʃāṭiʾ (m)	حارس شاطئ

TECHNICAL EQUIPMENT. TRANSPORT

Technical equipment

139. Computer

computer	kumbyūtir (m)	كمبيوتر
notebook, laptop	kumbyūtir maḥmūl (m)	كمبيوتر محمول
to turn on	ʃayyal	شغّل
to turn off	aɣlaq	أغلق
keyboard	lawḥat al mafātīḥ (f)	لوحة المفاتيح
key	miftāḥ (m)	مفتاح
mouse	fa'ra (f)	فأرة
mouse mat	wisādat fa'ra (f)	وسادة فأرة
button	zirr (m)	زرّ
cursor	mu'aʃʃir (m)	مؤشّر
monitor	ʃāʃa (f)	شاشة
screen	ʃāʃa (f)	شاشة
hard disk	qurṣ ṣalib (m)	قرص صلب
hard disk capacity	si'at taχzīn (f)	سعة تخزين
memory	ðākira (f)	ذاكرة
random access memory	ðākirat al wuṣūl al 'aʃwā'iy (f)	ذاكرة الوصول العشوائيّ
file	malaff (m)	ملفّ
folder	ḥāfiẓa (m)	حافظة
to open (vt)	fataḥ	فتح
to close (vt)	aɣlaq	أغلق
to save (vt)	ḥafaẓ	حفظ
to delete (vt)	masaḥ	مسح
to copy (vt)	nasaχ	نسخ
to sort (vt)	ṣannaf	صنّف
to transfer (copy)	naqal	نقل
programme	barnāmaʒ (m)	برنامج
software	barāmiʒ kumbyūtir (pl)	برامج كمبيوتر
programmer	mubarmiʒ (m)	مبرمج
to program (vt)	barmaʒ	برمج
hacker	hākir (m)	هاكر
password	kalimat as sirr (f)	كلمة السرّ
virus	virūs (m)	فيروس
to find, to detect	waʒad	وجد
byte	bayt (m)	بايت

megabyte	miʒabāyt (m)	ميجابايت
data	bayānāt (pl)	بيانات
database	qaʿidat bayānāt (f)	قاعدة بيانات

cable (USB, etc.)	kābil (m)	كابل
to disconnect (vt)	faṣal	فصل
to connect (sth to sth)	waṣṣal	وصّل

140. Internet. E-mail

Internet	intirnit (m)	إنترنت
browser	mutaṣaffiḥ (m)	متصفح
search engine	muḥarrik baḥθ (m)	محرّك بحث
provider	ʃarikat al intirnīt (f)	شركة الإنترنيت

webmaster	mudīr al mawqiʿ (m)	مدير الموقع
website	mawqiʿ iliktrūniy (m)	موقع إلكتروني
web page	ṣafḥat wīb (f)	صفحة ويب

| address (e-mail ~) | ʿunwān (m) | عنوان |
| address book | daftar al ʿanāwīn (m) | دفتر العناوين |

postbox	ṣundūq al barīd (m)	صندوق البريد
post	barīd (m)	بريد
full (adj)	mumtaliʾ	ممتلىء

message	risāla iliktrūniyya (f)	رسالة إلكترونيّة
incoming messages	rasa'il wārida (pl)	رسائل واردة
outgoing messages	rasa'il ṣādira (pl)	رسائل صادرة
sender	mursil (m)	مرسل
to send (vt)	arsal	أرسل
sending (of mail)	irsāl (m)	إرسال
receiver	mursal ilayh (m)	مرسل إليه
to receive (vt)	istalam	إستلم

| correspondence | murāsala (f) | مراسلة |
| to correspond (vi) | tarāsal | تراسل |

file	malaff (m)	ملفّ
to download (vt)	ḥammal	حمّل
to create (vt)	anʃaʾ	أنشأ
to delete (vt)	masaḥ	مسح
deleted (adj)	mamsūḥ	ممسوح

connection (ADSL, etc.)	ittiṣāl (m)	إتّصال
speed	surʿa (f)	سرعة
modem	mudim (m)	مودم
access	wuṣūl (m)	وصول
port (e.g. input ~)	maxraʒ (m)	مخرج

connection (make a ~)	ittiṣāl (m)	إتّصال
to connect to ... (vi)	ittaṣal	إتّصل
to select (vt)	ixtār	إختار
to search (for ...)	baḥaθ	بحث

Transport

aeroplane	ṭā'ira (f)	طائرة
air ticket	taðkirat ṭā'ira (f)	تذكرة طائرة
airline	ʃarikat ṭayarān (f)	شركة طيران
airport	maṭār (m)	مطار
supersonic (adj)	xāriq liṣ ṣawt	خارق للصوت
captain	qā'id aṭ ṭā'ira (m)	قائد الطائرة
crew	ṭāqim (m)	طاقم
pilot	ṭayyār (m)	طيّار
stewardess	muḍīfat ṭayarān (f)	مضيفة طيران
navigator	mallāḥ (m)	ملّاح
wings	aʒniḥa (pl)	أجنحة
tail	ðayl (m)	ذيل
cockpit	kabīna (f)	كابينة
engine	mutūr (m)	موتور
undercarriage (landing gear)	ʿaʒalāt al hubūṭ (pl)	عجلات الهبوط
turbine	turbīna (f)	تريبنة
propeller	mirwaḥa (f)	مروحة
black box	musaʒʒil aṭ ṭayarān (m)	مسجّل الطيران
yoke (control column)	ʿaʒalat qiyāda (f)	عجلة قيادة
fuel	wuqūd (m)	وقود
safety card	biṭāqat as salāma (f)	بطاقة السلامة
oxygen mask	qinā' uksiʒīn (m)	قناع أوكسيجين
uniform	libās muwaḥḥad (m)	لباس موحّد
lifejacket	sutrat naʒāt (f)	سترة نجاة
parachute	miẓallat hubūṭ (f)	مظلّة هبوط
takeoff	iqlā' (m)	إقلاع
to take off (vi)	aqla'at	أقلعت
runway	madraʒ aṭ ṭā'irāt (m)	مدرج الطائرات
visibility	ru'ya (f)	رؤية
flight (act of flying)	ṭayarān (m)	طيران
altitude	irtifā' (m)	إرتفاع
air pocket	ʒayb hawā'iy (m)	جيب هوائيّ
seat	maq'ad (m)	مقعد
headphones	sammā'āt ra'siya (pl)	سمّاعات رأسيّة
folding tray (tray table)	ṣīniyya qābila liṭ ṭayy (f)	صينية قابلة للطيّ
airplane window	ʃubbāk aṭ ṭā'ira (m)	شبّاك الطائرة
aisle	mamarr (m)	ممرّ

142. Train

train	qiṭār (m)	قطار
commuter train	qiṭār (m)	قطار
express train	qiṭār sarī (m)	قطار سريع
diesel locomotive	qāṭirat dīzil (f)	قاطرة ديزل
steam locomotive	qāṭira buxāriyya (f)	قاطرة بخاريّة
coach, carriage	ʿaraba (f)	عربة
buffet car	ʿarabat al maṭʿam (f)	عربة المطعم
rails	quḍubān (pl)	قضبان
railway	sikka ḥadīdiyya (f)	سكة حديديّة
sleeper (track support)	ʿāriḍa (f)	عارضة
platform (railway ~)	raṣīf (m)	رصيف
platform (~ 1, 2, etc.)	xaṭṭ (m)	خطّ
semaphore	simafūr (m)	سيمافور
station	maḥaṭṭa (f)	محطّة
train driver	sāʾiq (m)	سائق
porter (of luggage)	ḥammāl (m)	حمّال
carriage attendant	masʾūl ʿarabat al qiṭār (m)	مسؤول عربة القطار
passenger	rākib (m)	راكب
ticket inspector	kamsariy (m)	كمسريّ
corridor (in train)	mamarr (m)	ممرّ
emergency brake	farāmil aṭ ṭawāriʾ (pl)	فرامل الطوارئ
compartment	yurfa (f)	غرفة
berth	sarīr (m)	سرير
upper berth	sarīr ʿulwiy (m)	سرير علويّ
lower berth	sarīr sufliy (m)	سرير سفليّ
bed linen, bedding	ayṭiyat as sarīr (pl)	أغطية السرير
ticket	taðkira (f)	تذكرة
timetable	ʒadwal (m)	جدول
information display	lawḥat maʿlūmāt (f)	لوحة معلومات
to leave, to depart	yādar	غادر
departure (of a train)	muyādara (f)	مغادرة
to arrive (ab. train)	waṣal	وصل
arrival	wuṣūl (m)	وصول
to arrive by train	waṣal bil qiṭār	وصل بالقطار
to get on the train	rakib al qiṭār	ركب القطار
to get off the train	nazil min al qiṭār	نزل من القطار
train crash	hiṭām qiṭār (m)	حطام قطار
to derail (vi)	xaraʒ ʿan xaṭṭ sayrih	خرج عن خطّ سيره
steam locomotive	qāṭira buxāriyya (f)	قاطرة بخاريّة
stoker, fireman	ʿataʃʒiy (m)	عطشجيّ
firebox	furn al muḥarrik (m)	فرن المحرّك
coal	faḥm (m)	فحم

143. Ship

ship	safīna (f)	سفينة
vessel	safīna (f)	سفينة
steamship	bāxira (f)	باخرة
riverboat	bāxira nahriyya (f)	باخرة نهريّة
cruise ship	bāxira siyahiyya (f)	باخرة سياحيّة
cruiser	ṭarrād (m)	طرّاد
yacht	yaxt (m)	يخت
tugboat	qāṭira (f)	قاطرة
barge	ṣandal (m)	صندل
ferry	ʿabbāra (f)	عبّارة
sailing ship	safīna ʃirāʿiyya (m)	سفينة شراعيّة
brigantine	markab ʃirāʿiy (m)	مركب شراعيّ
ice breaker	muhaṭṭimat ʒalīd (f)	محطّمة جليد
submarine	ɣawwāṣa (f)	غوّاصة
boat (flat-bottomed ~)	markab (m)	مركب
dinghy (lifeboat)	zawraq (m)	زورق
lifeboat	qārib naʒāt (m)	قارب نجاة
motorboat	lanʃ (m)	لنش
captain	qubṭān (m)	قبطان
seaman	baḥḥār (m)	بحّار
sailor	baḥḥār (m)	بحّار
crew	ṭāqim (m)	طاقم
boatswain	raʾīs al bahḥāra (m)	رئيس البحّارة
ship's boy	ṣabiy as safīna (m)	صبي السفينة
cook	ṭabbāx (m)	طبّاخ
ship's doctor	ṭabīb as safīna (m)	طبيب السفينة
deck	saṭh as safīna (m)	سطح السفينة
mast	sāriya (f)	سارية
sail	ʃirāʿ (m)	شراع
hold	ʿambar (m)	عنبر
bow (prow)	muqaddama (m)	مقدّمة
stern	muʾaxirat as safīna (f)	مؤخرّة السفينة
oar	miʒðāf (m)	مجذاف
screw propeller	mirwaḥa (f)	مروحة
cabin	kabīna (f)	كابينة
wardroom	ɣurfat al istirāḥa (f)	غرفة الإسترّاحة
engine room	qism al ʾālāt (m)	قسم الآلات
bridge	burʒ al qiyāda (m)	برج القيادة
radio room	ɣurfat al lāsilkiy (f)	غرفة اللاسلكيّ
wave (radio)	mawʒa (f)	موجة
logbook	siʒil as safīna (m)	سجل السفينة
spyglass	minẓār (m)	منظار
bell	ʒaras (m)	جرس

flag	ʻalam (m)	علم
hawser (mooring ~)	ḥabl (m)	حبل
knot (bowline, etc.)	ʻuqda (f)	عقدة
deckrails	drabizīn (m)	درابزين
gangway	sullam (m)	سلّم
anchor	mirsāt (f)	مرساة
to weigh anchor	rafaʻ mirsāt	رفع مرساة
to drop anchor	rasa	رسا
anchor chain	silsilat mirsāt (f)	سلسلة مرساة
port (harbour)	mīnāʼ (m)	ميناء
quay, wharf	marsa (m)	مرسى
to berth (moor)	rasa	رسا
to cast off	aqlaʻ	أقلع
trip, voyage	riḥla (f)	رحلة
cruise (sea trip)	riḥla baḥriyya (f)	رحلة بحرية
course (route)	masār (m)	مسار
route (itinerary)	ṭarīq (m)	طريق
fairway (safe water channel)	maʒra milāḥiy (m)	مجرى ملاحيّ
shallows	miyāh ḍaḥla (f)	مياه ضحلة
to run aground	ʒanaḥ	جنح
storm	ʻāṣifa (f)	عاصفة
signal	iʃāra (f)	إشارة
to sink (vi)	ɣariq	غرق
Man overboard!	saqaṭ raʒul min as safīna!	سقط رجل من السفينة!
SOS (distress signal)	nidāʼ iɣāθa (m)	نداء إغاثة
ring buoy	ṭawq naʒāt (m)	طوق نجاة

144. Airport

airport	maṭār (m)	مطار
aeroplane	ṭāʼira (f)	طائرة
airline	ʃarikat ṭayarān (f)	شركة طيران
air traffic controller	marāqib al ḥaraka al ʒawwiyya (pl)	مراقب الحركة الجويّة
departure	muɣādara (f)	مغادرة
arrival	wuṣūl (m)	وصول
to arrive (by plane)	waṣal	وصل
departure time	waqt al muɣādara (m)	وقت المغادرة
arrival time	waqt al wuṣūl (m)	وقت الوصول
to be delayed	taʼaxxar	تأخّر
flight delay	taʼaxxur ar riḥla (m)	تأخّر الرحلة
information board	lawḥat al maʻlūmāt (f)	لوحة المعلومات
information	istiʻlāmāt (pl)	إستعلامات
to announce (vt)	aʻlan	أعلن

flight (e.g. next ~)	riḥla (f)	رحلة
customs	ʒamārik (pl)	جمارك
customs officer	muwaẓẓaf al ʒamārik (m)	موظّف الجمارك
customs declaration	taṣrīḥ ʒumrukiy (m)	تصريح جمركيّ
to fill in (vt)	mala'	ملأ
to fill in the declaration	mala' at taṣrīḥ	ملأ التصريح
passport control	taftīʃ al ʒawāzāt (m)	تفتيش الجوازات
luggage	aʃʃunaṭ (pl)	الشنط
hand luggage	ʃunaṭ al yad (pl)	شنط اليد
luggage trolley	ʿarabat ʃunaṭ (f)	عربة شنط
landing	hubūṭ (m)	هبوط
landing strip	mamarr al hubūṭ (m)	ممرّ الهبوط
to land (vi)	habaṭ	هبط
airstair (passenger stair)	sullam aṭ ṭā'ira (m)	سلّم الطائرة
check-in	tasʒīl (m)	تسجيل
check-in counter	makān at tasʒīl (m)	مكان التسجيل
to check-in (vi)	saʒʒal	سجّل
boarding card	biṭāqat ṣuʿūd (f)	بطاقة صعود
departure gate	bawwābat al muɣādara (f)	بوّابة المغادرة
transit	tranzīt (m)	ترانزيت
to wait (vt)	intaẓar	إنتظر
departure lounge	qā'at al muɣādara (f)	قاعة المغادرة
to see off	waddaʿ	ودّع
to say goodbye	waddaʿ	ودّع

145. Bicycle. Motorcycle

bicycle	darrāʒa (f)	درّاجة
scooter	skutir (m)	سكوتر
motorbike	darrāʒa nāriyya (f)	درّاجة ناريّة
to go by bicycle	rakib ad darrāʒa	ركب الدرّاجة
handlebars	miqwad (m)	مقود
pedal	dawwāsa (f)	دوّاسة
brakes	farāmil (pl)	فرامل
bicycle seat (saddle)	maqʿad (m)	مقعد
pump	ṭulumba (f)	طلمبة
pannier rack	raff al amti'a (m)	رفّ الأمتعة
front lamp	miṣbāḥ (m)	مصباح
helmet	xūða (f)	خوذة
wheel	ʿaʒala (f)	عجلة
mudguard	rafraf (m)	رفرف
rim	iṭār (m)	إطار
spoke	barmaq al ʿaʒala (m)	برمق العجلة

Cars

146.   Types of cars

car	sayyāra (f)	سيّارة
sports car	sayyāra riyāḍiyya (f)	سيّارة رياضيّة
limousine	limuzīn (m)	ليموزين
off-road vehicle	sayyārat ṭuruq waʿra (f)	سيارة طرق وعرة
drophead coupé (convertible)	kabriulīh (m)	كابريوليه
minibus	mikrubāṣ (m)	ميكروباص
ambulance	isʿāf (m)	إسعاف
snowplough	ӡarrāfat θalӡ (f)	جرّافة ثلج
lorry	ʃāḥina (f)	شاحنة
road tanker	nāqilat bitrūl (f)	ناقلة بترول
van (small truck)	ʿarabat naql (f)	عربة نقل
tractor unit	ӡarrār (m)	جرّار
trailer	maqṭūra (f)	مقطورة
comfortable (adj)	murīḥ	مريح
used (adj)	mustaʿmal	مستعمل

147.   Cars. Bodywork

bonnet	kabbūt (m)	كبّوت
wing	rafraf (m)	رفرف
roof	saqf (m)	سقف
windscreen	zuӡāӡ amāmiy (m)	زجاج أماميّ
rear-view mirror	mir'āt dāҳiliyya (f)	مرآة داخليّة
windscreen washer	munaẓẓif az zuӡāӡ (m)	منظّف الزجاج
windscreen wipers	massāḥāt (pl)	مسّاحات
side window	zuӡāӡ ӡānibiy (m)	زجاج جانبيّ
electric window	mākina zuӡāӡ (f)	ماكينة زجاج
aerial	hawā'iy (m)	هوائيّ
sunroof	nāfiðat as saqf (f)	نافذة السقف
bumper	miṣadd as sayyāra (m)	مصدّ السيارة
boot	ṣundūq as sayyāra (m)	صندوق السيّارة
roof luggage rack	raff saqf as sayyāra (m)	رفّ سقف السيّارة
door	bāb (m)	باب
door handle	ukrat al bāb (f)	أوكرة الباب
door lock	qifl al bāb (m)	قفل الباب
number plate	lawḥat raqm as sayyāra (f)	لوحة رقم السيارة
silencer	kātim aṣ ṣawt (m)	كاتم الصوت

| petrol tank | xazzān al banzīn (m) | خزّان البنزين |
| exhaust pipe | umbūb al 'ādim (m) | أنبوب العادم |

accelerator	yāz (m)	غاز
pedal	dawwāsa (f)	دوّاسة
accelerator pedal	dawwāsat al wuqūd (f)	دوّاسة الوقود

brake	farāmil (pl)	فرامل
brake pedal	dawwāsat al farāmil (m)	دوّاسة الفرامل
to brake (use the brake)	farmal	فرمل
handbrake	farmalat al yad (f)	فرملة اليد

clutch	ta'ʃīq (m)	تعشيق
clutch pedal	dawwāsat at ta'ʃīq (f)	دوّاسة التعشيق
clutch disc	qurṣ at ta'ʃīq (m)	قرص التعشيق
shock absorber	mumtaṣṣ liṣ ṣadamāt (m)	ممتصّ الصدمات

wheel	'aʒala (f)	عجلة
spare tyre	'aʒala iḥtiyāṭiyya (f)	عجلة احتياطيّة
tyre	iṭār (m)	إطار
wheel cover (hubcap)	yitā' miḥwar al 'aʒala (m)	غطاء محور العجلة

driving wheels	'aʒalāt al qiyāda (pl)	عجلات القيادة
front-wheel drive (as adj)	daf' amāmiy (m)	دفع أماميّ
rear-wheel drive (as adj)	daf' xalfiy (m)	دفع خلفيّ
all-wheel drive (as adj)	daf' rubā'iy (m)	دفع رباعيّ

gearbox	ṣundūq at turūs (m)	صندوق التروس
automatic (adj)	utumatīkiy	أوتوماتيكيّ
mechanical (adj)	yadawiy	يدويّ
gear lever	nāqil as sur'a (m)	ناقل السرعة

| headlamp | al miṣbāḥ al amāmiy (m) | المصباح الأماميّ |
| headlights | al maṣābīḥ al amāmiyya (pl) | المصابيح الأماميّة |

dipped headlights	al anwār al munxafiḍa (pl)	الأنوار المنخفضة
full headlights	al anwār al 'āliya (m)	الأنوار العالية
brake light	ḍū' al farāmil (m)	ضوء الفرامل

sidelights	aḍwā' ʒānibiyya (pl)	أضواء جانبيّة
hazard lights	aḍwā' at taḥðīr (pl)	أضواء التحذير
fog lights	aḍwā' aḍ ḍabāb (pl)	أضواء الضباب
turn indicator	iʃārat al in'iṭāf (f)	إشارة الإنعطاف
reversing light	miṣbāḥ ar ruʒū' lil xalf (m)	مصباح الرجوع للخلف

148. Cars. Passenger compartment

car interior	ṣālūn as sayyāra (m)	صالون السيّارة
leather (as adj)	min al ʒild	من الجلد
velour (as adj)	min al muxmal	من المخمل
upholstery	tanʒīd (m)	تنجيد

| instrument (gage) | ʒihāz (m) | جهاز |
| dashboard | lawḥat at taḥakkum (f) | لوحة التحكم |

speedometer	ʻaddād surʻa (m)	عدّاد سرعة
needle (pointer)	muʼaʃʃir (m)	مؤشّر
mileometer	ʻaddād al masāfāt (m)	عدّاد المسافات
indicator (sensor)	ʻaddād (m)	عدّاد
level	mustawa (m)	مستوى
warning light	lammbat inðār (f)	لمبة إنذار
steering wheel	miqwad (m)	مقود
horn	zāmūr (m)	زامور
button	zirr (m)	زرّ
switch	nāqil, miftāḥ (m)	ناقل، مفتاح
seat	maqʻad (m)	مقعد
backrest	misnad aẓ ẓahr (m)	مسند الظهر
headrest	masnad ar raʼs (m)	مسند الرأس
seat belt	ḥizām al amn (m)	حزام الأمن
to fasten the belt	rabaṭ al ḥizām	ربط الحزام
adjustment (of seats)	ḍabṭ (m)	ضبط
airbag	wisāda hawāʼiyya (f)	وسادة هوائيّة
air-conditioner	takyīf (m)	تكييف
radio	iðāʻa (f)	إذاعة
CD player	muʃayyil sidi (m)	مشغّل سي دي
to turn on	fataḥ, ʃayyal	فتح، شغّل
aerial	hawāʼiy (m)	هوائيّ
glove box	durʒ (m)	درج
ashtray	ṭaqṭūqa (f)	طقطوقة

149. Cars. Engine

engine	muḥarrik (m)	محرّك
motor	mutūr (m)	موتور
diesel (as adj)	dīzil	ديزل
petrol (as adj)	ʻalal banzīn	على البنزين
engine volume	siʻat al muḥarrik (f)	سعة المحرّك
power	qudra (f)	قدرة
horsepower	ḥiṣān (m)	حصان
piston	mikbas (m)	مكبس
cylinder	usṭuwāna (f)	أسطوانة
valve	ṣimām (m)	صمام
injector	ʒihāz baxxāx (f)	جهاز بخّاخ
generator (alternator)	muwallid (m)	مولّد
carburettor	karburātir (m)	كاربراتير
motor oil	zayt al muḥarrik (m)	زيت المحرّك
radiator	mubarrid al muḥarrik (m)	مبرّد المحرّك
coolant	mādda mubarrida (f)	مادّة مبرّدة
cooling fan	mirwaḥa (f)	مروحة
battery (accumulator)	baṭṭāriyya (f)	بطّاريّة
starter	miftāḥ at taʃyīl (m)	مفتاح التشغيل

ignition	niẓām taʃɣīl (m)	نظام تشغيل
sparking plug	ʃam'at al iḥtirāq (f)	شمعة الاحتراق
terminal (battery ~)	ṭaraf tawṣīl (m)	طرف توصيل
positive terminal	ṭaraf mūʒab (m)	طرف موجب
negative terminal	ṭaraf sālib (m)	طرف سالب
fuse	fāṣima (f)	فاصمة
air filter	miṣfāt al hawā' (f)	مصفاة الهواء
oil filter	miṣfāt az zayt (f)	مصفاة الزيت
fuel filter	miṣfāt al banzīn (f)	مصفاة البنزين

150. Cars. Crash. Repair

car crash	ḥādiθ sayyāra (f)	حادث سيّارة
traffic accident	ḥādiθ murūriy (m)	حادث مروريّ
to crash (into the wall, etc.)	iṣtadam	إصطدم
to get smashed up	taḥaṭṭam	تحطّم
damage	χasāra (f)	خسارة
intact (unscathed)	salīm	سليم
to break down (vi)	ta'aṭṭal	تعطّل
towrope	ḥabl as saḥb (m)	حبل السحب
puncture	θuqb (m)	ثقب
to have a puncture	faʃʃ	فش
to pump up	nafaχ	نفخ
pressure	ḍaɣṭ (m)	ضغط
to check (to examine)	iχtabar	إختبر
repair	iṣlāḥ (m)	إصلاح
garage (auto service shop)	warʃat iṣlāḥ as sayyārāt (f)	ورشة إصلاح السيّارات
spare part	qiṭ'at ɣiyār (f)	قطعة غيار
part	qiṭ'a (f)	قطعة
bolt (with nut)	mismār qalāwūz (m)	مسمار قلاووظ
screw (fastener)	burɣiy (m)	برغيّ
nut	ṣamūla (f)	صامولة
washer	ḥalqa (f)	حلقة
bearing (e.g. ball ~)	maḥmal (m)	محمل
tube	umbūba (f)	أنبوبة
gasket (head ~)	'azaqa (f)	عزقة
cable, wire	silk (m)	سلك
jack	rāfi'at sayyāra (f)	رافعة سيّارة
spanner	miftāḥ aṣ ṣawāmīl (m)	مفتاح الصواميل
hammer	miṭraqa (f)	مطرقة
pump	ṭulumba (f)	طلمبة
screwdriver	mifakk (m)	مفكّ
fire extinguisher	miṭfa'at ḥarīq (f)	مطفأة حريق
warning triangle	muθallaθ taḥðīr (m)	مثلّث تحذير
to stall (vi)	tawaqqaf	توقّف

stall (n)	tawaqquf (m)	توقّف
to be broken	kān maksūran	كان مكسورًا
to overheat (vi)	saxan bi ʃidda	سخن بشدّة
to be clogged up	kān masdūdan	كان مسدودًا
to freeze up (pipes, etc.)	taʒammad	تجمّد
to burst (vi, ab. tube)	infaʒar	إنفجر
pressure	daɣṭ (m)	ضغط
level	mustawa (m)	مستوى
slack (~ belt)	daʔīf	ضعيف
dent	baʕʒa (f)	بعجة
knocking noise (engine)	daqq (m)	دقّ
crack	ʃaqq (m)	شقّ
scratch	xadʃ (m)	خدش

151. Cars. Road

road	ṭarīq (m)	طريق
motorway	ṭarīq sarīʕ (m)	طريق سريع
highway	ṭarīq sarīʕ (m)	طريق سريع
direction (way)	ittiʒāh (m)	إتّجاه
distance	masāfa (f)	مسافة
bridge	ʒisr (m)	جسر
car park	mawqif as sayyārāt (m)	موقف السيّارات
square	maydān (m)	ميدان
road junction	taqāṭuʕ ṭuruq (m)	تقاطع طرق
tunnel	nafaq (m)	نفق
petrol station	maḥaṭṭat banzīn (f)	محطّة بنزين
car park	mawqif as sayyārāt (m)	موقف السيّارات
petrol pump	midaxxat banzīn (f)	مضخّة بنزين
auto repair shop	warʃat iṣlāḥ as sayyārāt (f)	ورشة إصلاح السيّارات
to fill up	malaʔ bil wuqūd	ملأ بالوقود
fuel	wuqūd (m)	وقود
jerrycan	ʒirikan (m)	جركن
asphalt, tarmac	asfalt (m)	أسفلت
road markings	ʕalāmāt aṭ ṭarīq (pl)	علامات الطريق
kerb	ḥāffat ar raṣīf (f)	حافّة الرصيف
crash barrier	sūr (m)	سور
ditch	qanāt (f)	قناة
roadside (shoulder)	ḥāffat aṭ ṭarīq (f)	حافّة الطريق
lamppost	ʕamūd nūr (m)	عمود نور
to drive (a car)	sāq	ساق
to turn (e.g., ~ left)	inʕaṭaf	إنعطف
to make a U-turn	istadār lil xalf	إستدار للخلف
reverse (~ gear)	ḥaraka ilal warāʔ (f)	حركة إلى الوراء
to honk (vi)	zammar	زمّر
honk (sound)	ṣawṭ az zāmūr (m)	صوت الزامور

to get stuck (in the mud, etc.)	waḥil	وحل
to spin the wheels	dawwar al ʿaʒala	دوّر العجلة
to cut, to turn off (vt)	awqaf	أوقف
speed	surʿa (f)	سرعة
to exceed the speed limit	taʒāwaz as surʿa al quṣwa	تجاوز السرعة القصوى
to give a ticket	faraḍ ɣarāma	فرض غرامة
traffic lights	iʃārāt al murūr (pl)	إشارات المرور
driving licence	ruxṣat al qiyāda (f)	رخصة قيادة
level crossing	maʿbar (m)	معبر
crossroads	taqāṭuʿ (m)	تقاطع
zebra crossing	maʿbar al muʃāt (m)	معبر المشاة
bend, curve	munʿaṭif (m)	منعطف
pedestrian precinct	makān muxaṣṣaṣ lil muʃāt (f)	مكان مخصّص للمشاة

PEOPLE. LIFE EVENTS

152. Holidays. Event

celebration, holiday	ʿīd (m)	عيد
national day	ʿīd waṭaniy (m)	عيد وطنيّ
public holiday	yawm al ʿuṭla ar rasmiyya (m)	يوم العطلة الرسمية
to commemorate (vt)	iḥtafal	إحتفل
event (happening)	ḥadaθ (m)	حدث
event (organized activity)	munasaba (f)	مناسبة
banquet (party)	walīma (f)	وليمة
reception (formal party)	ḥaflat istiqbāl (f)	حفلة إستقبال
feast	walīma (f)	وليمة
anniversary	ðikra sanawiyya (f)	ذكرى سنويّة
jubilee	yubīl (m)	يوبيل
to celebrate (vt)	iḥtafal	إحتفل
New Year	ra's as sana (m)	رأس السنة
Happy New Year!	kull sana wa anta ṭayyib!	كلّ سنة وأنت طيَب!
Father Christmas	baba nuwīl (m)	بابا نويل
Christmas	ʿīd al mīlād (m)	عيد الميلاد
Merry Christmas!	ʿīd mīlād saʿīd!	عيد ميلاد سعيد!
Christmas tree	ʃaʒarat ra's as sana (f)	شجرة رأس السنة
fireworks (fireworks show)	al'āb nāriyya (pl)	ألعاب ناريّة
wedding	zifāf (m)	زفاف
groom	ʿarīs (m)	عريس
bride	ʿarūsa (f)	عروسة
to invite (vt)	da'a	دعا
invitation card	biṭāqat da'wa (f)	بطاقة دعوة
guest	ḍayf (m)	ضيف
to visit (~ your parents, etc.)	zār	زار
to meet the guests	istaqbal aḍ ḍuyūf	إستقبل الضيوف
gift, present	hadiyya (f)	هديّة
to give (sth as present)	qaddam	قدّم
to receive gifts	istalam al hadāya	إستلم الهدايا
bouquet (of flowers)	bāqat zuhūr (f)	باقة زهور
congratulations	tahnī'a (f)	تهنئة
to congratulate (vt)	hanna'	هنّأ
greetings card	biṭāqat tahnī'a (f)	بطاقة تهنئة
to send a postcard	arsal biṭāqat tahni'a	أرسل بطاقة تهنئة
to get a postcard	istalam biṭāqat tahnī'a	إستلم بطاقة تهنئة

toast	naxb (m)	نخب
to offer (a drink, etc.)	dayyaf	ضيّف
champagne	ʃambāniya (f)	شمبانيا
to enjoy oneself	istamtaʿ	إستمتع
merriment (gaiety)	farah (m)	فرح
joy (emotion)	saʿāda (f)	سعادة
dance	rāqiṣa (f)	رقصة
to dance (vi, vt)	raqaṣ	رقص
waltz	vāls (m)	فالس
tango	tāngu (m)	تانجو

153. Funerals. Burial

cemetery	maqbara (f)	مقبرة
grave, tomb	qabr (m)	قبر
cross	ṣalīb (m)	صليب
gravestone	ʃāhid al qabr (m)	شاهد القبر
fence	sūr (m)	سور
chapel	kanīsa saɣīra (f)	كنيسة صغيرة
death	mawt (m)	موت
to die (vi)	māt	مات
the deceased	al mutawaffi (m)	المتوفّي
mourning	hidād (m)	حداد
to bury (vt)	dafan	دفن
undertakers	bayt al ʒanāzāt (m)	بيت الجنازات
funeral	ʒanāza (f)	جنازة
wreath	iklīl (m)	إكليل
coffin	tābūt (m)	تابوت
hearse	sayyārat naql al mawta (f)	سيّارة نقل الموتى
shroud	kafan (m)	كفن
funeral procession	ʒanāza (f)	جنازة
funerary urn	qārūra li hifz ramād al mawta (f)	قارورة لحفظ رماد الموتى
crematorium	mahraqat ʒuθaθ al mawta (f)	محرقة جثث الموتى
obituary	naʿiy (m)	نعيّ
to cry (weep)	baka	بكى
to sob (vi)	nahab	نحب

154. War. Soldiers

platoon	faṣīla (f)	فصيلة
company	sariyya (f)	سريّة
regiment	fawʒ (m)	فوج
army	ʒayʃ (m)	جيش

division	firqa (f)	فرقة
section, squad	waḥda (f)	وحدة
host (army)	ʒayʃ (m)	جيش
soldier	ʒundiy (m)	جنديّ
officer	ḍābiṭ (m)	ضابط
private	ʒundiy (m)	جنديّ
sergeant	raqīb (m)	رقيب
lieutenant	mulāzim (m)	ملازم
captain	naqīb (m)	نقيب
major	rā'id (m)	رائد
colonel	ʿaqīd (m)	عقيد
general	ʒinirāl (m)	جنرال
sailor	baḥḥār (m)	بحّار
captain	qubṭān (m)	قبطان
boatswain	raʾīs al baḥḥāra (m)	رئيس البحّارة
artilleryman	madfaʿiy (m)	مدفعيّ
paratrooper	ʒundiy al maẓallāt (m)	جنديّ المظلّلات
pilot	ṭayyār (m)	طيّار
navigator	mallāḥ (m)	ملّاح
mechanic	mikanīkiy (m)	ميكانيكيّ
pioneer (sapper)	muhandis ʿaskariy (m)	مهندس عسكريّ
parachutist	miẓalliy (m)	مظلّيّ
reconnaissance scout	mustakʃif (m)	مستكشف
sniper	qannāṣ (m)	قنّاص
patrol (group)	dawriyya (f)	دوريّة
to patrol (vt)	qām bi dawriyya	قام بدوريّة
sentry, guard	ḥāris (m)	حارس
warrior	muḥārib (m)	محارب
patriot	waṭaniy (m)	وطنيّ
hero	baṭal (m)	بطل
heroine	baṭala (f)	بطلة
traitor	χā'in (m)	خائن
to betray (vt)	χān	خان
deserter	hārib min al ʒayʃ (m)	هارب من الجيش
to desert (vi)	harab min al ʒayʃ	هرب من الجيش
mercenary	ma'ʒūr (m)	مأجور
recruit	ʒundiy ʒadīd (m)	جنديّ جديد
volunteer	mutaṭawwiʿ (m)	متطوّع
dead (n)	qatīl (m)	قتيل
wounded (n)	ʒarīḥ (m)	جريح
prisoner of war	asīr (m)	أسير

155. War. Military actions. Part 1

war	ḥarb (f)	حرب
to be at war	ḥārab	حارب

civil war	ḥarb ahliyya (f)	حرب أهلّية
treacherously (adv)	γadran	غدرًا
declaration of war	i'lān ḥarb (m)	إعلان حرب
to declare (~ war)	a'lan	أعلن
aggression	'udwān (m)	عدوان
to attack (invade)	haʒam	هجم

to invade (vt)	iḥtall	إحتلّ
invader	muḥtall (m)	محتلّ
conqueror	fātiḥ (m)	فاتح

defence	difā' (m)	دفاع
to defend (a country, etc.)	dāfa'	دافع
to defend (against …)	dāfa' 'an nafsih	دافع عن نفسه

enemy	'aduww (m)	عدوّ
foe, adversary	χaṣm (m)	خصم
enemy (as adj)	'aduww	عدوّ

| strategy | istratiʒiyya (f) | إستراتيجيّة |
| tactics | taktīk (m) | تكتيك |

order	amr (m)	أمر
command (order)	amr (m)	أمر
to order (vt)	amar	أمر
mission	muhimma (f)	مهمّة
secret (adj)	sirriy	سرّيّ

| battle | ma'raka (f) | معركة |
| combat | qitāl (m) | قتال |

attack	huʒūm (m)	هجوم
charge (assault)	inqiḍāḍ (m)	إنقضاض
to storm (vt)	inqaḍḍ	إنقضّ
siege (to be under ~)	ḥiṣār (m)	حصار

| offensive (n) | huʒūm (m) | هجوم |
| to go on the offensive | haʒam | هجم |

| retreat | insiḥāb (m) | إنسحاب |
| to retreat (vi) | insaḥab | إنسحب |

| encirclement | iḥāṭa (f) | إحاطة |
| to encircle (vt) | aḥāṭ | أحاط |

bombing (by aircraft)	qaṣf (m)	قصف
to drop a bomb	asqaṭ qumbula	أسقط قنبلة
to bomb (vt)	qaṣaf	قصف
explosion	infiʒār (m)	إنفجار

shot	ṭalaqa (f)	طلقة
to fire (~ a shot)	aṭlaq an nār	أطلق النار
firing (burst of ~)	iṭlāq an nār (m)	إطلاق النار

| to aim (to point a weapon) | ṣawwab | صوّب |
| to point (a gun) | ṣawwab | صوّب |

to hit (the target)	aṣāb al hadaf	أصاب الهدف
to sink (~ a ship)	aɣraq	أغرق
hole (in a ship)	θuqb (m)	ثقب
to founder, to sink (vi)	ɣariq	غرق

front (war ~)	ʒabha (f)	جبهة
evacuation	iχlā' aṭ ṭawāri' (m)	إخلاء الطوارئ
to evacuate (vt)	aχla	أخلى

trench	χandaq (m)	خندق
barbed wire	aslāk ʃā'ika (pl)	أسلاك شائكة
barrier (anti tank ~)	ḥāʒiz (m)	حاجز
watchtower	burʒ muraqaba (m)	برج مراقبة

military hospital	mustaʃfa 'askariy (m)	مستشفى عسكريّ
to wound (vt)	ʒaraḥ	جرح
wound	ʒurḥ (m)	جرح
wounded (n)	ʒarīḥ (m)	جريح
to be wounded	uṣīb bil ʒirāḥ	أصيب بالجراح
serious (wound)	χaṭīr	خطير

156. Weapons

weapons	asliḥa (pl)	أسلحة
firearms	asliḥa nāriyya (pl)	أسلحة ناريّة
cold weapons (knives, etc.)	asliḥa bayḍā' (pl)	أسلحة بيضاء

chemical weapons	asliḥa kīmyā'iyya (pl)	أسلحة كيميائيّة
nuclear (adj)	nawawiy	نوويّ
nuclear weapons	asliḥa nawawiyya (pl)	أسلحة نوويّة

bomb	qumbula (f)	قنبلة
atomic bomb	qumbula nawawiyya (f)	قنبلة نوويّة

pistol (gun)	musaddas (m)	مسدّس
rifle	bunduqiyya (f)	بندقيّة
submachine gun	bunduqiyya huʒūmiyya (f)	بندقيّة هجوميّة
machine gun	raʃʃāʃ (m)	رشّاش

muzzle	fūha (f)	فوهة
barrel	sabṭāna (f)	سبطانة
calibre	'iyār (m)	عيار

trigger	zinād (m)	زناد
sight (aiming device)	muṣawwib (m)	مصوّب
magazine	maχzan (m)	مخزن
butt (shoulder stock)	'aqab al bunduqiyya (m)	عقب البندقيّة

hand grenade	qumbula yadawiyya (f)	قنبلة يدويّة
explosive	mawādd mutafaʒʒira (pl)	موادّ متفجّرة

bullet	ruṣāṣa (f)	رصاصة
cartridge	χarṭūʃa (f)	خرطوشة
charge	ḥaʃwa (f)	حشوة

ammunition	ðaχā'ir (pl)	ذخائر
bomber (aircraft)	qāðifat qanābil (f)	قاذفة قنابل
fighter	ṭā'ira muqātila (f)	طائرة مقاتلة
helicopter	hiliukūbtir (m)	هليكوبتر
anti-aircraft gun	madfaθ muḍādd liṭ ṭa'irāṭ (m)	مدفع مضادٌ للطائرات
tank	dabbāba (f)	دبّابة
tank gun	madfaʿ ad dabbāba (m)	مدفع الدبّابة
artillery	madfaʿiyya (f)	مدفعيّة
gun (cannon, howitzer)	madfaʿ (m)	مدفع
to lay (a gun)	ṣawwab	صوّب
shell (projectile)	qaðīfa (f)	قذيفة
mortar bomb	qumbula hāwun (f)	قنبلة هاون
mortar	hāwun (m)	هاون
splinter (shell fragment)	ʃaẓiyya (f)	شظيّة
submarine	ɣawwāṣa (f)	غوّاصة
torpedo	ṭurbīd (m)	طوربيد
missile	ṣārūχ (m)	صاروخ
to load (gun)	ḥaʃa	حشا
to shoot (vi)	aṭlaq an nār	أطلق النار
to point at (the cannon)	ṣawwab	صوّب
bayonet	ḥarba (f)	حربة
rapier	ʃīʃ (m)	شيش
sabre (e.g. cavalry ~)	sayf munḥani (m)	سيف منحن
spear (weapon)	rumḥ (m)	رمح
bow	qaws (m)	قوس
arrow	sahm (m)	سهم
musket	muskīt (m)	مسكيت
crossbow	qaws mustaʿraḍ (m)	قوس مستعرض

157. Ancient people

primitive (prehistoric)	bidā'iy	بدائيّ
prehistoric (adj)	ma qabl at tarīχ	ما قبْل التاريخ
ancient (~ civilization)	qadīm	قديم
Stone Age	al ʿaṣr al ḥaʒariy (m)	العصر الحجريّ
Bronze Age	al ʿaṣr al brunziy (m)	العصر البرونزيّ
Ice Age	al ʿaṣr al ʒalīdiy (m)	العصر الجليديّ
tribe	qabīla (f)	قبيلة
cannibal	'ākil laḥm al baʃar (m)	آكل لحم البشر
hunter	ṣayyād (m)	صيّاد
to hunt (vi, vt)	iṣṭād	إصطاد
mammoth	mamūθ (m)	ماموث
cave	kahf (m)	كهف
fire	nār (f)	نار
campfire	nār muχayyam (m)	نار مخيّم

cave painting	rasm fil kahf (m)	رسم في الكهف
tool (e.g. stone axe)	adāt (f)	أداة
spear	rumḥ (m)	رمح
stone axe	fa's haʒariy (m)	فأس حجريّ
to be at war	ḥārab	حارب
to domesticate (vt)	daʒʒan	دجّن
idol	ṣanam (m)	صنم
to worship (vt)	'abad	عبد
superstition	xurāfa (f)	خرافة
rite	mansak (m)	منسك
evolution	taṭawwur (m)	تطوّر
development	numuww (m)	نموّ
disappearance (extinction)	ixtifā' (m)	إختفاء
to adapt oneself	takayyaf	تكيّف
archaeology	'ilm al 'āθār (m)	علم الآثار
archaeologist	'ālim'āθār (m)	عالِم آثار
archaeological (adj)	aθariy	أثري
excavation site	mawqi' ḥafr (m)	موقع حفر
excavations	tanqīb (m)	تنقيب
find (object)	iktiʃāf (m)	إكتشاف
fragment	qiṭ'a (f)	قطعة

158. Middle Ages

people (ethnic group)	ʃa'b (m)	شعب
peoples	ʃu'ūb (pl)	شعوب
tribe	qabīla (f)	قبيلة
tribes	qabā'il (pl)	قبائل
barbarians	al barābira (pl)	البرابرة
Gauls	al γalyūn (pl)	الغاليون
Goths	al qūṭiyyūn (pl)	القوطيّون
Slavs	as silāf (pl)	السلاف
Vikings	al vaykinγ (pl)	الفايكينغ
Romans	ar rūmān (pl)	الرومان
Roman (adj)	rumāniy	رومانيّ
Byzantines	bizanṭiyyūn (pl)	بيزنطيّون
Byzantium	bīzanṭa (f)	بيزنطة
Byzantine (adj)	bizanṭiy	بيزنطيّ
emperor	imbiraṭūr (m)	إمبراطور
leader, chief (tribal ~)	za'īm (m)	زعيم
powerful (~ king)	qawiy	قويّ
king	malik (m)	ملك
ruler (sovereign)	ḥākim (m)	حاكم
knight	fāris (m)	فارس
feudal lord	iqṭā'iy (m)	إقطاعيّ

feudal (adj)	iqtā'iy	إقطاعيّ
vassal	muqta' (m)	مقطع
duke	dūq (m)	دوق
earl	īrl (m)	إيرل
baron	barūn (m)	بارون
bishop	usquf (m)	أسقف
armour	dir' (m)	درع
shield	turs (m)	ترس
sword	sayf (m)	سيف
visor	ḥāffa amāmiyya lil χūða (f)	حافة أماميّة للخوذة
chainmail	dir' az zarad (m)	درع الزرد
Crusade	ḥamla ṣalībiyya (f)	حملة صليبيّة
crusader	ṣalībiy (m)	صليبيّ
territory	arḍ (f)	أرض
to attack (invade)	haʒam	هجم
to conquer (vt)	fataḥ	فتح
to occupy (invade)	iḥtall	إحتلّ
siege (to be under ~)	ḥiṣār (m)	حصار
besieged (adj)	muḥāṣar	محاصر
to besiege (vt)	ḥāṣar	حاصر
inquisition	maḥākim at taftīʃ (pl)	محاكم التفتيش
inquisitor	mufattiʃ (m)	مفتّش
torture	ta'ðīb (m)	تعذيب
cruel (adj)	qās	قاس
heretic	hartūqiy (m)	هرطوقيّ
heresy	hartaqa (f)	هرطقة
seafaring	as safar bil baḥr (m)	السفر بالبحر
pirate	qurṣān (m)	قرصان
piracy	qarṣana (f)	قرصنة
boarding (attack)	muhāʒmat safīna (f)	مهاجمة سفينة
loot, booty	ɣanīma (f)	غنيمة
treasure	kunūz (pl)	كنوز
discovery	iktiʃāf (m)	إكتشاف
to discover (new land, etc.)	iktaʃaf	إكتشف
expedition	ba'θa (f)	بعثة
musketeer	fāris (m)	فارس
cardinal	kardināl (m)	كاردينال
heraldry	ʃi'ārāt an nabāla (pl)	شعارات النبالة
heraldic (adj)	χāṣṣ bi ʃi'ārāt an nabāla	خاصّ بشعارات النبالة

159. Leader. Chief. Authorities

king	malik (m)	ملك
queen	malika (f)	ملكة
royal (adj)	malakiy	ملكيّ

kingdom	mamlaka (f)	مملكة
prince	amīr (m)	أمير
princess	amīra (f)	أميرة
president	raīs (m)	رئيس
vice-president	nā'ib ar raīs (m)	نائب الرئيس
senator	'uḍw maʒlis aʃ ʃuyūχ (m)	عضو مجلس الشيوخ
monarch	'āhil (m)	عاهل
ruler (sovereign)	ḥakim (m)	حاكم
dictator	diktatūr (m)	ديكتاتور
tyrant	ṭāɣiya (f)	طاغية
magnate	ra'smāliy kabīr (m)	رأسمالي كبير
director	mudīr (m)	مدير
chief	raīs (m)	رئيس
manager (director)	mudīr (m)	مدير
boss	raīs (m), mudīr (m)	رئيس، مدير
owner	ṣāḥib (m)	صاحب
leader	zaīm (m)	زعيم
head (~ of delegation)	raīs (m)	رئيس
authorities	suluṭāt (pl)	سلطات
superiors	ru'asā' (pl)	رؤساء
governor	muḥāfiẓ (m)	محافظ
consul	qunṣul (m)	قنصل
diplomat	diblumāsiy (m)	دبلوماسيّ
mayor	raīs al baladiyya (m)	رئيس البلديّة
sheriff	ʃarīf (m)	شريف
emperor	imbiraṭūr (m)	إمبراطور
tsar, czar	qayṣar (m)	قيصر
pharaoh	fir'awn (m)	فرعون
khan	χān (m)	خان

160. Breaking the law. Criminals. Part 1

bandit	qāṭi' ṭarīq (m)	قاطع طريق
crime	ʒarīma (f)	جريمة
criminal (person)	muʒrim (m)	مجرم
thief	sāriq (m)	سارق
to steal (vi, vt)	saraq	سرق
stealing, theft	sirqa (f)	سرقة
to kidnap (vt)	χaṭaf	خطف
kidnapping	χaṭf (m)	خطف
kidnapper	χāṭif (m)	خاطف
ransom	fidya (f)	فدية
to demand ransom	ṭalab fidya	طلب فدية
to rob (vt)	nahab	نهب
robbery	nahb (m)	نهب

robber	nahhāb (m)	نهّاب
to extort (vt)	balṭaʒ	بلطج
extortionist	balṭaʒiy (m)	بلطجيّ
extortion	balṭaʒa (f)	بلطجة
to murder, to kill	qatal	قتل
murder	qatl (m)	قتل
murderer	qātil (m)	قاتل
gunshot	ṭalaqat nār (f)	طلقة نار
to fire (~ a shot)	aṭlaq an nār	أطلق النار
to shoot to death	qatal bir ruṣāṣ	قتل بالرصاص
to shoot (vi)	aṭlaq an nār	أطلق النار
shooting	iṭlāq an nār (m)	إطلاق النار
incident (fight, etc.)	ḥādiθ (m)	حادث
fight, brawl	ʿirāk (m)	عراك
Help!	sāʿidni	ساعدني!
victim	ḍaḥiyya (f)	ضحيّة
to damage (vt)	atlaf	أتلف
damage	xasāra (f)	خسارة
dead body, corpse	ʒuθθa (f)	جثّة
grave (~ crime)	ʿanīf	عنيف
to attack (vt)	haʒam	هجم
to beat (to hit)	ḍarab	ضرب
to beat up	ḍarab	ضرب
to take (rob of sth)	salab	سلب
to stab to death	ṭaʿan ḥatta al mawt	طعن حتّى الموت
to maim (vt)	ʃawwah	شوّه
to wound (vt)	ʒaraḥ	جرح
blackmail	balṭaʒa (f)	بلطجة
to blackmail (vt)	ibtazz	إبتزّ
blackmailer	mubtazz (m)	مبتزّ
protection racket	naṣb (m)	نصب
racketeer	naṣṣāb (m)	نصّاب
gangster	raʒul ʿiṣāba (m)	رجل عصابة
mafia	māfia (f)	مافيا
pickpocket	naʃʃāl (m)	نشّال
burglar	liṣṣ buyūt (m)	لصّ بيوت
smuggling	tahrīb (m)	تهريب
smuggler	muharrib (m)	مهرّب
forgery	tazwīr (m)	تزوير
to forge (counterfeit)	zawwar	زوّر
fake (forged)	muzawwar	مزوّر

161. Breaking the law. Criminals. Part 2

rape	iɣtiṣāb (m)	إغتصاب
to rape (vt)	iɣtaṣab	إغتصب

rapist	muɣtaṣib (m)	مغتصب
maniac	mahwūs (m)	مهووس
prostitute (fem.)	ʿāhira (f)	عاهرة
prostitution	daʿāra (f)	دعارة
pimp	qawwād (m)	قوّاد
drug addict	mudmin muxaddirāt (m)	مدمن مخدّرات
drug dealer	tāʒir muxaddirāt (m)	تاجر مخدّرات
to blow up (bomb)	faʒʒar	فجّر
explosion	infiʒār (m)	إنفجار
to set fire	afʿal an nār	أشعل النار
arsonist	muʃʿil ḥarīq (m)	مشعل حريق
terrorism	irhāb (m)	إرهاب
terrorist	irhābiy (m)	إرهابيّ
hostage	rahīna (m)	رهينة
to swindle (deceive)	iḥtāl	إحتال
swindle, deception	iḥtiyāl (m)	إحتيال
swindler	muḥtāl (m)	محتال
to bribe (vt)	raʃa	رشا
bribery	irtiʃāʾ (m)	إرتشاء
bribe	raʃwa (f)	رشوة
poison	samm (m)	سمّ
to poison (vt)	sammam	سمّم
to poison oneself	sammam nafsahu	سمّم نفسه
suicide (act)	intiḥār (m)	إنتحار
suicide (person)	muntaḥir (m)	منتحر
to threaten (vt)	haddad	هدّد
threat	tahdīd (m)	تهديد
to make an attempt	ḥāwal iɣtiyāl	حاول الإغتيال
attempt (attack)	muḥāwalat iɣtiyāl (f)	محاولة إغتيال
to steal (a car)	saraq	سرق
to hijack (a plane)	ixtaṭaf	إختطف
revenge	intiqām (m)	إنتقام
to avenge (get revenge)	intaqam	إنتقم
to torture (vt)	ʿaððab	عذّب
torture	taʿðīb (m)	تعذيب
to torment (vt)	ʿaððab	عذّب
pirate	qurṣān (m)	قرصان
hooligan	wabaʃ (m)	وبش
armed (adj)	musallaḥ	مسلّح
violence	ʿunf (m)	عنف
illegal (unlawful)	ɣayr qānūniy	غير قانونيّ
spying (espionage)	taʒassas (m)	تجسّس
to spy (vi)	taʒassas	تجسّس

162. Police. Law. Part 1

justice	qaḍā' (m)	قضاء
court (see you in ~)	maḥkama (f)	محكمة
judge	qāḍi (m)	قاض
jurors	muḥallafūn (pl)	محلّفون
jury trial	qaḍā' al muḥallafīn (m)	قضاء المحلّفين
to judge, to try (vt)	ḥakam	حكم
lawyer, barrister	muḥāmi (m)	محام
defendant	mudda'a 'alayh (m)	مدّعى عليه
dock	qafṣ al ittihām (m)	قفص الإتّهام
charge	ittihām (m)	إتّهام
accused	muttaham (m)	متّهم
sentence	ḥukm (m)	حكم
to sentence (vt)	ḥakam	حكم
guilty (culprit)	muðnib (m)	مذنب
to punish (vt)	'āqab	عاقب
punishment	'uqūba (f), 'iqāb (m)	عقوبة, عقاب
fine (penalty)	ɣarāma (f)	غرامة
life imprisonment	siʒn mada al ḥayāt (m)	سجن مدى الحياة
death penalty	'uqūbat 'i'dām (f)	عقوبة إعدام
electric chair	kursiy kaharabā'iy (m)	كرسيّ كهربائيّ
gallows	maʃnaqa (f)	مشنقة
to execute (vt)	a'dam	أعدم
execution	i'dām (m)	إعدام
prison	siʒn (m)	سجن
cell	zinzāna (f)	زنزانة
escort (convoy)	ḥirāsa (f)	حراسة
prison officer	ḥāris siʒn (m)	حارس سجن
prisoner	saʒīn (m)	سجين
handcuffs	aṣfād (pl)	أصفاد
to handcuff (vt)	ṣaffad	صفّد
prison break	hurūb min as siʒn (m)	هروب من السجن
to break out (vi)	harab	هرب
to disappear (vi)	iχtafa	إختفى
to release (from prison)	aχla sabīl	أخلى سبيل
amnesty	'afw 'āmm (m)	عفو عامّ
police	ʃurṭa (f)	شرطة
police officer	ʃurṭiy (m)	شرطيّ
police station	qism ʃurṭa (m)	قسم شرطة
truncheon	hirāwat aʃ ʃurṭiy (f)	هراوة الشرطيّ
megaphone (loudhailer)	būq (m)	بوق
patrol car	sayyārat dawriyyāt (f)	سيّارة دوريّات

siren	ṣaffārat inðār (f)	صفّارة إنذار
to turn on the siren	aṭlaq sirīna	أطلق سرينة
siren call	ṣawt sirīna (m)	صوت سرينة
crime scene	masraḥ al ʒarīma (m)	مسرح الجريمة
witness	ʃāhid (m)	شاهد
freedom	ḥurriyya (f)	حرّية
accomplice	ʃarīk fil ʒarīma (m)	شريك في الجريمة
to flee (vi)	harab	هرب
trace (to leave a ~)	aθar (m)	أثر

163. Police. Law. Part 2

search (investigation)	baḥθ (m)	بحث
to look for ...	baḥaθ	بحث
suspicion	ʃubha (f)	شبهة
suspicious (e.g., ~ vehicle)	maʃbūh	مشبوه
to stop (cause to halt)	awqaf	أوقف
to detain (keep in custody)	iʻtaqal	إعتقل
case (lawsuit)	qaḍiyya (f)	قضيّة
investigation	taḥqīq (m)	تحقيق
detective	muḥaqqiq (m)	محقّق
investigator	mufattiʃ (m)	مفتّش
hypothesis	riwāya (f)	رواية
motive	dāfiʻ (m)	دافع
interrogation	istiʒwāb (m)	إستجواب
to interrogate (vt)	istaʒwab	إستجوب
to question (~ neighbors, etc.)	istanṭaq	إستنطق
check (identity ~)	faḥṣ (m)	فحص
round-up (raid)	ʒamʻ (m)	جمع
search (~ warrant)	taftīʃ (m)	تفتيش
chase (pursuit)	muṭārada (f)	مطاردة
to pursue, to chase	ṭārad	طارد
to track (a criminal)	tābaʻ	تابع
arrest	iʻtiqāl (m)	إعتقال
to arrest (sb)	iʻtaqal	إعتقل
to catch (thief, etc.)	qabaḍ	قبض
capture	qabḍ (m)	قبض
document	waθīqa (f)	وثيقة
proof (evidence)	dalīl (m)	دليل
to prove (vt)	aθbat	أثبت
footprint	baṣma (f)	بصمة
fingerprints	baṣamāt al aṣābiʻ (pl)	بصمات الأصابع
piece of evidence	dalīl (m)	دليل
alibi	dafʻ bil ɣayba (f)	دفع بالغيبة
innocent (not guilty)	barīʼ	بريء
injustice	ẓulm (m)	ظلم

unjust, unfair (adj)	ɣayr 'ādil	غير عادل
criminal (adj)	iʒrāmiy	إجرامي
to confiscate (vt)	ṣādar	صادر
drug (illegal substance)	muxaddirāt (pl)	مخدرات
weapon, gun	silāḥ (m)	سلاح
to disarm (vt)	ʒarrad min as silāḥ	جرّد من السلاح
to order (command)	amar	أمر
to disappear (vi)	ixtafa	إختفى
law	qānūn (m)	قانون
legal, lawful (adj)	qānūniy, ʃar'iy	قانوني، شرعي
illegal, illicit (adj)	ɣayr qanūny, ɣayr ʃar'i	غير قانوني، غير شرعي
responsibility (blame)	mas'ūliyya (f)	مسؤوليّة
responsible (adj)	mas'ūl (m)	مسؤول

NATURE

The Earth. Part 1

164. Outer space

space	faḍā' (m)	فضاء
space (as adj)	faḍā'iy	فضائيّ
outer space	faḍā' (m)	فضاء
world	'ālam (m)	عالم
universe	al kawn (m)	الكون
galaxy	al maʒarra (f)	المجرّة
star	naʒm (m)	نجم
constellation	burʒ (m)	برج
planet	kawkab (m)	كوكب
satellite	qamar ṣinā'iy (m)	قمر صناعيّ
meteorite	haʒar nayzakiy (m)	حجر نيزكيّ
comet	muðannab (m)	مذنّب
asteroid	kuwaykib (m)	كويكب
orbit	madār (m)	مدار
to revolve (~ around the Earth)	dār	دار
atmosphere	al ɣilāf al ʒawwiy (m)	الغلاف الجوّيّ
the Sun	aʃ ʃams (f)	الشمس
solar system	al maʒmū'a aʃ ʃamsiyya (f)	المجموعة الشمسيّة
solar eclipse	kusūf aʃ ʃams (m)	كسوف الشمس
the Earth	al arḍ (f)	الأرض
the Moon	al qamar (m)	القمر
Mars	al mirrīχ (m)	المرّيخ
Venus	az zahra (f)	الزهرة
Jupiter	al muʃtari (m)	المشتري
Saturn	zuhal (m)	زحل
Mercury	'aṭārid (m)	عطارد
Uranus	urānus (m)	اورانوس
Neptune	nibtūn (m)	نبتون
Pluto	blūtu (m)	بلوتو
Milky Way	darb at tabbāna (m)	درب التبّانة
Great Bear (Ursa Major)	ad dubb al akbar (m)	الدبّ الأكبر
North Star	naʒm al 'quṭb (m)	نجم القطب
Martian	sākin al mirrīχ (m)	ساكن المرّيخ
extraterrestrial (n)	faḍā'iy (m)	فضائيّ

alien	faḍā'iy (m)	فضائيّ
flying saucer	ṭabaq ṭā'ir (m)	طبق طائر
spaceship	markaba faḍā'iyya (f)	مركبة فضائيّة
space station	maḥaṭṭat faḍā' (f)	محطّة فضاء
blast-off	inṭilāq (m)	إنطلاق
engine	mutūr (m)	موتور
nozzle	manfaθ (m)	منفث
fuel	wuqūd (m)	وقود
cockpit, flight deck	kabīna (f)	كابينة
aerial	hawā'iy (m)	هوائيّ
porthole	kuwwa mustadīra (f)	كوّة مستديرة
solar panel	lawḥ ʃamsiy (m)	لوح شمسيّ
spacesuit	baðlat al faḍā' (f)	بذلة الفضاء
weightlessness	in'idām al wazn (m)	إنعدام الوزن
oxygen	uksiʒīn (m)	أكسجين
docking (in space)	rasw (m)	رسو
to dock (vi, vt)	rasa	رسا
observatory	marṣad (m)	مرصد
telescope	tiliskūp (m)	تلسكوب
to observe (vt)	rāqab	راقب
to explore (vt)	istakʃaf	إستكشف

165. The Earth

the Earth	al arḍ (f)	الأرض
the globe (the Earth)	al kura al arḍiyya (f)	الكرة الأرضيّة
planet	kawkab (m)	كوكب
atmosphere	al ɣilāf al ʒawwiy (m)	الغلاف الجوّيّ
geography	ʒuɣrāfiya (f)	جغرافيا
nature	ṭabī'a (f)	طبيعة
globe (table ~)	namūðaʒ lil kura al arḍiyya (m)	نموذج للكرة الأرضيّة
map	χarīṭa (f)	خريطة
atlas	aṭlas (m)	أطلس
Europe	urūbba (f)	أوروبّا
Asia	'āsiya (f)	آسيا
Africa	afrīqiya (f)	أفريقيا
Australia	usturāliya (f)	أستراليا
America	amrīka (f)	أمريكا
North America	amrīka aʃ ʃimāliyya (f)	أمريكا الشماليّة
South America	amrīka al ʒanūbiyya (f)	أمريكا الجنوبيّة
Antarctica	al quṭb al ʒanūbiy (m)	القطب الجنوبيّ
the Arctic	al quṭb aʃ ʃimāliy (m)	القطب الشماليّ

166. Cardinal directions

north	ʃimāl (m)	شمال
to the north	ilaʃ ʃimāl	إلى الشمال
in the north	fiʃ ʃimāl	في الشمال
northern (adj)	ʃimāliy	شماليّ
south	ʒanūb (m)	جنوب
to the south	ilal ʒanūb	إلى الجنوب
in the south	fil ʒanūb	في الجنوب
southern (adj)	ʒanūbiy	جنوبيّ
west	ɣarb (m)	غرب
to the west	ilal ɣarb	إلى الغرب
in the west	fil ɣarb	في الغرب
western (adj)	ɣarbiy	غربيّ
east	ʃarq (m)	شرق
to the east	ilaʃ ʃarq	إلى الشرق
in the east	fiʃ ʃarq	في الشرق
eastern (adj)	ʃarqiy	شرقيّ

167. Sea. Ocean

sea	baḥr (m)	بحر
ocean	muḥīṭ (m)	محيط
gulf (bay)	xalīʒ (m)	خليج
straits	maḍīq (m)	مضيق
land (solid ground)	barr (m)	برّ
continent (mainland)	qārra (f)	قارّة
island	ʒazīra (f)	جزيرة
peninsula	ʃibh ʒazīra (f)	شبه جزيرة
archipelago	maʒmūʕat ʒuzur (f)	مجموعة جزر
bay, cove	xalīʒ (m)	خليج
harbour	mīnāʼ (m)	ميناء
lagoon	buḥayra ʃāṭiʼa (f)	بحيرة شاطئة
cape	raʼs (m)	رأس
atoll	ʒazīra marʒāniyya istiwāʼiyya (f)	جزيرة مرجانيّة إستوائيّة
reef	ʃiʕāb (pl)	شعاب
coral	murʒān (m)	مرجان
coral reef	ʃiʕāb marʒāniyya (pl)	شعاب مرجانيّة
deep (adj)	ʼamīq	عميق
depth (deep water)	ʕumq (m)	عمق
abyss	mahwāt (f)	مهواة
trench (e.g. Mariana ~)	xandaq (m)	خندق
current (Ocean ~)	tayyār (m)	تيّار
to surround (bathe)	aḥāṭ	أحاط

shore	sāḥil (m)	ساحل
coast	sāḥil (m)	ساحل
flow (flood tide)	madd (m)	مدّ
ebb (ebb tide)	ʒazr (m)	جزر
shoal	miyāh ḍaḥla (f)	مياه ضحلة
bottom (~ of the sea)	qāʿ (m)	قاع
wave	mawʒa (f)	موجة
crest (~ of a wave)	qimmat mawʒa (f)	قمّة موجة
spume (sea foam)	zabad al baḥr (m)	زبد البحر
storm (sea storm)	ʿāṣifa (f)	عاصفة
hurricane	iʿṣār (m)	إعصار
tsunami	tsunāmi (m)	تسونامي
calm (dead ~)	hudūʾ (m)	هدوء
quiet, calm (adj)	hādiʾ	هادئ
pole	quṭb (m)	قطب
polar (adj)	quṭby	قطبيّ
latitude	ʿarḍ (m)	عرض
longitude	ṭūl (m)	طول
parallel	mutawāzi (m)	متواز
equator	χaṭṭ al istiwāʾ (m)	خط الإستواء
sky	samāʾ (f)	سماء
horizon	ufuq (m)	أفق
air	hawāʾ (m)	هواء
lighthouse	manāra (f)	منارة
to dive (vi)	ɣāṣ	غاص
to sink (ab. boat)	ɣariq	غرق
treasure	kunūz (pl)	كنوز

168. Mountains

mountain	ʒabal (m)	جبل
mountain range	silsilat ʒibāl (f)	سلسلة جبال
mountain ridge	qimam ʒabaliyya (pl)	قمم جبليّة
summit, top	qimma (f)	قمّة
peak	qimma (f)	قمّة
foot (~ of the mountain)	asfal (m)	أسفل
slope (mountainside)	munḥadar (m)	منحدر
volcano	burkān (m)	بركان
active volcano	burkān naʃiṭ (m)	بركان نشط
dormant volcano	burkān χāmid (m)	بركان خامد
eruption	θawrān (m)	ثوران
crater	fūhat al burkān (f)	فوهة البركان
magma	māɣma (f)	ماغما
lava	ḥumam burkāniyya (pl)	حمم بركانيّة

molten (~ lava)	munṣahira	منصهرة
canyon	tal‘a (m)	تلعة
gorge	wādi ḍayyiq (m)	واد ضيّق
crevice	ʃaqq (m)	شقّ
abyss (chasm)	hāwiya (f)	هاوية
pass, col	mamarr ʒabaliy (m)	ممرّ جبليّ
plateau	haḍba (f)	هضبة
cliff	ʒurf (m)	جرف
hill	tall (m)	تلّ
glacier	nahr ʒalīdiy (m)	نهر جليديّ
waterfall	ʃallāl (m)	شلّال
geyser	fawwāra ḥārra (m)	فوّارة حارّة
lake	buḥayra (f)	بحيرة
plain	sahl (m)	سهل
landscape	manẓar ṭabīʿiy (m)	منظر طبيعيّ
echo	ṣada (m)	صدى
alpinist	mutasalliq al ʒibāl (m)	متسلّق الجبال
rock climber	mutasalliq ṣuxūr (m)	متسلّق صخور
to conquer (in climbing)	taɣallab ‘ala	تغلّب على
climb (an easy ~)	tasalluq (m)	تسلّق

169. Rivers

river	nahr (m)	نهر
spring (natural source)	‘ayn (m)	عين
riverbed (river channel)	maʒra an nahr (m)	مجرى النهر
basin (river valley)	ḥawḍ (m)	حوض
to flow into ...	ṣabb fi ...	صبّ في...
tributary	rāfid (m)	رافد
bank (river ~)	ḍiffa (f)	ضفّة
current (stream)	tayyār (m)	تيّار
downstream (adv)	f ittiʒāh maʒra an nahr	في إتجاه مجرى النهر
upstream (adv)	ḍidd at tayyār	ضد التيّار
inundation	ɣamr (m)	غمر
flooding	fayaḍān (m)	فيضان
to overflow (vi)	fāḍ	فاض
to flood (vt)	ɣamar	غمر
shallow (shoal)	miyāh ḍaḥla (f)	مياه ضحلة
rapids	munḥadar an nahr (m)	منحدر النهر
dam	sadd (m)	سدّ
canal	qanāt (f)	قناة
reservoir (artificial lake)	xazzān māʾiy (m)	خزّان مائيّ
sluice, lock	hawīs (m)	هويس
water body (pond, etc.)	masṭaḥ māʾiy (m)	مسطح مائيّ
swamp (marshland)	mustanqaʿ (m)	مستنقع

bog, marsh	mustanqa' (m)	مستنقع
whirlpool	dawwāma (f)	دوّامة
stream (brook)	ȝadwal mā'iy (m)	جدول مائيّ
drinking (ab. water)	aʃ ʃurb	الشرب
fresh (~ water)	'aðb	عذب
ice	ȝalīd (m)	جليد
to freeze over (ab. river, etc.)	taȝammad	تجمّد

170. Forest

forest, wood	ɣāba (f)	غابة
forest (as adj)	ɣāba	غابة
thick forest	ɣāba kaθīfa (f)	غابة كثيفة
grove	ɣāba ṣaɣīra (f)	غابة صغيرة
forest clearing	minṭaqa uzīlat minha al aʃȝār (f)	منطقة أزيلت منها الأشجار
thicket	aȝama (f)	أجمة
scrubland	ʃuȝayrāt (pl)	شجيرات
footpath (troddenpath)	mamarr (m)	ممرّ
gully	wādi ḍayyiq (m)	واد ضيّق
tree	ʃaȝara (f)	شجرة
leaf	waraqa (f)	ورقة
leaves (foliage)	waraq (m)	ورق
fall of leaves	tasāquṭ al awrāq (m)	تساقط الأوراق
to fall (ab. leaves)	saqaṭ	سقط
top (of the tree)	ra's (m)	رأس
branch	ɣuṣn (m)	غصن
bough	ɣuṣn (m)	غصن
bud (on shrub, tree)	bur'um (m)	برعم
needle (of the pine tree)	ʃawka (f)	شوكة
fir cone	kūz aṣ ṣanawbar (m)	كوز الصنوبر
tree hollow	ȝawf (m)	جوف
nest	'uʃʃ (m)	عشّ
burrow (animal hole)	ȝuḥr (m)	جحر
trunk	ȝið' (m)	جذع
root	ȝiðr (m)	جذر
bark	liḥā' (m)	لحاء
moss	ṭuḥlub (m)	طحلب
to uproot (remove trees or tree stumps)	iqtala'	إقتلع
to chop down	qaṭa'	قطع
to deforest (vt)	azāl al ɣābāt	أزال الغابات
tree stump	ȝið' aʃ ʃaȝara (m)	جذع الشجرة

campfire	nār muχayyam (m)	نار مخيّم
forest fire	ḥarīq ɣāba (m)	حريق غابة
to extinguish (vt)	aṭfa'	أطفأ
forest ranger	ḥāris al ɣāba (m)	حارس الغابة
protection	ḥimāya (f)	حماية
to protect (~ nature)	ḥama	حمى
poacher	sāriq aṣ ṣayd (m)	سارق الصيد
steel trap	maṣyada (f)	مصيدة
to gather, to pick (vt)	ʒamaʿ	جمع
to lose one's way	tāh	تاه

171. Natural resources

natural resources	θarawāt ṭabīʿiyya (pl)	ثروات طبيعيّة
minerals	maʿādin (pl)	معادن
deposits	makāmin (pl)	مكامن
field (e.g. oilfield)	ḥaql (m)	حقل
to mine (extract)	istaχraʒ	إستخرج
mining (extraction)	istiχrāʒ (m)	إستخراج
ore	χām (m)	خام
mine (e.g. for coal)	manʒam (m)	منجم
shaft (mine ~)	manʒam (m)	منجم
miner	ʿāmil manʒam (m)	عامل منجم
gas (natural ~)	ɣāz (m)	غاز
gas pipeline	χaṭṭ anābīb ɣāz (m)	خط أنابيب غاز
oil (petroleum)	nafṭ (m)	نفط
oil pipeline	anābīb an nafṭ (pl)	أنابيب النفط
oil well	bi'r an nafṭ (m)	بئر النفط
derrick (tower)	ḥaffāra (f)	حفّارة
tanker	nāqilat an nafṭ (f)	ناقلة النفط
sand	raml (m)	رمل
limestone	ḥaʒar kalsiy (m)	حجر كـلسيّ
gravel	ḥaṣa (m)	حصى
peat	χaθθ faḥm nabātiy (m)	خثّ فحم نباتيّ
clay	ṭīn (m)	طين
coal	faḥm (m)	فحم
iron (ore)	ḥadīd (m)	حديد
gold	ðahab (m)	ذهب
silver	fiḍḍa (f)	فضّة
nickel	nikil (m)	نيكل
copper	nuḥās (m)	نحاس
zinc	zink (m)	زنك
manganese	manɣanīz (m)	منغنيز
mercury	zi'baq (m)	زئبق
lead	ruṣāṣ (m)	رصاص
mineral	maʿdan (m)	معدن

crystal	ballūra (f)	بلّورة
marble	ruẖām (m)	رخام
uranium	yurānuim (m)	يورانيوم

The Earth. Part 2

172. Weather

weather	ṭaqs (m)	طقس
weather forecast	naʃra ʒawwiyya (f)	نشرة جوّيّة
temperature	ḥarāra (f)	حرارة
thermometer	tirmūmitr (m)	ترمومتر
barometer	barūmitr (m)	بارومتر
humid (adj)	raṭib	رطب
humidity	ruṭūba (f)	رطوبة
heat (extreme ~)	ḥarāra (f)	حرارة
hot (torrid)	ḥārr	حارّ
it's hot	al ʒaww ḥārr	الجوّ حارّ
it's warm	al ʒaww dāfi'	الجوّ دافئ
warm (moderately hot)	dāfi'	دافئ
it's cold	al ʒaww bārid	الجوّ بارد
cold (adj)	bārid	بارد
sun	ʃams (f)	شمس
to shine (vi)	aḍā'	أضاء
sunny (day)	muʃmis	مشمس
to come up (vi)	ʃaraq	شرق
to set (vi)	ɣarab	غرب
cloud	saḥāba (f)	سحابة
cloudy (adj)	ɣā'im	غائم
rain cloud	saḥābat maṭar (f)	سحابة مطر
somber (gloomy)	ɣā'im	غائم
rain	maṭar (m)	مطر
it's raining	innaha tamṭur	إنّها تمطر
rainy (~ day, weather)	mumṭir	ممطر
to drizzle (vi)	raðð	رذّ
pouring rain	maṭar munhamir (f)	مطر منهمر
downpour	maṭar ɣazīr (m)	مطر غزير
heavy (e.g. ~ rain)	ʃadīd	شديد
puddle	birka (f)	بركة
to get wet (in rain)	ibtall	إبتلّ
fog (mist)	ḍabāb (m)	ضباب
foggy	muḍabbab	مضبّب
snow	θalʒ (m)	ثلج
it's snowing	innaha taθluʒ	إنّها تثلج

173. Severe weather. Natural disasters

thunderstorm	ʻāṣifa raʻdiyya (f)	عاصفة رعديّة
lightning (~ strike)	barq (m)	برق
to flash (vi)	baraq	برق
thunder	raʻd (m)	رعد
to thunder (vi)	raʻad	رعد
it's thundering	tarʻad as samā'	ترعد السماء
hail	maṭar bard (m)	مطر برد
it's hailing	tamṭur as samā' bardan	تمطر السماء بردًا
to flood (vt)	ɣamar	غمر
flood, inundation	fayaḍān (m)	فيضان
earthquake	zilzāl (m)	زلزال
tremor, shoke	hazza arḍiyya (f)	هزّة أرضيّة
epicentre	markaz az zilzāl (m)	مركز الزلزال
eruption	θawrān (m)	ثوران
lava	ḥumam burkāniyya (pl)	حمم بركانيّة
twister, tornado	iʻṣār (m)	إعصار
typhoon	ṭūfān (m)	طوفان
hurricane	iʻṣār (m)	إعصار
storm	ʻāṣifa (f)	عاصفة
tsunami	tsunāmi (m)	تسونامي
cyclone	iʻṣār (m)	إعصار
bad weather	ṭaqs sayyi' (m)	طقس سيّء
fire (accident)	ḥarīq (m)	حريق
disaster	kāriθa (f)	كارثة
meteorite	ḥaʒar nayzakiy (m)	حجر نيزكيّ
avalanche	inhiyār θalʒiy (m)	إنهيار ثلجيّ
snowslide	inhiyār θalʒiy (m)	إنهيار ثلجيّ
blizzard	ʻāṣifa θalʒiyya (f)	عاصفة ثلجيّة
snowstorm	ʻāṣifa θalʒiyya (f)	عاصفة ثلجيّة

Fauna

174. Mammals. Predators

predator	ḥayawān muftaris (m)	حيوان مفترس
tiger	namir (m)	نمر
lion	asad (m)	أسد
wolf	ði'b (m)	ذئب
fox	θaʻlab (m)	ثعلب
jaguar	namir amrīkiy (m)	نمر أمريكيّ
leopard	fahd (m)	فهد
cheetah	namir ṣayyād (m)	نمر صيّاد
black panther	namir aswad (m)	نمر أسود
puma	būma (m)	بوما
snow leopard	namir aθ θulūʒ (m)	نمر الثلوج
lynx	waʃaq (m)	وشق
coyote	qayūṭ (m)	قيوط
jackal	ibn 'āwa (m)	ابن آوى
hyena	ḍabuʻ (m)	ضبع

175. Wild animals

animal	ḥayawān (m)	حيوان
beast (animal)	ḥayawān (m)	حيوان
squirrel	sinʒāb (m)	سنجاب
hedgehog	qumfuð (m)	قنفذ
hare	arnab barriy (m)	أرنب برّيّ
rabbit	arnab (m)	أرنب
badger	ɣarīr (m)	غرير
raccoon	rākūn (m)	راكون
hamster	qidād (m)	قداد
marmot	marmuṭ (m)	مرموط
mole	xuld (m)	خلد
mouse	fa'r (m)	فأر
rat	ʒura ð (m)	جرذ
bat	xuffāʃ (m)	خفّاش
ermine	qāqum (m)	قاقم
sable	sammūr (m)	سمّور
marten	dalaq (m)	دلق
weasel	ibn ʻirs (m)	إبن عرس
mink	mink (m)	منك

beaver	qundus (m)	قندس
otter	quḍā'a (f)	قضاعة
horse	ḥiṣān (m)	حصان
moose	mūz (m)	موظ
deer	ayyil (m)	أيَل
camel	ʒamal (m)	جمل
bison	bisūn (m)	بيسون
wisent	θawr barriy (m)	ثور بريّ
buffalo	ʒāmūs (m)	جاموس
zebra	ḥimār zarad (m)	حمار زرد
antelope	ẓabiy (m)	ظبي
roe deer	yaḥmūr (m)	يحمور
fallow deer	ayyil asmar urubbiy (m)	أيَل أسمر أوروبّيَ
chamois	ʃamwāh (f)	شاموه
wild boar	xinzīr barriy (m)	خنزير بريَ
whale	ḥūt (m)	حوت
seal	fuqma (f)	فقمة
walrus	faẓẓ (m)	فظَ
fur seal	fuqmat al firā' (f)	فقمة الفراء
dolphin	dilfīn (m)	دلفين
bear	dubb (m)	دبّ
polar bear	dubb quṭbiy (m)	دبّ قطبيَ
panda	bānda (m)	باندا
monkey	qird (m)	قرد
chimpanzee	ʃimbanzi (m)	شيمبانزي
orangutan	urangutān (m)	أورنغوتان
gorilla	ɣurīlla (f)	غوريلا
macaque	qird al makāk (m)	قرد المكاك
gibbon	ʒibbūn (m)	جيبون
elephant	fīl (m)	فيل
rhinoceros	xartīt (m)	خرتيت
giraffe	zarāfa (f)	زرافة
hippopotamus	faras an nahr (m)	فرس النهر
kangaroo	kanɣar (m)	كنغر
koala (bear)	kuala (m)	كوالا
mongoose	nims (m)	نمس
chinchilla	ʃinʃla (f)	شنشيلة
skunk	ẓaribān (m)	ظربان
porcupine	nīṣ (m)	نيص

176. Domestic animals

cat	qiṭṭa (f)	قطَة
tomcat	ðakar al qiṭṭ (m)	ذكر القطَ
dog	kalb (m)	كلب

horse	ḥiṣān (m)	حصان
stallion (male horse)	faḥl al xayl (m)	فحل الخيل
mare	unθa al faras (f)	أنثى الفرس

cow	baqara (f)	بقرة
bull	θawr (m)	ثور
ox	θawr (m)	ثور

sheep (ewe)	xarūf (f)	خروف
ram	kabʃ (m)	كبش
goat	māʿiz (m)	ماعز
billy goat, he-goat	ðakar al māʿið (m)	ذكر الماعز

| donkey | ḥimār (m) | حمار |
| mule | baɣl (m) | بغل |

pig	xinzīr (m)	خنزير
piglet	xannūṣ (m)	خنّوص
rabbit	arnab (m)	أرنب

| hen (chicken) | daʒāʒa (f) | دجاجة |
| cock | dīk (m) | ديك |

duck	baṭṭa (f)	بطّة
drake	ðakar al baṭṭ (m)	ذكر البطّ
goose	iwazza (f)	إوزّة

| tom turkey, gobbler | dīk rūmiy (m) | ديك روميّ |
| turkey (hen) | daʒāʒ rūmiy (m) | دجاج روميّ |

domestic animals	ḥayawānāt dawāʒin (pl)	حيوانات دواجن
tame (e.g. ~ hamster)	alīf	أليف
to tame (vt)	allaf	ألّف
to breed (vt)	rabba	ربّى

farm	mazraʿa (f)	مزرعة
poultry	ṭuyūr dāʒina (pl)	طيور داجنة
cattle	māʃiya (f)	ماشية
herd (cattle)	qaṭīʿ (m)	قطيع

stable	isṭabl xayl (m)	إسطبل خيل
pigsty	ḥaẓīrat al xanāzīr (f)	حظيرة الخنازير
cowshed	zirībat al baqar (f)	زريبة البقر
rabbit hutch	qunn al arānib (m)	قنّ الأرانب
hen house	qunn ad daʒāʒ (m)	قن الدجاج

177. Dogs. Dog breeds

dog	kalb (m)	كلب
sheepdog	kalb raʿy (m)	كلب رعي
German shepherd	kalb ar rāʿi al almāniy (m)	كلب الراعي الألمانيّ
poodle	būdli (m)	بودل
dachshund	daʃhund (m)	دشهند
bulldog	bulduɣ (m)	بلدغ

boxer	buksir (m)	بوكسر
mastiff	mastīf (m)	ماستيف
Rottweiler	rut vāylir (m)	روت فايلر
Doberman	dubirmān (m)	دوبرمان

basset	bāsit (m)	باسيت
bobtail	bubteyl (m)	بوبتيل
Dalmatian	kalb dalmāsiy (m)	كلب دلماسي
cocker spaniel	kukkir spaniil (m)	كوكر سبانييل

| Newfoundland | nyu faundland (m) | نيوفاوندلاند |
| Saint Bernard | san birnār (m) | سنبرنار |

husky	haski (m)	هاسكي
Chow Chow	tʃaw tʃaw (m)	تشاوتشاو
spitz	ʃbītz (m)	شبيتز
pug	bāk (m)	باك

178. Sounds made by animals

barking (n)	nubāḥ (m)	نباح
to bark (vi)	nabaḥ	نبح
to miaow (vi)	mā'	ماء
to purr (vi)	χarχar	خرخر

to moo (vi)	χār	خار
to bellow (bull)	χār	خار
to growl (vi)	damdam	دمدم

howl (n)	'uwā' (m)	عواء
to howl (vi)	'awa	عوى
to whine (vi)	'awa	عوى

to bleat (sheep)	ma'ma'	مأمأ
to oink, to grunt (pig)	qaba'	قبع
to squeal (vi)	ṣāḥ	صاح

to croak (vi)	naqq	نقّ
to buzz (insect)	ṭann	طنّ
to chirp (crickets, grasshopper)	zaqzaq	زقزق

179. Birds

bird	ṭā'ir (m)	طائر
pigeon	ḥamāma (f)	حمامة
sparrow	'uṣfūr (m)	عصفور
tit (great tit)	qurquf (m)	قرقف
magpie	'aq'aq (m)	عقعق

| raven | ɣurāb aswad (m) | غراب أسود |
| crow | ɣurāb (m) | غراب |

jackdaw	zāɣ (m)	زاغ
rook	ɣurāb al qayẓ (m)	غراب القيظ
duck	baṭṭa (f)	بطّة
goose	iwazza (f)	إوزّة
pheasant	tadarruʒ (m)	تدرج
eagle	nasr (m)	نسر
hawk	bāz (m)	باز
falcon	ṣaqr (m)	صقر
vulture	raɣam (m)	رخم
condor (Andean ~)	kundūr (m)	كندور
swan	timma (m)	تمّة
crane	kurkiy (m)	كركي
stork	laqlaq (m)	لقلق
parrot	babaɣā' (m)	ببغاء
hummingbird	ṭannān (m)	طنّان
peacock	ṭāwūs (m)	طاووس
ostrich	na'āma (f)	نعامة
heron	balaʃūn (m)	بلشون
flamingo	nuḥām wardiy (m)	نحام ورديّ
pelican	baʒa'a (f)	بجعة
nightingale	bulbul (m)	بلبل
swallow	sunūnū (m)	سنونو
thrush	sumna (m)	سمنة
song thrush	summuna muɣarrida (m)	سمنة مغرّدة
blackbird	ʃaḥrūr aswad (m)	شحرور أسود
swift	samāma (m)	سمامة
lark	qubbara (f)	قبّرة
quail	sammān (m)	سمّان
woodpecker	naqqār al ɣaʃab (m)	نقّار الخشب
cuckoo	waqwāq (m)	وقواق
owl	būma (f)	بومة
eagle owl	būm urāsiy (m)	بوم أوراسيّ
wood grouse	dīk il ɣalanʒ (m)	ديك الخلنج
black grouse	ṭayhūʒ aswad (m)	طيهوج أسود
partridge	ḥaʒal (m)	حجل
starling	zurzūr (m)	زرزور
canary	kanāriy (m)	كناريّ
hazel grouse	ṭayhūʒ il bunduq (m)	طيهوج البندق
chaffinch	ʃurʃūr (m)	شرشور
bullfinch	diɣnāʃ (m)	دغناش
seagull	nawras (m)	نورس
albatross	al qaṭras (m)	القطرس
penguin	biṭrīq (m)	بطريق

180. Birds. Singing and sounds

to sing (vi)	ɣanna	غنّى
to call (animal, bird)	nāda	نادى
to crow (cock)	ṣāḥ	صاح
cock-a-doodle-doo	kukukuku	كوكوكوكو
to cluck (hen)	qaraq	قرق
to caw (crow call)	naʿaq	نعق
to quack (duck call)	baṭbaṭ	بطبط
to cheep (vi)	ṣaʾṣaʾ	صأصأ
to chirp, to twitter	zaqzaq	زقزق

181. Fish. Marine animals

bream	abramīs (m)	أبراميس
carp	ʃabbūṭ (m)	شبّوط
perch	farχ (m)	فرخ
catfish	qarmūṭ (m)	قرموط
pike	samak al karāki (m)	سمك الكراكي
salmon	salmūn (m)	سلمون
sturgeon	ḥafʃ (m)	حفش
herring	rinʒa (f)	رنجة
Atlantic salmon	salmūn aṭlasiy (m)	سلمون أطلسيّ
mackerel	usqumriy (m)	أسقمريّ
flatfish	samak mufalṭaḥ (f)	سمك مفلطح
zander, pike perch	samak sandar (m)	سمك سندر
cod	qudd (m)	قدّ
tuna	tūna (f)	تونة
trout	salmūn muraqqaṭ (m)	سلمون مرقّط
eel	ḥankalīs (m)	حنكليس
electric ray	raʿād (m)	رعّاد
moray eel	murāy (m)	موراي
piranha	birāna (f)	بيرانا
shark	qirʃ (m)	قرش
dolphin	dilfīn (m)	دلفين
whale	ḥūt (m)	حوت
crab	salṭaʿūn (m)	سلطعون
jellyfish	qindīl al baḥr (m)	قنديل البحر
octopus	uχṭubūṭ (m)	أخطبوط
starfish	naʒmat al baḥr (f)	نجمة البحر
sea urchin	qumfuð al baḥr (m)	قنفذ البحر
seahorse	ḥiṣān al baḥr (m)	فرس البحر
oyster	maḥār (m)	مَحار
prawn	ʒambari (m)	جمبريّ

| lobster | istakūza (f) | إستكوزا |
| spiny lobster | karkand ʃāik (m) | كركند شائك |

182. Amphibians. Reptiles

| snake | θu'bān (m) | ثعبان |
| venomous (snake) | sāmm | سامّ |

viper	af'a (f)	أفعى
cobra	kūbra (m)	كوبرا
python	biθūn (m)	بيثون
boa	buwā' (f)	بواء

grass snake	θu'bān al 'uʃb (m)	ثعبان العشب
rattle snake	af'a al ʒalʒala (f)	أفعى الجلجلة
anaconda	anakūnda (f)	أناكوندا

lizard	siħliyya (f)	سحليّة
iguana	iɣwāna (f)	إغوانة
monitor lizard	waral (m)	ورل
salamander	samandar (m)	سمندر
chameleon	ħirbā' (f)	حرباء
scorpion	'aqrab (m)	عقرب

turtle	sulaħfāt (f)	سلحفاة
frog	difda' (m)	ضفدع
toad	difda' aṭ ṭīn (m)	ضفدع الطين
crocodile	timsāħ (m)	تمساح

183. Insects

insect	ħaʃara (f)	حشرة
butterfly	farāʃa (f)	فراشة
ant	namla (f)	نملة
fly	ðubāba (f)	ذبابة
mosquito	namūsa (f)	ناموسة
beetle	χunfusa (f)	خنفسة

wasp	dabbūr (m)	دبّور
bee	naħla (f)	نحلة
bumblebee	naħla ṭannāna (f)	نحلة طنّانة
gadfly (botfly)	na'ra (f)	نعرة

| spider | 'ankabūt (m) | عنكبوت |
| spider's web | nasīʒ 'ankabūt (m) | نسيج عنكبوت |

dragonfly	ya'sūb (m)	يعسوب
grasshopper	ʒarād (m)	جراد
moth (night butterfly)	'itta (f)	عتّة

| cockroach | ṣurṣūr (m) | صرصور |
| tick | qurāda (f) | قرادة |

flea	buryūθ (m)	برغوث
midge	baʿūḍa (f)	بعوضة
locust	ʒarād (m)	جراد
snail	ḥalzūn (m)	حلزون
cricket	ṣarrār al layl (m)	صرّار الليل
firefly	yarāʿa muḍīʾa (f)	يراعة مضيئة
ladybird	daʿsūqa (f)	دعسوقة
cockchafer	xunfusa kabīra (f)	خنفسة كبيرة
leech	ʿalaqa (f)	علقة
caterpillar	yasrūʿ (m)	يسروع
earthworm	dūda (f)	دودة
larva	yaraqa (f)	يرقة

184. Animals. Body parts

beak	minqār (m)	منقار
wings	aʒniḥa (pl)	أجنحة
foot (of the bird)	riʒl (f)	رجل
feathers (plumage)	rīʃ (m)	ريش
feather	rīʃa (f)	ريشة
crest	tāʒ (m)	تاج
gills	xayāʃīm (pl)	خياشيم
spawn	bayḍ as samak (pl)	بيض السمك
larva	yaraqa (f)	يرقة
fin	ziʿnifa (f)	زعنفة
scales (of fish, reptile)	ḥarāfiʃ (pl)	حرافش
fang (canine)	nāb (m)	ناب
paw (e.g. cat's ~)	qadam (f)	قدم
muzzle (snout)	xaṭm (m)	خطم
mouth (cat's ~)	fam (m)	فم
tail	ðayl (m)	ذيل
whiskers	ʃawārib (pl)	شوارب
hoof	ḥāfir (m)	حافر
horn	qarn (m)	قرن
carapace	dirʿ (m)	درع
shell (mollusk ~)	maḥāra (f)	محارة
eggshell	qiʃrat bayḍa (f)	قشرة بيضة
animal's hair (pelage)	ʃaʿr (m)	شعر
pelt (hide)	ʒild (m)	جلد

185. Animals. Habitats

habitat	mawṭin (m)	موطن
migration	hiʒra (f)	هجرة
mountain	ʒabal (m)	جبل

reef	ʃiʻāb (pl)	شعاب
cliff	ʒurf (m)	جرف
forest	ɣāba (f)	غابة
jungle	adɣāl (pl)	أدغال
savanna	savānna (f)	سافانّا
tundra	tundra (f)	تندرا
steppe	sahb (m)	سهب
desert	ṣaḥrāʼ (f)	صحراء
oasis	wāḥa (f)	واحة
sea	baḥr (m)	بحر
lake	buḥayra (f)	بحيرة
ocean	muḥīṭ (m)	محيط
swamp (marshland)	mustanqaʻ (m)	مستنقع
freshwater (adj)	al miyāh al ʻaðba	المياه العذبة
pond	birka (f)	بركة
river	nahr (m)	نهر
den (bear's ~)	wakr (m)	وكر
nest	ʻuʃʃ (m)	عشّ
tree hollow	ʒawf (m)	جوف
burrow (animal hole)	ʒuḥr (m)	جحر
anthill	ʻuʃʃ naml (m)	عشّ نمل

Flora

186. Trees

tree	ʃaʒara (f)	شجرة
deciduous (adj)	nafḍiyya	نفضيّة
coniferous (adj)	ṣanawbariyya	صنوبريّة
evergreen (adj)	dāʾimat al xuḍra	دائمة الخضرة
apple tree	ʃaʒarat tuffāḥ (f)	شجرة تفّاح
pear tree	ʃaʒarat kummaθra (f)	شجرة كمّثرى
cherry tree	ʃaʒarat karaz (f)	شجرة كرز
plum tree	ʃaʒarat barqūq (f)	شجرة برقوق
birch	batūla (f)	بتولا
oak	ballūṭ (f)	بلّوط
linden tree	ʃaʒarat zayzafūn (f)	شجرة زيزفون
aspen	ḥawr raʒrāʒ (m)	حور رجراج
maple	qayqab (f)	قيقب
spruce	ratinaʒ (f)	راتينج
pine	ṣanawbar (f)	صنوبر
larch	arziyya (f)	أرزيّة
fir tree	tannūb (f)	تنّوب
cedar	arz (f)	أرز
poplar	ḥawr (f)	حور
rowan	ɣubayrāʾ (f)	غبيراء
willow	ṣafṣāf (f)	صفصاف
alder	ʒār il māʾ (m)	جار الماء
beech	zān (m)	زان
elm	dardār (f)	دردار
ash (tree)	marān (f)	مران
chestnut	kastanāʾ (f)	كستناء
magnolia	maɣnūliya (f)	مغنوليا
palm tree	naxla (f)	نخلة
cypress	sarw (f)	سرو
mangrove	ayka sāḥiliyya (f)	أيكة ساحليّة
baobab	bāubāb (f)	باوباب
eucalyptus	ukaliptus (f)	أوكاليبتوس
sequoia	siqūya (f)	سيكويا

187. Shrubs

bush	ʃuʒayra (f)	شجيرة
shrub	ʃuʒayrāt (pl)	شجيرات

grapevine	karma (f)	كرمة
vineyard	karam (m)	كرم
raspberry bush	tūt al ʿullayq al aḥmar (m)	توت العليق الأحمر
redcurrant bush	kiʃmiʃ aḥmar (m)	كشمش أحمر
gooseberry bush	ʿinab aθ θaʿlab (m)	عنب الثعلب
acacia	sanṭ (f)	سنط
barberry	amīr barīs (m)	أمير باريس
jasmine	yāsmīn (m)	ياسمين
juniper	ʿarʿar (m)	عرعر
rosebush	ʃuʒayrat ward (f)	شجيرة ورد
dog rose	ward ʒabaliy (m)	ورد جبليّ

188. Mushrooms

mushroom	fuṭr (f)	فطر
edible mushroom	fuṭr ṣāliḥ lil akl (m)	فطر صالح للأكل
poisonous mushroom	fuṭr sāmm (m)	فطر سامّ
cap	ṭarbūʃ al fuṭr (m)	طربوش الفطر
stipe	sāq al fuṭr (m)	ساق الفطر
cep, penny bun	fuṭr bulīṭ ma'kūl (m)	فطر بوليط مأكول
orange-cap boletus	fuṭr aḥmar (m)	فطر أحمر
birch bolete	fuṭr bulīṭ (m)	فطر بوليط
chanterelle	fuṭr kwīzi (m)	فطر كويزي
russula	fuṭr russūla (m)	فطر روسّولا
morel	fuṭr al ɣūʃna (m)	فطر الغوشنة
fly agaric	fuṭr amānīt aṭ ṭā'ir as sāmm (m)	فطر أمانيت الطائر السامّ
death cap	fuṭr amānīt falusyāniy as sāmm (m)	فطر أمانيت فالوسياني السامّ

189. Fruits. Berries

fruit	θamra (f)	ثمرة
fruits	θamr (m)	ثمر
apple	tuffāḥa (f)	تفّاحة
pear	kummaθra (f)	كمّثرى
plum	barqūq (m)	برقوق
strawberry (garden ~)	farawla (f)	فراولة
cherry	karaz (m)	كرز
grape	ʿinab (m)	عنب
raspberry	tūt al ʿullayq al aḥmar (m)	توت العليق الأحمر
blackcurrant	ʿinab aθ θaʿlab al aswad (m)	عنب الثعلب الأسود
redcurrant	kiʃmiʃ aḥmar (m)	كشمش أحمر
gooseberry	ʿinab aθ θaʿlab (m)	عنب الثعلب
cranberry	tūt aḥmar barriy (m)	توت أحمر برّيّ

orange	burtuqāl (m)	برتقال
tangerine	yūsufiy (m)	يوسفي
pineapple	ananās (m)	أناناس
banana	mawz (m)	موز
date	tamr (m)	تمر

lemon	laymūn (m)	ليمون
apricot	miʃmiʃ (f)	مشمش
peach	durrāq (m)	دراق
kiwi	kiwi (m)	كيوي
grapefruit	zinbāʿ (m)	زنباع

berry	ḥabba (f)	حبّة
berries	ḥabbāt (pl)	حبّات
cowberry	ʿinab aθ θawr (m)	عنب الثور
wild strawberry	farāwla barriyya (f)	فراولة برّية
bilberry	ʿinab al aḥrāʒ (m)	عنب الأحراج

190. Flowers. Plants

| flower | zahra (f) | زهرة |
| bouquet (of flowers) | bāqat zuhūr (f) | باقة زهور |

rose (flower)	warda (f)	وردة
tulip	tulīb (f)	توليب
carnation	qurumful (m)	قرنفل
gladiolus	dalbūθ (f)	دلبوث

cornflower	turunʃāh (m)	ترنشاه
harebell	ʒarīs (m)	جريس
dandelion	hindibāʾ (f)	هندباء
camomile	babunʒ (m)	بابونج

aloe	aluwwa (m)	ألوّة
cactus	ṣabbār (m)	صبّار
rubber plant, ficus	tīn (m)	تين

lily	sawsan (m)	سوسن
geranium	ibrat ar rāʿi (f)	إبرة الراعي
hyacinth	zanbaq (f)	زنبق

mimosa	mimūza (f)	ميموزا
narcissus	narʒis (f)	نرجس
nasturtium	abu χanʒar (f)	أبو خنجر

orchid	saḥlab (f)	سحلب
peony	fawniya (f)	فاوانيا
violet	banafsaʒ (f)	بنفسج

pansy	banafsaʒ muθallaθ (m)	بنفسج مثلّث
forget-me-not	ʾāðān al faʾr (pl)	آذان الفأر
daisy	uqhuwān (f)	أقحوان
poppy	χaʃχāʃ (f)	خشخاش
hemp	qinnab (m)	قنب

mint	na'nā' (m)	نعناع
lily of the valley	sawsan al wādi (m)	سوسن الوادي
snowdrop	zahrat al laban (f)	زهرة اللبن
nettle	qarrāṣ (m)	قرّاص
sorrel	ḥammāḍ (m)	حمّاض
water lily	nilūfar (m)	نيلوفر
fern	saraxs (m)	سرخس
lichen	uʃna (f)	أشنة
conservatory (greenhouse)	daffa (f)	دفيئة
lawn	'uʃb (m)	عشب
flowerbed	ʒunaynat zuhūr (f)	جنينة زهور
plant	nabāt (m)	نبات
grass	'uʃb (m)	عشب
blade of grass	'uʃba (f)	عشبة
leaf	waraqa (f)	ورقة
petal	waraqat az zahra (f)	ورقة الزهرة
stem	sāq (f)	ساق
tuber	darnat nabāt (f)	درنة نبات
young plant (shoot)	nabta saɣīra (f)	نبتة صغيرة
thorn	ʃawka (f)	شوكة
to blossom (vi)	nawwar	نوّر
to fade, to wither	ðabal	ذبل
smell (odour)	rā'iḥa (f)	رائحة
to cut (flowers)	qaṭa'	قطع
to pick (a flower)	qaṭaf	قطف

191. Cereals, grains

grain	ḥubūb (pl)	حبوب
cereal crops	maḥāṣīl al ḥubūb (pl)	محاصيل الحبوب
ear (of barley, etc.)	sumbula (f)	سنبلة
wheat	qamḥ (m)	قمح
rye	ʒāwdār (m)	جاودار
oats	ʃūfān (m)	شوفان
millet	duxn (m)	دخن
barley	ʃa'īr (m)	شعير
maize	ðura (f)	ذرّة
rice	urz (m)	أرز
buckwheat	ḥinṭa sawdā' (f)	حنطة سوداء
pea plant	bisilla (f)	بسلّة
kidney bean	faṣūliya (f)	فاصوليا
soya	fūl aṣ ṣūya (m)	فول الصويا
lentil	'adas (m)	عدس
beans (pulse crops)	fūl (m)	فول

REGIONAL GEOGRAPHY

192. Politics. Government. Part 1

politics	siyāsa (f)	سياسة
political (adj)	siyāsiy	سياسيّ
politician	siyāsiy (m)	سياسي
state (country)	dawla (f)	دولة
citizen	muwāṭin (m)	مواطن
citizenship	ʒinsiyya (f)	جنسيّة
national emblem	ʃiʿār waṭaniy (m)	شعار وطنيّ
national anthem	naʃīd waṭaniy (m)	نشيد وطنيّ
government	ḥukūma (f)	حكومة
head of state	ra's ad dawla (m)	رأس الدولة
parliament	barlamān (m)	برلمان
party	ḥizb (m)	حزب
capitalism	ra'smāliyya (f)	رأسماليّة
capitalist (adj)	ra'smāliy	رأسماليّ
socialism	iʃtirākiyya (f)	إشتراكيّة
socialist (adj)	iʃtirākiy	إشتراكيّ
communism	ʃuyūʿiyya (f)	شيوعيّة
communist (adj)	ʃuyūʿiy	شيوعيّ
communist (n)	ʃuyūʿiy (m)	شيوعي
democracy	dimuqraṭiyya (f)	ديموقراطيّة
democrat	dimuqrāṭiy (m)	ديموقراطيّ
democratic (adj)	dimuqrāṭiy	ديموقراطيّ
Democratic party	al ḥizb ad dimukrāṭiy (m)	الحزب الديموقراطيّ
liberal (n)	libirāliy (m)	ليبراليّ
Liberal (adj)	libirāliy	ليبراليّ
conservative (n)	muḥāfiẓ (m)	محافظ
conservative (adj)	muḥāfiẓ	محافظ
republic (n)	ʒumhūriyya (f)	جمهوريّة
republican (n)	ʒumhūriy (m)	جمهوريّ
Republican party	al ḥizb al ʒumhūriy (m)	الحزب الجمهوريّ
elections	intiχābāt (pl)	إنتخابات
to elect (vt)	intaχab	إنتخب
elector, voter	nāχib (m)	ناخب
election campaign	ḥamla intiχābiyya (f)	حملة إنتخابيّة
voting (n)	taṣwīt (m)	تصويت
to vote (vi)	ṣawwat	صوّت

suffrage, right to vote	ḥaqq al intixāb (m)	حقّ الإنتخاب
candidate	muraʃʃaḥ (m)	مرشّح
to run for (~ President)	raʃʃaḥ nafsahu	رشّح نفسه
campaign	ḥamla (f)	حملة
opposition (as adj)	muʿāriḍ	معارض
opposition (n)	muʿāraḍa (f)	معارضة
visit	ziyāra (f)	زيارة
official visit	ziyāra rasmiyya (f)	زيارة رسميّة
international (adj)	duwaliy	دوليّ
negotiations	mubāḥaθāt (pl)	مباحثات
to negotiate (vi)	aʒra mubāḥaθāt	أجرى مباحثات

193. Politics. Government. Part 2

society	muʒtamaʿ (m)	مجتمع
constitution	dustūr (m)	دستور
power (political control)	sulṭa (f)	سلطة
corruption	fasād (m)	فساد
law (justice)	qānūn (m)	قانون
legal (legitimate)	qānūniy	قانونيّ
justice (fairness)	ʿadāla (f)	عدالة
just (fair)	ʿādil	عادل
committee	laʒna (f)	لجنة
bill (draft law)	maʃrūʿ qānūn (m)	مشروع قانون
budget	mīzāniyya (f)	ميزانيّة
policy	siyāsa (f)	سياسة
reform	iṣlāḥ (m)	إصلاح
radical (adj)	radikāliy	راديكاليّ
power (strength, force)	quwwa (f)	قوّة
powerful (adj)	qawiy	قويّ
supporter	mu'ayyid (m)	مؤيّد
influence	ta'θīr (m)	تأثير
regime (e.g. military ~)	niẓām ḥukm (m)	نظام حكم
conflict	xilāf (m)	خلاف
conspiracy (plot)	mu'āmara (f)	مؤامرة
provocation	istifzāz (m)	إستفزاز
to overthrow (regime, etc.)	asqaṭ	أسقط
overthrow (of a government)	isqāṭ (m)	إسقاط
revolution	θawra (f)	ثورة
coup d'état	inqilāb (m)	إنقلاب
military coup	inqilāb ʿaskariy (m)	انقلاب عسكريّ
crisis	azma (f)	أزمة
economic recession	rukūd iqtiṣādiy (m)	ركود إقتصاديّ

demonstrator (protester)	mutaẓāhir (m)	متظاهر
demonstration	muẓāhara (f)	مظاهرة
martial law	al aḥkām al 'urfiyya (pl)	الأحكام العرفيّة
military base	qa'ida 'askariyya (f)	قاعدة عسكريّة

| stability | istiqrār (m) | إستقرار |
| stable (adj) | mustaqirr | مستقرّ |

| exploitation | istiɣlāl (m) | إستغلال |
| to exploit (workers) | istaɣall | إستغلّ |

racism	'unṣuriyya (f)	عنصريّة
racist	'unṣuriy (m)	عنصريّ
fascism	fāʃiyya (f)	فاشيّة
fascist	fāʃiy (m)	فاشيّ

194. Countries. Miscellaneous

foreigner	aʒnabiy (m)	أجنبيّ
foreign (adj)	aʒnabiy	أجنبيّ
abroad (in a foreign country)	fil χāriʒ	في الخارج

emigrant	nāziḥ (m)	نازح
emigration	nuziḥ (m)	نزوح
to emigrate (vi)	nazūḥ	نزح

the West	al ɣarb (m)	الغرب
the East	aʃ ʃarq (m)	الشرق
the Far East	aʃ ʃarq al aqṣa (m)	الشرق الأقصى

civilization	ḥaḍāra (f)	حضارة
humanity (mankind)	al baʃariyya (f)	البشريّة
the world (earth)	al 'ālam (m)	العالم
peace	salām (m)	سلام
worldwide (adj)	'ālamiy	عالميّ

homeland	waṭan (m)	وطن
people (population)	ʃa'b (m)	شعب
population	sukkān (pl)	سكّان
people (a lot of ~)	nās (pl)	ناس
nation (people)	umma (f)	أمّة
generation	ʒīl (m)	جيل

territory (area)	arḍ (f)	أرض
region	mintaqa (f)	منطقة
state (part of a country)	wilāya (f)	ولاية

tradition	taqlīd (m)	تقليد
custom (tradition)	'āda (f)	عادة
ecology	'ilm al bī'a (m)	علم البيئة

Indian (Native American)	hindiy aḥmar (m)	هنديّ أحمر
Gypsy (masc.)	ɣaʒariy (m)	غجريّ
Gypsy (fem.)	ɣaʒariyya (f)	غجريّة

Gypsy (adj)	ɣaʒariy	غجريّ
empire	imbiraṭuriyya (f)	أمبراطوريّة
colony	musta'mara (f)	مستعمرة
slavery	'ubūdiyya (f)	عبوديّة
invasion	ɣazw (m)	غزو
famine	maʒāʿa (f)	مجاعة

195. Major religious groups. Confessions

religion	dīn (m)	دين
religious (adj)	dīniy	دينيّ
faith, belief	ʾīmān (m)	إيمان
to believe (in God)	ʾāman	آمن
believer	mu'min (m)	مؤمن
atheism	al ilḥād (m)	الإلحاد
atheist	mulḥid (m)	ملحد
Christianity	al masīḥiyya (f)	المسيحيّة
Christian (n)	masīḥiy (m)	مسيحيّ
Christian (adj)	masīḥiy	مسيحيّ
Catholicism	al kaθūlikiyya (f)	الكاثوليكيّة
Catholic (n)	kaθulīkiy (m)	كاثوليكيّ
Catholic (adj)	kaθulīkiy	كاثوليكيّ
Protestantism	al brutistantiyya (f)	البروتستانتية
Protestant Church	al kanīsa al brutistantiyya (f)	الكنيسة البروتستانتيّة
Protestant (n)	brutistantiy (m)	بروتستانتيّ
Orthodoxy	urθuðuksiyya (f)	الأرثوذكسيّة
Orthodox Church	al kanīsa al urθuðuksiyya (f)	الكنيسة الأرثوذكسيّة
Orthodox (n)	urθuðuksiy (m)	أرثوذكسيّ
Presbyterianism	maʃīχiyya (f)	المشيخيّة
Presbyterian Church	al kanīsa al maʃīχiyya (f)	الكنيسة المشيخيّة
Presbyterian (n)	maʃīχiy (m)	مشيخيّ
Lutheranism	al kanīsa al luθiriyya (f)	الكنيسة اللوثريّة
Lutheran (n)	luθiriy (m)	لوثريّ
Baptist Church	al kanīsa al ma'madāniyya (f)	الكنيسة المعمدانيّة
Baptist (n)	ma'madāniy (m)	معمدانيّ
Anglican Church	al kanīsa al anʒlikāniyya (f)	الكنيسة الإنجليكانيّة
Anglican (n)	anʒlikāniy (m)	أنجليكانيّ
Mormonism	al murumūniyya (f)	المورمونيّة
Mormon (n)	masīḥiy murmūn (m)	مسيحيّ مرمون
Judaism	al yahūdiyya (f)	اليهوديّة
Jew (n)	yahūdiy (m)	يهوديّ
Buddhism	al būðiyya (f)	البوذيّة
Buddhist (n)	būðiy (m)	بوذيّ

Hinduism	al hindūsiyya (f)	الهندوسيّة
Hindu (n)	hindūsiy (m)	هندوسي
Islam	al islām (m)	الإسلام
Muslim (n)	muslim (m)	مسلم
Muslim (adj)	islāmiy	إسلاميّ
Shiah Islam	al maðhab aʃ ʃ'iy (m)	المذهب الشيعيّ
Shiite (n)	ʃ'iy (m)	شيعيّ
Sunni Islam	al maðhab as sunniy (m)	المذهب السنّيّ
Sunnite (n)	sunniy (m)	سنّيّ

196. Religions. Priests

priest	qissīs (m), kāhin (m)	قسّيس, كاهن
the Pope	al bāba (m)	البابا
monk, friar	rāhib (m)	راهب
nun	rāhiba (f)	راهبة
pastor	qissīs (m)	قسّيس
abbot	raˀīs ad dayr (m)	رئيس الدير
vicar (parish priest)	viqār (m)	فيقار
bishop	usquf (m)	أسقف
cardinal	kardināl (m)	كاردينال
preacher	tabʃīr (m)	تبشير
preaching	xutba (f)	خطبة
parishioners	raˈiyyat al abraʃiyya (f)	رعية الأبرشيّة
believer	mu'min (m)	مؤمن
atheist	mulhid (m)	ملحد

197. Faith. Christianity. Islam

Adam	'ādam (m)	آدم
Eve	hawā' (f)	حوّاء
God	allah (m)	الله
the Lord	ar rabb (m)	الربّ
the Almighty	al qadīr (m)	القدير
sin	ðamb (m)	ذنب
to sin (vi)	aðnab	أذنب
sinner (masc.)	muðnib (m)	مذنب
sinner (fem.)	muðniba (f)	مذنبة
hell	al ʒahīm (f)	الجحيم
paradise	al ʒanna (f)	الجنّة
Jesus	yasūˈ (m)	يسوع
Jesus Christ	yasūˈ al masīh (m)	يسوع المسيح

the Holy Spirit	ar rūḥ al qudus (m)	الروح القدس
the Saviour	al masīḥ (m)	المسيح
the Virgin Mary	maryam al 'aðrā' (f)	مريم العذراء
the Devil	aʃ ʃayṭān (m)	الشيطان
devil's (adj)	ʃayṭāniy	شيطانيّ
Satan	aʃ ʃayṭān (m)	الشيطان
satanic (adj)	ʃayṭāniy	شيطانيّ
angel	malāk (m)	ملاك
guardian angel	malāk ḥāris (m)	ملاك حارس
angelic (adj)	malā'ikiy	ملائكيّ
apostle	rasūl (m)	رسول
archangel	al malak ar ra'īsiy (m)	الملك الرئيسي
the Antichrist	al masīḥ ad daʒʒāl (m)	المسيح الدجّال
Church	al kanīsa (f)	الكنيسة
Bible	al kitāb al muqaddas (m)	الكتاب المقدّس
biblical (adj)	tawrātiy	توراتيّ
Old Testament	al 'ahd al qadīm (m)	العهد القديم
New Testament	al 'ahd al ʒadīd (m)	العهد الجديد
Gospel	inʒīl (m)	إنجيل
Holy Scripture	al kitāb al muqaddas (m)	الكتاب المقدّس
Heaven	al ʒanna (f)	الجنّة
Commandment	waṣiyya (f)	وصيّة
prophet	nabiy (m)	نبيّ
prophecy	nubū'a (f)	نبوءة
Allah	allah (m)	الله
Mohammed	muḥammad (m)	محمّد
the Koran	al qur'ān (m)	القرآن
mosque	masʒid (m)	مسجد
mullah	mulla (m)	ملّا
prayer	ṣalāt (f)	صلاة
to pray (vi, vt)	ṣalla	صلّى
pilgrimage	ḥaʒʒ (m)	حجّ
pilgrim	ḥāʒʒ (m)	حاجّ
Mecca	makka al mukarrama (f)	مكة المكرّمة
church	kanīsa (f)	كنيسة
temple	ma'bad (m)	معبد
cathedral	katidrā'iyya (f)	كاتدرائيّة
Gothic (adj)	qūṭiy	قوطيّ
synagogue	kanīs ma'bad yahūdiy (m)	كنيس معبد يهوديّ
mosque	masʒid (m)	مسجد
chapel	kanīsa ṣaɣīra (f)	كنيسة صغيرة
abbey	dayr (m)	دير
convent	dayr (m)	دير
monastery	dayr (m)	دير
bell (church ~s)	ʒaras (m)	جرس

bell tower	burӡ al ӡaras (m)	برج الجرس
to ring (ab. bells)	daqq	دق
cross	ṣalīb (m)	صليب
cupola (roof)	qubba (f)	قبّة
icon	ʼīkūna (f)	ايقونة
soul	nafs (f)	نفس
fate (destiny)	maṣīr (m)	مصير
evil (n)	ʃarr (m)	شرّ
good (n)	χayr (m)	خير
vampire	maṣṣāṣ dimā' (m)	مصّاص دماء
witch (evil ~)	sāḥira (f)	ساحرة
demon	ʃayṭān (m)	شيطان
spirit	rūḥ (m)	روح
redemption (giving us ~)	takfīr (m)	تكفير
to redeem (vt)	kaffar 'an	كفّر عن
church service	qaddās (m)	قدّاس
to say mass	alqa χuṭba bil kanīsa	ألقى خطبة بالكنيسة
confession	i'tirāf (m)	إعتراف
to confess (vi)	i'taraf	إعترف
saint (n)	qiddīs (m)	قدّيس
sacred (holy)	muqaddas (m)	مقدّس
holy water	mā' muqaddas (m)	ماء مقدّس
ritual (n)	ṭuqūs (pl)	طقوس
ritual (adj)	ṭuqūsiy	طقوسيّ
sacrifice	ðabīḥa (f)	ذبيحة
superstition	χurāfa (f)	خرافة
superstitious (adj)	mu'min bil χurāfāt (m)	مؤمن بالخرافات
afterlife	al 'āχira (f)	الآخرة
eternal life	al ḥayāt al abadiyya (f)	الحياة الأبدية

MISCELLANEOUS

198. Various useful words

background (green ~)	xalfiyya (f)	خَلفيّة
balance (of the situation)	tawāzun (m)	توازن
barrier (obstacle)	ḥāʒiz (m)	حاجز
base (basis)	asās (m)	أساس
beginning	bidāya (f)	بداية
category	fiʾa (f)	فئة
cause (reason)	sabab (m)	سبب
choice	ixtiyār (m)	إختيار
coincidence	ṣudfa (f)	صدفة
comfortable (~ chair)	murīḥ	مريح
comparison	muqārana (f)	مقارنة
compensation	taʿwīḍ (m)	تعويض
degree (extent, amount)	daraʒa (f)	درجة
development	tanmiya (f)	تنمية
difference	farq (m)	فرق
effect (e.g. of drugs)	taʾθīr (m)	تأثير
effort (exertion)	ʒuhd (m)	جهد
element	ʿunṣur (m)	عنصر
end (finish)	nihāya (f)	نهاية
example (illustration)	miθāl (m)	مثال
fact	ḥaqīqa (f)	حقيقة
frequent (adj)	mutakarrir (m)	متكرّر
growth (development)	numuww (m)	نموّ
help	musāʿada (f)	مساعدة
ideal	miθāl (m)	مثال
kind (sort, type)	nawʿ (m)	نوع
labyrinth	tayh (m)	تيه
mistake, error	xaṭaʾ (m)	خطأ
moment	laḥza (f)	لحظة
object (thing)	mawḍūʿ (m)	موضوع
obstacle	ʿaqba (f)	عقبة
original (original copy)	aṣl (m)	أصل
part (~ of sth)	ʒuzʾ (m)	جزء
particle, small part	ʒuzʾ (m)	جزء
pause (break)	istirāḥa (f)	إستراحة
position	mawqif (m)	موقف
principle	mabdaʾ (m)	مبدأ
problem	muʃkila (f)	مشكلة
process	ʿamaliyya (f)	عمليّة

progress	taqaddum (m)	تقدّم
property (quality)	χaṣṣa (f)	خاصّة
reaction	radd fiʿl (m)	ردّ فعل
risk	muχāṭara (f)	مخاطرة

secret	sirr (m)	سرّ
series	silsila (f)	سلسلة
shape (outer form)	ʃakl (m)	شكل
situation	ḥāla (f), waḍʿ (m)	حالة, وضع
solution	ḥall (m)	حلّ

standard (adj)	qiyāsiy	قياسيّ
standard (level of quality)	qiyās (m)	قياس
stop (pause)	istirāḥa (f)	إستراحة
style	uslūb (m)	أسلوب

system	niẓām (m)	نظام
table (chart)	ʒadwal (m)	جدول
tempo, rate	surʿa (f)	سرعة
term (word, expression)	muṣṭalaḥ (m)	مصطلح
thing (object, item)	ʃayʾ (m)	شيء

truth (e.g. moment of ~)	ḥaqīqa (f)	حقيقة
turn (please wait your ~)	dawr (m)	دور
type (sort, kind)	nawʿ (m)	نوع
urgent (adj)	ʿāʒil	عاجل
urgently	ʿāʒilan	عاجلا

utility (usefulness)	manfaʿa (f)	منفعة
variant (alternative)	ʃakl muχtalif (m)	شكل مختلف
way (means, method)	ṭarīqa (f)	طريقة
zone	mintaqa (f)	منطقة

www.ingramcontent.com/pod-product-compliance
Lightning Source LLC
LaVergne TN
LVHW051340080426
835509LV00020BA/3222